To Donna M. Van Blarcom, my love.

To my Mom and Dad, Concetta and Joseph Cascio. To the archive!

Contents

PREFACE

*T*he focus of this book is on 1776, the primary year of Revolutionary fervor in New York. This was a year full of indecision, taking sides, debate, division, preparation, troop massing, a Declaration, a great battle, troop movements, grand amphibious operations and the beginning of a long British military occupation. Western Queens County, the future eleven-square-mile Long Island City, would experience or be affected by all the above actions.

Most military action in lower New York Province occurred in 1776. The battle for New York took place here, from Staten Island to the Battle of Long Island in August 1776. From the British army and its Hessian auxiliaries preparing and staging on Queens County farmlands and in Newtown homes, it would invade New York Island. The British enemy massed on Newtown Creek to bring the war to New York City. The British Royal Navy patrolled the East River to bring the strength of empire to these western Long Island shores and through the Hell Gate. The instruments of total war marched and rolled across the roads and grounds of the future Long Island City in 1776. Cannonballs, bayonets and gold and silver coin caches were found here decades later. Many colonial houses stood long enough to be photographed for posterity's sake; most homes were gone by the 1920s. Some of the ancient Dutch and English colonial road patterns are still in use, and the tidal waterways are still formidable hazards to smooth and safe river navigation.

The year 1775 belonged to Boston. After April 1776, the Revolutionary War's focus became New York City and the highly strategic Long Island, from Brooklyn's terminal moraine high ground to Queens's Hell Gate.

The year 1776 was that of revolution on Long Island, especially here in the future Long Island City. This year is also chosen to show its absolute importance to the formation of the new and vital United States of America. Failure and defeat and occupation here did not lead to total defeat. Instead, they helped the Americans forge a greater resolve and earn the strength of character that officers and soldiers alike would need to push ever forward toward victory on the battlefields from New Jersey to Pennsylvania, Upstate New York, the Carolinas and, finally, Yorktown, Virginia.

Although the British did not evacuate western Queens County and New York City until November 1783, the war and its harsh, uninterrupted occupation began here in August 1776. All of the future Long Island City and its surrounding waterways were under British and Hessian control for seven long years.

The author was a staff sergeant in the United States Army in Hessen, West Germany, and in seven U.S. states. He has added his knowledge of history and tactics and has proposed a number of scenarios where a decision had to be made in a moment. Advice to those ready to dismiss or critique a decision or sacrifice: Judge all these men and women with compassion and care. You were not there in 1776.

The author uses 1776 as pushback against cancel culture and intentional American historical diminishment, as a counter to those who wish to dilute or disregard the honorable sacrifices and the great strides that the Americans made. They were creating, out of the oppressive and draconian monarchies of the world, a new and fairer form of government by the people. Yes, there were flaws in America's founding, such as severely limited voting for non-white males and the reprehensible institution of slavery. But these unjust issues could not be properly addressed without, first and foremost, a stable form of republican government. The rectification of all other issues had to wait. A new nation must first crawl before it can stand and stand before it can walk. Independence from Great Britain first. To American independence! Huzzah!

Richard Melnick
March 6, 2023

ACKNOWLEDGEMENTS

Thank you, God.

Thanks to Steven Melnick; Loretta Fields; Joseph Cascio Jr.; my late sister, Christa Melnick; the late Mrs. Theresa Arenaro; Elsie Pagan; and Rosalia Palazzo.

Many thanks to:

J. Banks Smither, acquisitions editor at The History Press

Dave Nelson, an American Revolution historian, researcher, and proofreader

Karen E. Van Blarcom, for formatting, proofreading and coffee

Elizabeth Winner, proofreading and editing

The Greater Astoria Historical Society (GAHS; founded 1985) Board of Directors:

Robert Singleton (a descendant of John Hart, signer of the Declaration of Independence),

Debbie Van Cura and DeeAnne Gorman (see https://astorialic. org for GAHS)

Kevin Walsh, GAHS board member, founder of Forgotten New York (see https://forgotten-ny.com)

Matt LaRose, GAHS trustee from 2006 to 2019

Thomas Jackson (1950–2006)

Former GAHS presidents Al Ronzoni and Marie Carella

Walter Kehoe, Steve Villafane and the late Gloria Elias

Frank Carrado (1930–2019), Korean War veteran and great
friend of GAHS

George Delis, a founder, in 1977, of the early historical society

Corey Kilgannon, *New York Times*

Brian Kilmeade, *Fox News* and radio podcasts

John Batchelor, WOR 710 AM New York City radio and podcasts

Dr. Jeffrey Kroessler (1952–2023), formerly of John Jay College
in New York City

Marion Duckworth Smith of the Lent-Riker-Smith house

Vincent F. Seyfried, prolific Queens historian (1918–2012)

David Morse, American actor

Julio Fernandez, for photographs of Continental currency, U.S.
currency, commemorative coinage and maps

Erik Huber, image archivist, Queens Library Archives, Central
Library (QBPL), Jamaica, New York

Lauren Robinson, metadata and rights and reproductions
specialist, Museum of the City of New York

Nadezhda Allen, executive director (until 2019), and Kelsey Brow,
curator, (Rufus) King Manor, Jamaica, Queens, New York

Christian Poepken M.A., Hessisches Landesarchiv-Hessisches
Staatsarchiv Marburg, Deutschland (Germany)

Jacqueline Masseo, Fraunces Tavern Museum

St. Joseph's Roman Catholic Church, Astoria, New York

American Revolution Round Table of New York (see www.arrt-ny.org)

ARRTNY friends:

  Brilliant author and historian the late Tom Fleming (1927–
  2017)

  Dr. David Jacobs, ARRTNY chairman

  John Buchanan

  Jon Carriel

  Fred Cookinham

  Dr. Joanne Grasso

  Lynne Saginaw

  Chris Thuilot

  Julia Bedard

  A good number of ARRTNY members are acclaimed authors,
  historians and educators; all are, of course, American
  Revolution enthusiasts. Huzzah!

Barnet Schecter, author of *The Battle for New York* (2002)

Jeff Richman, the Green-Wood Cemetery historian
John Gallagher (1937–2002), author of *The Battle of Brooklyn, 1776* (1995)

My eight years in the United States Army and New York Army National Guard made me appreciate my great country. Let freedom ring. I salute the United States military veterans that I have known from my family:

Chester "Jack" Melnicki (1912–1968), corporal, U.S. Army, World War II

Leoluca "Louis" Cascio (1895–1979), U.S. Army, 1916

Michael Fields (1954–2017), U.S. Army

Donald F. Van Blarcom (1930–2014), sergeant, U.S. Army

Madeline Arenaro (1931–2009), U.S. Marine Corps (USMC)

Marie Arenaro (1923–2015), USMC

Luigi DeLeo (1893–1968), served in the Italian army in Libya, north Africa, 1911–16, opposing the ancient Ottoman Turks. His son, my uncle Carmine DeLeo (1926–2020), served in the U.S. Army in 1945–46 and in post–World War II occupied Japan in 1946.

Many thanks to:

Astoria, New York, Purple Heart recipients Jerry Kril; Rocco Moretto (1924–2018); Aldo Zirli (1934–2018); and Luke Gasparre (1924–2020). Catholic War Veterans of Astoria Ed Babor (d. 2021) and Tony Meloni

Gary Agopian, Juan Gil, Haimchandra Nand Kumar, Roberto Torres, George Pote Jr., Union 32 BJ SEIU

Jerome Carre, for a detailed translation of two important 1776 French maps of Hell Gate and East River

Fernando Gonzalez Alcaniz

Chris Brown

Andrew Finch

Irene Haberkorn

Gary Levine

Ryan McMahon

Robert Nachtrieb

Michael Nahon

Corey Cregar-Webster

The late Mark Von Kreuter (1962–2020)

Sally Bishop
Dr. Kevin Jovanovic
Steven Mezzio
Joseph Sforzo
Harald Stavenas
Tuesday Sondafone-Toomey
Grenville Cuyler (1938–February 1, 2020). The old Cuyler's Alley in lower Manhattan (de-mapped in 1968) was named after his ancient Dutch New York family.
Jeffrey L.A. Brown (1960–2008)
U.S. military men of note, the fathers of friends: William Murphy, John Christel, James W. Meyers, Frank Arculeo and Ralph Klepsch. God bless all these fine men who answered their country's call to serve and fight.
Corporal Robert A. Hendriks, U.S. Marines, twenty-five, the eldest son of a school friend. Corporal Hendriks was killed while serving in Afghanistan on April 8, 2019. Freedom is not free.

Thank you to a new United States Marine, my awesome grandnephew Lance Corporal Devin Perez. God bless your service to our great country.

Thank you to the American presidents during this book-writing process, Donald J. Trump and Joseph R. Biden Jr. God bless America.

And thank you to my old friends from the good town of my upbringing, Carle Place, Long Island, New York: Tom Murphy, Paul Murphy, Bob Christel, Steve Christel, Jim Meyers and Tom Arculeo.

"No easy way to be free."[1]

Chapter 1

EARLY HISTORY OF THE
FUTURE LONG ISLAND CITY

*W*estern Queens County on New York's Long Island was observed by European sailors in April 1614 when Dutch sea captain, explorer and fur trader Adriaen Block sailed north up the East River (Oost Riviere). Captain Block sailed through the treacherous Hell Gate (anglicized from Hellegat, Dutch for "bright passage"). This narrow rock- and reef-filled tidal strait was a great hindrance to sea navigation. Block and his crew sailed to the eastern end of the East River at Throgs Neck into the Long Island Sound and beyond. Block established that Long Island was just that: an island.

The East River is a tidal strait sixteen miles (fourteen nautical miles) long that connects Upper New York Bay to the Long Island Sound. The waterways surrounding the eleven-square-mile Long Island City, from south to north, are: Newtown Creek, Dutch Kills, Anable Basin, the East Channel of the East River, Hallett's Cove, Hell Gate, Pot Cove and, to the east of Lawrence Point, Luyster (Steinway) Creek, Rikers Island Channel and Bowery Bay. Beyond Rikers Island lie Flushing Bay and the eastern East River out to the Long Island Sound. The future Long Island City waterfront lay at a very strategic point along the East River, the back door to New York City.

Relevant to the Newtown of 1776, the important map on the following page shows the approximate boundaries of all the Dutch land grants, called "ground briefs," in the Dutch colony of New Netherland. The map shows a small Riker's Island, now more than four times its original size. Both

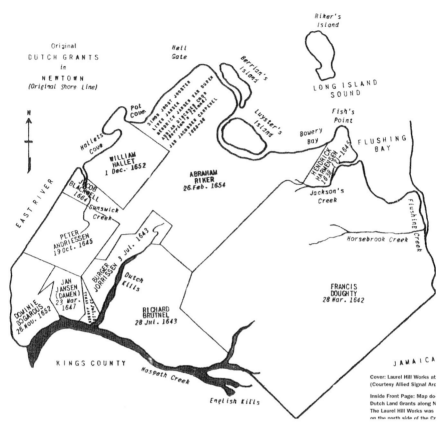

The "Original Dutch Grants in Newtown" (1638–1664) map reveals the first land purchases in western Newtown. In 1776, these grantees' descendants fought for liberty. *Public domain. Queens Borough Public Library (QBPL).*

Berrian's (Berrien's) and Luyster's Islands are now landfilled to the Queens County, Long Island "mainland."

A few families of the original land grantees made their homes here into 1776 and beyond. Hallet(t), Riker, Blackwell, Fish and Berrian all played roles as Patriots in Newtown. Many families were divided in their support of the opposing ideologies: Whig versus Tory, Patriot against Loyalist, Rebel against Royalist, family against family. Flee now, cousin, or I may have to sound the alarm.

The Province of New York (1664–1783) was an English proprietary colony and, in later years, a royal colony, and New York City was the seat of the province's government. New York was one of the original thirteen colonies in British America on the Eastern Seaboard of the North American continent. British Canada, to the north, would fight for its mother country, Great Britain. British officers, troops and weaponry would soon have to travel from England to Boston, Massachusetts, and elsewhere, over three thousand miles across the Atlantic Ocean. The average sea journey took one month; many lasted longer due to the variety of obstacles that did befall the seafarers of yore.

Place Names

The Long Island City area was part of the Maspeth Native American tribal lands. Rockaway, Matinecock and Canarsie tribes populated local lands and plied the rough waters in their tulipwood canoes. The 1630s and 1640s Dutch "Out Plantations" on Long Island along the East River gave way to the English land grants. Hallett's Cove hamlet existed from 1652 until well after the Revolution. The British county system in the Province of New York was created in 1683. Queens, Kings and Suffolk were the three counties on Long Island during the American Revolution. Bordering Queens County were Kings County to the south and west and Suffolk County to the east. Nearby, across the East River, were New York County—primarily made up of York (Manhattan) Island and its surrounding, lesser islands—and Westchester County, to the north, on the continental mainland of North America. Note that Nassau and Bronx Counties did not exist in 1776. Queens County was divided into five towns: Newtown, Flushing, Jamaica, Hempstead and Oyster Bay.

Long after the Revolution, some of the area within the town of Newtown became, in 1839, the village of Astoria. In 1870, Astoria became part of the larger, eleven-square mile Long Island City. The incorporated Long Island City lasted for twenty-eight years. Locally, the modern Long Island City is no longer an incorporated civic or political entity; it is a district name within the borough of Queens in the city of New York since it was created in 1898. The old town of Newtown existed from circa 1652 to 1898. The Newtown name is still in use for, to name a few, a high school, a subway station and a historical society.

Hallett's Cove in 1776 was a small community on the East River, in the town of Newtown, in western Queens County, on Long Island, in British New York Province. Hallett's Cove is now a section of Astoria, in Long Island City, in the borough of Queens, on Long Island, in the city of New York, in the state of New York. Got that? These 1776 names will be used to

The main gate of the 1703 Lawrence Cemetery. Along part of Old Bowery Road, the dedicated caretaker has enlightened scores of researchers, visitors and passersby since the 1960s. *R. Melnick photo.*

bring that period back into the modern historical record. Current reference points will be provided to give the reader a precise modern locale and a greater sense of place.

The historic 1703 Lawrence Cemetery along the Old Bowery Road is now on 20th Road and 35th Street in Astoria. Major Jonathan Lawrence is buried here, having served in the Long Island militia from 1775 to 1776, from exile in the New York Provincial Congress and in the New York State Senate from 1777 to 1783. Officially the Lawrence Manor Burial Ground, the graveyard received interments until 1975. The northwestern point of Long Island north of Hell Gate is Lawrence Point, and 29th Street in Astoria was formerly Lawrence Street.

Old Bowery Road ran east to west linking the East River to Bowery Bay Road, which ran north to Bowery Bay and south to Newtown Creek. Portions of the colonial and strategic Old Bowery Road still exist as 20th Road, from 46th Street, one-way traffic westbound, across Steinway Street to 31st Street. The ancient layout and interesting route are fairly nondescript, save for some fine late-1800s houses. To walk the road gives one a feeling of the former character of those olden days: the rolling hills, the slight turns in the road.

On May 1, 1707, the sovereign nation "the Kingdom of Great Britain" was established as Scotland, England and the part of the English island called Wales, unified by the Act of Union 1707. What was English in terms of national identity and possession was now British. In 1776, it was the British that were coming.

In 1718, the Alsop Family Burial Ground received its first interment. The Hallett Family Burial Ground at Main Street in Astoria received interments starting circa 1724 until 1861; the bodies have since been relocated. Both of these burial grounds would hold brave men and women of 1776.

The core center of the surviving Lent-Riker-Smith house may date from as far back as 1654. The current house was built in 1729; the plaque affixed to the grand home reads, "Landmarks of New York. Lent Homestead. This colonial Dutch farmhouse, probably built in 1729 by Abraham Lent, grandson of Abraham Riker, is one of the oldest in New York City."[2] The accessible salt waters of Bowery Bay ebb and flood behind the house. This pastoral scene has not changed much since 1776.

Three miles away, the Jacob Blackwell house along the East River was built circa 1730. The extant large Dutch door, in the learned care of the Greater Astoria Historical Society, dates from circa 1765.

The Moore-Jackson Family Burial Ground had its first interment in 1733. An old, gray, weatherworn sign attached to the border fence on 54th Street, Woodside, gives way to a new, larger sign placed inside the fence. A Captain Samuel Moore farmhouse built close by in 1684 was the home of Nathaniel Moore, a Loyalist, when Revolutionary hostilities came to Long Island in

Circa 1729. Lent-Riker-Smith house. A splendid nineteenth-century painting by William R. Miller of the extant ancient house. Jacobus Lent owned the house in Revolutionary 1776. *Courtesy Marion Duckworth Smith.*

August 1776. A different Captain Samuel Moore house stood to the north on Old Bowery Road, owned in 1776 by Patriot colonel Jeromus Remsen. Others buried in the 1733 graveyard were named Blackwell, Berrien, Fish, Rapelye and Hallett; all would play roles in the Revolutionary upheaval. Augustine Moore died in 1769 and was buried here; his gloriously extant gravestone is at the far left in the photo on the facing page (see "A.M."). Some of the headstones were moved or resituated by the U.S. government's Works Progress Administration in 1936.

The Moore-Jackson Cemetery, shown on the facing page, is in Woodside, just outside of this book's Long Island City parameters. 51st Street in Woodside runs along the line of Bowery Bay Road for a short stretch, an important strategic military sector in the local history of western Newtown. The fragile gravestones survived near disaster as many trees were felled during Superstorm Sandy in late October 2012. Thick fallen trees lay but inches from the existing, fully intact stones, exposing the fragile nature of old cemeteries. The cemetery grounds are neatly and effectively cared for by the Queens Historical Society and smart neighborhood stewardship. In 1776, there was to be major activity at this Nathaniel Moore house.

America was founded and built on faith in God. The St. James Church in Newtown, today at 86-02 Broadway in Elmhurst, was erected in 1735.

1733. Moore-Jackson Cemetery. When it was a Tory property during the Revolutionary War, the buried predecessors of house occupant Nathaniel Moore were more likely to be respected than trod on. *R. Melnick photo.*

Established in 1704, this house of worship is now a Church of England mission church. The Anglican Church, then synonymous with the Church of England, was and is of the Episcopal polity. Based on their interpretation of the Bible and the word of God, Anglicans differed from the independence-leaning Presbyterians, as these two factions of Christianity played subtle, if not major, roles in the Revolution.

In 1745–46, the Jacobite Rebellion occurred, the last rebellion on the British Isles. History has proven that the British look back to Culloden Moor, in Scotland, where the final battle took place. This event gives one historical perspective. "King George II, bound by the Rule of Law, repulsed the Scots and Bonnie Prince Charlie" and their one final armed attempt at gaining Scottish independence from England, from Great Britain. The Scottish rebellion was crushed, and Great Britain remained intact. As for having to confront and stop the American rebellion, "King George III knew this. He had to crush the insurrection."[3] King George III decided to heed the warnings of 1746 and attempted to forcefully suppress the American rebellion.

The "Old" St. James Episcopal Church was built in 1735. It is one of a very few Revolutionary War–era structures still intact in the former town of Newtown. *Donna M. Van Blarcom photo.*

Ferry service was established from Hallett's Cove crossing the East River to Horn's Hook on York (Manhattan) Island in 1753. On the Queens County side, ferry landings were either at the southwestern edge of the Astoria peninsula or in the calmer and less turbulent Hallett's Cove.

THE SEVEN YEARS' WAR (1756–63) between France and Great Britain is referred to as the French and Indian War (1754–63) to help define its North American activities. Many American and British soldiers of the Revolutionary War, including George Washington, Jacob Blackwell and William Howe, honed their leadership skills, earned their stripes and saw battle and death in the French and Indian War. King George III came to power in 1760. The great British victory over the French in 1763 won access to a continent but at a heavy price, which would be borne on colonial shoulders over the next twelve years. Local Newtown, Queens County veterans of the war were Colonel Blackwell and Colonel Jeromus Remsen, both of whom commanded local militia regiments. The Treaty of Paris of 1763 officially ended the French and Indian War. France surrendered its terrestrial possessions in North America to Great Britain and Spain. Britain was assured of regional colonial and maritime supremacy. On September 1, 1764, the British Parliament passed the Currency Act, which prevented the colonies from issuing paper money. Commerce in Newtown would be greatly affected. This, paired with the Sugar Act, angered colonists, who began to protest. The British were monetarily strapped by the great expenses and excesses of the late war with France. The king and Parliament began to disproportionately tax Britain's North American colonies, causing consternation and upheaval.

In 1765, Francis Lewis, a Welshman in British America and once a prisoner of war carried to France, purchased a handsome estate and moved his family to Whitestone, Queens County, Long Island.

The American Revolution Round Table of New York (ARRTNY) in 2015 reenacted the Stamp Act protests of November 1765. The 250th anniversary of this historically important battle of wills and loyalties had scholars, authors, educators and learned enthusiasts speak on the subject. The author has been an ARRTNY member, in good standing, since 2014. The protest took place at the Bowling Green, a park at the bottom of Broadway, north of the old fort site in 1765. The controversial Stamp Act placed duties payable to the British Crown on fifty-five types of documents. On November 1, 1765, the Stamp Act went into effect, and this British act of Parliament may have tipped the scales irreversibly toward rebellion. The prohibitive and punitive economic laws deeply affected Newtowners as well. "No taxation without representation" became a rallying cry. Other acts by the British Parliament that stirred the ire of American colonists were the 1765 Quartering Act, the 1766 Declaratory Act and the 1767 Townshend Acts.

The famous song "Yankee Doodle" was written in 1765.

Dr. Richard Shuckburg took an English ditty and improvised nonsense lyrics "Yankee"—Indian [Native American] for "English," and "doodle"—a collapse of "do little," to taunt colonial troops during the French and Indian War. British soldiers embraced the mockery, deriding colonists even on Sunday by standing outside church windows and out-singing the hymns.[4]

This well-known song would be sung loudly in western Newtown and all of Queens County, and we will revisit it in January 1776.

ON MARCH 5, 1770, agitated and surrounded British soldiers fired muskets into a rough Boston, Massachusetts crowd, killing five, in an incident Patriots termed the "Boston Massacre." This event was very important at the time and resonated strongly with most Whigs and Patriots. To combat the Tea Act, American colonists staged the Boston Tea Party on December 16, 1773, confiscating and throwing British tea into Boston Harbor. The colonists did not want to pay taxes to the British king and government if they were not represented in the British Parliament. The popular rallying cry of "no taxation without representation" became louder. A participant in the Tea Party and, later, a leader of Continental artillery was Ebenezer Stevens of Massachusetts. He wrote of his recollections of the Boston Tea Party, which many historians believe to be accurate. Colonel, later General, Stevens would, some years after the war, reside in Hallett's Cove.

The eleven-square-mile area of Long Island City is composed of distinct sections. The names of the places have changed through three languages and four nations: Lenape, the Native American language; Dutch from the Netherlands; English from England/Great Britain; and English in the United States. In 1776, these names included Hallett's Cove, Bowery Bay and Dutch Kills, all in the western portion of the town of Newtown, in western Queens County on Long Island in the British Province of New York.

Chapter 2

1774–1775

From Rebellion to War

*I*n the British North American colonies, the year 1774 began under the audacity of the recent December 16, 1773 Boston Tea Party. A revolutionary fervor began to strike the iron hot in wintry New England. The steam of cooling metals for muskets and swords did not cloud the spectacles and minds of the continent's greatest thinkers.

Men of means saw that bold words must result in greater actions. These British subjects, soon to be the first Americans, were also skilled doers in their respective colonial fields, the various trades that provided sustenance to the colonists. They were learned men, men of letters and scholarship. Those seeking liberty were also working men, ordinary men, some not formally educated and some on the lower rungs of society but all highly motivated. Many of the men in the city of New York worked very hard to achieve their place in the colony. Newtown residents in Queens County were no exception. Many Newtowners served the needs of the Crown in a variety of capacities. The question that many would soon have to answer was: Would the British North American colonies revolt against their mother country? Had Mother Britain not taken the greatest care to provide her subjects with land, opportunity and safety?

The year 1774 was the beginning of the final phase of misunderstandings between the king and his American subjects. The colonists were to unite and agitate for drastic change. The king's options to counter insurrection were few. Negotiation was a poor option. Continued punitive economic acts and measures might not work. The next option was to use force to defeat the impending revolt. Remember the Jacobites at Culloden. The revolutionaries must be crushed. From March through June 1774, Great Britain passed punitive laws, the Coercive Acts, to respond to the defiant Boston Tea Party. These Coercive Acts by the British Parliament were referred to as the Intolerable Acts by the subject American colonists. Queens County men and their wives were set to take sides in the heated political discussion. Important to local Newtown politics was that "the rumblings of the Revolution were beginning to be felt. Colonel Jeromus Remsen was accordingly placed at the head of the Town." On April 5, 1774, at a public town meeting, the town leaders "also voted that Jeromus Remsen Junr. shall be Supervisor."[5]

More protests ensued, as did the calling for and formulation of the First Continental Congress, which was to convene in Philadelphia, Pennsylvania, at a later date. New England was not the only hotbed for treasonous thinking. Some in New York City and Long Island were having thoughts and meetings concerning opposition to the Crown's crippling policies. Noteworthy is the June 21, 1774 Huntington Declaration of Rights. Huntington, on Long Island, was to the east across the old Queens County border, in Suffolk County. As in all cases involving the rebellion, words would have to be followed by action. These activities caught the eyes of Newtowners who began to lean toward advocating for anti-governmental measures. On hearing of the Huntington declaration, many Newtowners had their passions on the subject roused.

On September 5, 1774, fifty-six delegates from all of the thirteen colonies (except Georgia) met in Philadelphia to convene the First Continental Congress. There the delegates debated, opposed and then formulated their petition against the Intolerable Acts and issued the Declaration of Resolves on October 14, 1774. The delegates from the Province of New York to the 1774 Continental Congress were Isaac Low, John Alsop, John Jay, Philip Livingston, James Duane, William Floyd, Henry Wisner, John Haring and Simon Boerum. John Alsop of New York City and of the Newtown, Queens Alsop family, was a delegate to the congress in 1774. Some of these names live on in local New York and Long Island history.

On December 10, 1774, an important document (facing page) was created to establish lines of communication in the province. The improvement of clandestine communications between the American colonies was necessary. Unguarded conversation could lead to charges of treason. According to the document, by "the Spirited and well adapted resolves," the gentlemen would form committees of correspondence in New York Province and strictly follow the laws and orders put forth by the Continental Congress.

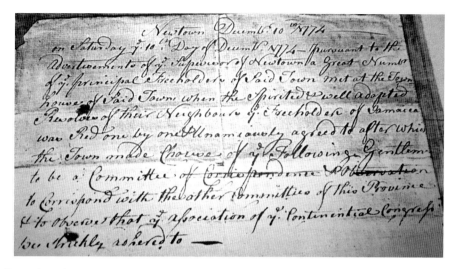

December 10, 1774 document. Significant events include Jacob Blackwell attending the December 10, 1774 meeting in Newtown to create a "Committee of Correspondence." *Public domain. Courtesy Greater Astoria Historical Society (GAHS).*

Seventeen men were elected to correspond in the name of Newtown for the cause of liberty. These were the major Newtown men involved in this enterprise:

> *Jacob Blackwell, Jonathan Lawrence, John Albertis, Richard Alsop, Esq., Samuel Moore, Abm. Brinckerhoff, Daniel Rapalje, Esq., William Furman, James Way, Philip Edsall, William Howard, Samuel Morrell, Thomas Lawrence, Jeromus Remsen, jr.; Jonathan Coe, Daniel Lawrence, Samuel Riker,*
> *This Committee did not meet till December 29th, (owing to the small-pox in Col. Blackwell's family,)*
> *Signed by order of the Committee, JACOB BLACKWELL, Chairman.*[6]

Most of the seventeen Patriots faced the utmost difficulties. There was, of course, opposition to the Patriot cause by the Tories and Loyalists and people wanting British protection. Silence could not remain neutral. The local Loyalists were against these resolves put forth by the Newtown freeholders. Within six months, they would object to the newly formed Whig New York Provincial Congress.

The author suggests that if one was disinclined to choose a side in the imminent armed struggle, one would flock to whomever was in power at that time. To clarify, an ardent supporter of one side may become much less enthused about the cause when an opposing force is marching down their road toward their home, possessions and family. The winds of political integrity will soon carry the smell of gunpowder.

Regardless of a Newtowner's stance on the question of independency or their allegiance to their king, strong grievances with the Crown did exist. How they were to be addressed was soon to be answered. How to obtain redress, and the proper and lawful means to do so, was paramount to any questioning of the British king's authority. To cross a strong monarch and his faithful military leaders might mean dismissal or imprisonment. As is common, the weaker party disapproved of the contrarian assembled committees and congresses. Tories refused to honor any laws against the king put forth by the illegal rebel congress.

> But a majority scouted such moderation, and no sooner had the resolutions of Congress been received at Newtown than these hastened, at the call of their supervisor, Jeromus Remsen jr., to adopt their recommendations. A large number assembled at the town-house, and seventeen persons were appointed to act as a committee of correspondence, and to see that the association formed by Congress be strictly adhered to within the limits of the town.[7]

With a Tory majority in nearly all of Queens County, the courageous yet outnumbered Newtown Patriots could not sell their cause to most of the population.

> Although meeting with much opposition the friends of liberty in Newtown responded to a call of the New York committee, inviting them to send a representative to a convention to be held in that city for the purpose of choosing delegates to a second general Congress.[8]

The competition for the hearts and minds of men and women was in full force. The issue could not leave one noncommittal. A man could speak treason in the company of like-minded others. Spies among them might be quick to reveal their perceived treachery. When the object of treasonous and slanderous activities decides to send an army into your town, talk becomes cheap. Newtown and Queens County Loyalists, as would be expected, were very much against the election of deputies for a Continental Congress. Being loyal to the British Crown, the Royalists/Loyalists/Tories issued a paper, the *Queens County Freeholder*, which stated strong arguments against any portion of loyalty to a rebel congress. The local Queens Whigs, in a strong attempt to counter the Loyalist publication, presented an appeal to the Loyalist freeholders of Newtown. This plan did not work. Queens County, as a whole, voted against sending deputies to the Continental Congress by a measure of three to one. In Newtown, the Whigs prevailed, but their efforts were foiled by the majority vote against deputies by Queens County. Of importance to Newtown and to the future Long Island City, seven prominent Loyalist inhabitants were Nathaniel Moore, John Moore Sr. and John Moore Jr., Captain Samuel Hallett, William Weyman, John Shoals and Captain Jeromus Rapelje.

The Patriot Newtown militia consisted of two beats, units of a company size of roughly 100 men: the North Beat and the South Beat. The North Beat, consisting of 107 men, was formed under Captain Jonathan Lawrence, and the South Beat was placed under the command of Captain Abraham Remsen and had 86 men. The Remsen family served the American cause very well. The majority of Newtown Remsens hailed from Whitepot, now a part of Forest Hills.

The Lawrence family of western Newtown served the cause of liberty in many capacities. Captain Richard Lawrence commanded forty-four men in a Newtown troop of light horse, later commanded by his brother, Captain Daniel Lawrence. Light horsemen were lightly armed cavalrymen, carrying swords and a pistol or two or a musket, who were made to move quickly to skirmish or to convey information from house to house, town to town. Light horsemen, or dragoons, whether British or American, could cover ground more quickly than any other combatants of the time and were able to track down fleeing troops or disrupt infantry forming for battle.

John Alsop (1724–1794) served in the New York delegation to the Continental Congress. British boots stomped the wooden floors of the captured Alsop houses. *Public domain. Max Rosenthal, lithographer. Date unknown.*

Other members of this light horse troop were Samuel Riker as second lieutenant, Jonathan Coe as cornet and Peter Rapelje as quartermaster. All the above names were those of prominent western Newtown people, where members of some families, such as the Rapeljes, overwhelmingly served the British cause of empire and king.

In 1643, the Alsops began farming in Newtown, and their Protestant Alsop family burial ground has been extant since 1718. John Alsop (1724–1794) had a home in western Newtown, and his successful mercantile business was located on York Island (Manhattan). His roots in our area of study make this prominent citizen and Patriot most worthy of our attention. John Alsop's spouse was Mary Frogat Alsop; their issue was one daughter, Mary Alsop (1769–1819), who is mentioned later in this book. In 1774, John Alsop was elected to represent New York Province as a delegate to the First Continental Congress in Philadelphia, from September to October 1774. His service with that august body continued into 1776.

1775

A letter of January 12, 1775, from Newtown, presented to the ruling British authorities fierce opposition to the resolves put forth by the Whigs, whose allegiance was to the Continental Congress. The local Loyalists wrote:

> *We, the subscribers, were no way concerned in certain resolves signed by Jacob Blackwell, Chairman, entered into by some inhabitants of Newtown, approving the proceedings of the Continental Congress; neither do we acknowledge any other representatives but the General Assembly of the Province. Signed by 58 persons.*[9]

Nathaniel Moore was a Loyalist during the American Revolution. Placing an advertisement in the widely circulated *Rivington's Gazette*, a Tory New York newspaper, Moore and other Newtowners disapproved of any instructions and actions put forth by the rebel Continental Congress.

Often, in rebellious times, the name of one man being similar to that of another may implicate the former as being a part of a perceived wrongdoing when that person is innocent. The clearing of one's name after the negative association is often difficult, as others may be quick to impugn future statements from the wrongly accused. Guilt by mere accusation was often enough to tarnish a reputation or destroy a business. One man petitioned Congress "to be restored to the good opinion of the friends of Liberty." In order to get his name removed from the "List of Delinquents" in Queens County, published in New York newspapers, and not to be considered "an enemy of his country," one Mr. Suydam submitted this petition to Congress for reinstatement. This letter was signed: "Hendrick Suydam, Miller, living at

JOSEPH HALLETT

Along with Colonel Jacob Blackwell, Joseph Hallett was a strong local Newtown Patriot. His family home and property at Hallett's Cove would suffer under British military might. *Public domain. Register of the Society of Sons of the Revolution, Connecticut, 1896.*

Newtown, L.I."[10] This gentleman ran the tidal gristmill on the Sunswick Creek at Hallett's Cove; during the Revolutionary War, it was called Suydam's Mill.

Joseph Hallett III was born in the family home on January 26, 1731, at Hallett's Cove, part of the town of Newtown. The old house stood on the grounds that are now the Hallets Cove Playground. His father, Joseph Hallett II, married Lydia Alsop of the eminent Newtown Alsop family. Joseph III is known to have started the gristmill at Sunswick Creek with Jacob Blackwell and Nathaniel Hazard in the 1750s. Elizabeth Hazard Hallett (1743–1814) of the equally prominent Hazard clan was Joseph's wife. Joseph Hallett, a shipping merchant and land investor, had a main residence on Pearl Street in New York City, but his country home was at Hallett's Cove. Joseph III "maintained a home at Hallet's Point, where he inherited an estate from his Grandfather, Joseph (1678–1750). His father, also named Joseph (1704–1731), died of smallpox at age 27 when Joseph was an infant."[11]

Joseph III, a strong Patriot, served the New York Provincial Congress on the Committee of Safety (1774–76) and was a member of the New York Committee of One Hundred, which formed on May 1, 1775. Hallett served his new nation as a deputy to the First, Second and Third New York Provincial Congresses, 1775–76. "His name is associated with the most zealous patriots in support of the War for Independence."[12] Hallett was also a trustee in the Presbyterian Church on Wall Street in New York City and was buried there on his death.

The Grand Union flag was used in 1776 and 1777 as an ensign and as a garrison flag. It is believed to be the first flag flown by American Continental forces, in Massachusetts, on January 1, 1776.

This flag is considered the first unofficial American Flag because it was never sanctioned by Congress....It seems likely that this flag shows the duality of American Independence and continued allegiance to the Crown.[13]

29

The Grand Union flag is considered to be the first national flag, adopted in December 1775. It flew proudly, and some Grand Union flags were captured at the Battle of Long Island. *Fraunces Tavern Museum flag, R. Melnick photo.*

One might wonder why the Americans would raise a flag containing the British Union Jack in its canton (upper corner), when the former was attempting to become independent from the latter.

> *It expressed the thought of the times and the political situation in the colonies, which at that time still acknowledged their allegiance to Great Britain.* [The] *idea was to show* [a] *sign of colonial allegiance to the crown while maintaining the rights of the United Colonies.*[14]

This flag was later carried proudly into battle by Continental army troops in August 1776. Other great American flags would soon be flown and followed by highly motivated and sufficiently armed men seeking to live free.

Revolutionary ideas turned into armed conflict on April 19, 1775. As Massachusetts Minutemen and the British redcoats stood well armed across from each other on the open Lexington Green, no one is really sure whose musket fired the first shot. Later that day, six miles down the road in Concord, local militiamen, in a composed and orderly fashion, acting under orders to protect their town from British regulars, fired "the shot heard 'round the world." And so began an armed revolution.

Drawn up in the committee chamber in New York on April 26, 1775, the document below lists numerous Queens citizens as well as other prominent New Yorkers. Many here helped promote rebellion, such as Philip Livingston, John Jay, Alexander McDougall, John Lasher and Hercules Mulligan. Note that the old British *s* here looks like an *f*, as is seen in "Alsop," "Livingston," "Remsen," et al. These men served the political, military or espionage side of the effort to shed the yoke of British tyranny and to found a new republic.

An April 26, 1775 document contained the local names of Alsop, Hallett, Lewis and Berrien, Queens County citizens friendly to the cause of liberty. *Public domain. Library of Congress, courtesy PICRYL.*

On May 10, 1775, the Second Continental Congress convened in Philadelphia for its opening meeting. Local Queens delegates attending were John Alsop and Francis Lewis, both of whom had homes and offices in New York City on lower York Island.

The First Provincial Congress, convened in New York City, pledged obedience to the Continental Congress on May 22, 1775. Although representing the city and county of New York, the Queens County and Hallett's Cove resident Joseph Hallett served in this august body. Other delegates with secondary links to western Newtown were John Morin Scott and John Sloss Hobart. The Continental army was created by the Second Continental Congress on June 14, 1775. For "purposes of common defense," this force would soon become the American or the United States Army. Huzzah! The next day, June 15, 1775, Colonel George Washington of Virginia was appointed commander in chief of the Continental army, becoming General Washington.

On June 17, 1775, British forces, in a Pyrrhic victory, captured the Charlestown peninsula at the Battle of Bunker Hill outside of Boston, in the colony of Massachusetts Bay. One distinguished American soldier depicted in the painting below is Major General Israel Putnam (far left), who would

The Death of General Warren at the Battle of Bunker's Hill, June 17, 1775, by John Trumbull. Three British officers portrayed here would be in Newtown in 1776. *Public domain. Museum of Fine Arts, Boston.*

play a future role on western Long Island in 1776. British lieutenant general William Howe (top, center), in the hat, wields a sword; to the right is Lieutenant General Henry Clinton, without a hat and with his sword raised high, and Lieutenant Lord Rawdon, holding the large British ensign (flag). These British leaders would be coming to Newtown and Queens County in 1776.

General John Burgoyne, referring to the conspicuous courage of Francis, Lord Rawdon (1754–1826), during the action at Bunker Hill, commented, "Lord Rawdon has this day stamped his fame for life."[15] Bunker Hill weighed heavily on the mind of one of its highest-ranking participants, Lieutenant General Howe. This British victory would greatly affect his decisions fourteen months later at New York.

In 1775, Samuel Moore III, Jacob Rapelye, George Brinckerhoff, Jonathan Lawrence, Samuel Riker and Dow van Dine were all local Newtown municipal officers and overseers. "These were fiery spirits, either for or against the Revolution."[16] The hostilities had begun in April and June 1775. An American declaration of independence from Great Britain was a year away.[17]

General George Washington assumed command of his Continental army on July 3, 1775. Two days later, the Second Continental Congress issued its Olive Branch Petition offering America's loyalty to Great Britain.

However, the petition was rejected by King George III, as he authorized officials of the British Empire "to use their utmost Endeavors to withstand and suppress such Rebellion."[18] The king would soon prove that he was deadly serious about crushing the insurrection. On August 23, 1775, King George III issued a Proclamation of Rebellion declaring the American colonists as traitors against his absolute authority over them.

Of the forty-eight colonial signers, the "New-York" delegates who signed the Olive Branch Petition were Philip Livingston, James Duane, John Alsop, Francis Lewis, John Jay, Robert Livingston Jr., Lewis Morris, William Floyd and Henry Wisner. John Alsop and his relatives, including a Richard Alsop, lived at or visited the Alsop family homestead near Newtown Creek. Francis Lewis resided at his estate in nearby Whitestone, part of the neighboring town of Flushing. The above would have more parchment to sign.

A local college law student and friend of Alexander Hamilton, Nicholas Fish became an officer in Malcom's New York Regiment, a state militia unit, first as a lieutenant and then as a captain. This was prior to the recent conflagration in Massachusetts. Acting on recent 1775 events, "at the commencement of hostilities between this country and Great Britain,

Nicholas Fish [resigned his militia service and] entered the American service with the commission of major."[19] Local Patriot Nicholas Fish was now a major in the Continental army.

As 1775 plodded on, the Continental (later U.S.) navy was founded on October 13. American ships would be built outside the British lines, along the entire Eastern Seaboard, from New Hampshire to Georgia. A member of the local Lawrence family would soon serve ably aboard a Continental navy warship.

Important to the chronology of 1775 events is that all Queens County delegates voted at Jamaica, Long Island, on November 7, 1775. The question of whether to actively oppose the Crown or not was at stake. The Patriot and Whig cause of liberty was voted down three to one. The Tories would have their way, for now.

The Continental (later U.S.) marines were established on November 10, 1775. By November 1775, the town of Newtown from the Flushing and Jamaica lines to the East River was about to become immersed in the warming cauldron of armed revolution.

A Patriot company commander from Suffolk County, William Williams, was sent to Queens County to enforce the laws of the Continental Congress and to confiscate Loyalist weapons. After a few days, he gave up and reported to the Provincial Congress:

> *The people conceal all their arms that are of any value; many declare that they know nothing about the Congress, nor do they care anything for the orders of Congress, and say they would sooner lose their lives than give up their arms; and that they would blow any man's brains out that should attempt to take them.*[20]

Queens County's support of the British king, based on the tenor of this quotation, was quite evident.

In December 1775, Queens County did not elect to send any delegates or deputies to the convention of the colony of New York, the Whig Provincial Congress. Queens County remained unrepresented in the provincial congress then meeting in New York City and was deemed to be in open contempt of the authority of the congress of New York and of the Continental Congress in Philadelphia. According to Joseph Tiedemann,

In Queens County on Long Island, in the critical years of 1775 and 1776, the Whigs never succeeded in discrediting royal authority or establishing the legitimacy of their own extralegal political institutions. As a result, Patriots from outside the county felt compelled to attempt subduing the area by force.[21]

The winter encampment of Continental army troops at Cambridge and the siege of Boston, Massachusetts, occurred from December 1775 to April 1776. Besides Massachusetts men, newly established Continental army units and outside militia served at Cambridge. The last day, December 31, of a tumultuous year, 1775, witnessed the death of American general Richard Montgomery in battle at Quebec, British Canada. A Captain Abraham Riker from Newtown fought at Quebec during the invasion of Canada and was present during the death of General Montgomery.

TERMS

American Revolution (1765–89/1801) versus Revolutionary War (1775–1783)

The notable Revolutionary scholar and New York City tour guide Fred Cookinham of the American Revolution Round Table of New York helps us to distinctly define the two different terms "American Revolution" and the "Revolutionary War."

The term "American Revolution" [can be a definition] for the whole era, or process, of the breakdown of royal power and the setting up of the new Constitution and federal government, and state constitutions and governments, of the United States. The word "revolution" means "one full turn." The Stamp Act Crisis of 1765 marks the first major crack in American loyalty to the Crown. The ratification of the new [U.S.] Constitution in 1788 might be considered the fulfillment of the process of revolution, but I like to think of 1801, and the inauguration of Thomas Jefferson as U.S. president, as the completion of the "one full turn." That marked a peaceful transition of power not only from one president to another, as Washington to Adams in 1797, but from one party to another: from the Federalist Party [of John Adams] to the Democratic-Republican Party [of Jefferson]. This was the final proof of the stability of the new system, so it completed the turn from a stable royal system to a new stable system of republican government.[22]

It is common to use the term "Revolutionary War" for the period of organized fighting between the Battles of Lexington and Concord, Massachusetts, on April 19, 1775, and the October 19, 1781 British defeat at Yorktown, Virginia. The term "Revolutionary War" may hereby extend not to the Treaty of Paris on September 3, 1783, but to the actual British departure from New York, on Evacuation Day, November 25, 1783. That would conclude the war by having the last of the British regular army and all the evacuating Loyalists out of New York, for good. The British were gone. The war was won.

> *But I would use the term "War for Independence" for that portion of the war after independence was declared on July 4, 1776. At that point it became a war of one nation against another nation, even though one of those nations did not yet recognize the existence of the other.*[23]

Massachusetts Continental Congressman, Founding Father and future second U.S. president John Adams helps to clarify the issue:

> *The Revolution was effected before the War commenced. The Revolution was in the minds and hearts of the people; a change in their religious sentiments of their duties and obligations.…This radical change in the principles, opinions, sentiments, and affections of the people, was the real American Revolution.*[24]

The Enemies/Opposing Forces

Political and ideological forces clash before guns crack and soldiers smash.

Those seeking independence from British rule in British North America were called the Whigs, Patriots, revolutionaries, rebels, Damned Rebels, Continentals, Colonials, Yankees, Presbyterians, American Whigs, insignificant provincials, rabble. The colonial provincial, then state, militias unified and became the Continental army, serving the United Colonies before they declared on July 4, 1776, that they were to become the United States of America.

Of lexiconic interest is the terminology used by one force to discredit the other's person and cause. King George III's response to the 1775 Olive Branch Petition referred to the rebellious colonials as "the unhappy and deluded multitude," in addition to other terms. His proclamation, received by and read in front of the Continental Congress on October 26, 1775, confirmed the king's ambition to suppress such rebellion. "For those who persist in this treason," it read, referring to, primarily, the signers of the Olive Branch Petition and the military men who had brought arms against the British Empire.[25]

VERSUS

The British colonists in America that supported the British monarch and empire were the Tories, Loyalists, Royalists, Episcopalians and the British colonial citizens loyal to their king. The officers and soldiers were known as the King's Men, the Regulars, Redcoats, Lobsters, Lobster Backs, Bloody Backs or the King's Troop. The term "disaffected" referred to the population that was currently on the losing side of the political and military situation in that region. The Loyalist mission was clear: to help the British defeat the American rebels and restore all thirteen colonies back to the complete peaceful control of the British Empire. Their belief was strong that the Crown Colony of New York should and would remain so.

Western Queens County, in 1776, had hamlets and settlements named Hallett's Cove, Hell Gate Neck, Lawrence Point, Bowery Bay, Middletown (this name was not in full use until 1800), Dutch Kills and Hunter's Point. The maps presented in this book will reveal the Long Island City names of 1776.

The New York Provincial Congress (1775–77) was a pro-American body, an alternative to the conservative Royalist New York Assembly. During this time, a number of Queens and Newtown Whigs were members of the provincial congress, which would include Joseph Hallett, John Alsop, Jonathan Lawrence and the most influential Queens County resident, Francis Lewis.

Of great importance was the military mission of Colonel Nathaniel Heard. His New Jersey militia was sent to Queens County to obey the following orders, issued in November 1775 by the Continental Congress in Philadelphia: to "take with him five or six hundred Minute Men, under discreet officers, and three companies of Regulars from Lord Sterling, and disarm every person in Queens county who voted against sending Deputies" and to confiscate their arms and to offer them oaths of loyalty.[26] If anyone refused compliance, they would be arrested. Heard's goal was to arrest the twenty-six most prominent Tories "as principal men among the disaffected."[27] This harsh order concluded that any such persons who voted against deputies, anyone not a friend to the American cause, would be denied all rights within the United Colonies. In addition to travel restrictions, the order stipulated that all Tories loyal to the king shall "be put out of the protection of the United Colonies, and that all trade and intercourse with them cease."[28]

Definitions aside, the struggle was real; what was to come was as real as your blood on your hand. The rebellious colonists were from every echelon of American society, from the highly educated Continental Congress to the lowest tier of citizen or personage, the undereducated, nonlandowning, working-class enlisted soldier.

Chapter 3

January–June 1776

Prelude to Action

*I*deas from the wise must be clarified and codified by written words. Written words inform and inflame, enlighten and inspire and enrage. The printed word gets around. This is where words must lead to action. Verbal sparring skills cannot stop slashing swords and musket balls. On January 1, 1776, the Continental army was reorganized in accordance with a congressional resolution that placed American forces under George Washington. On that New Year's Day, the Continental army was laying siege to Boston, which had been occupied by the British army since 1768. The British colonial governor of the Province of New York in 1776 was William Tryon (1729–1788), who had served as governor from 1771 to 1774 and again from 1775 to 1780.

The painting on the following page represents the magnitude of what King George III and the British had brought to these rebellious American shores. The historic and meaningful symbols of great power abound. The might, range and supremacy of the British Royal Navy were well known. Shown are the king and his crown, his army officers on horseback, his feared grenadiers, encampment tents and Royal Navy ships of the line, all on their way to America. British naval dominance over eastern North America and the north Atlantic Ocean was undeniable.

Here we enter the pivotal year of 1776, when great American minds were to create a document and a new American army tried to defend its position in New York. Kings and Queens Counties were mostly Tory yet home to not a few ardent Patriots, who will be discussed going forward. Forces were mustering, ideas were being put forth and decisions had to be made. Where do you stand on the question of independency?

King George III painted by Benjamin West in 1779. The British war machine, king, army and navy, is represented well. Parallels to 1776 are many. *Public domain. Courtesy Royal Collection Trust, www.rct.uk.*

Very noteworthy in this revolutionary trek, on January 10, 1776, the pamphlet *Common Sense* was published. Thomas Paine's work impressed and inspired many to fight for independence from British rule.

Colonel Nathaniel Heard (1730–1792) was a leading Woodbridge, New Jersey Patriot during the Revolutionary War. In January 1776, Colonel Heard and his New Jersey militia were "ordered by the Continental Congress to march to Long Island to disarm and arrest Tories."[29] He was sent at the request of the New York Provincial Congress because there were not enough rebellious New Yorkers to muster to do this difficult job.

On January 19, 1776, six hundred New Jersey militia led by Colonel Heard crossed the North (Hudson) River to New York Island. At Horn's Hook (now Gracie Point), they crossed the East River on the Hell Gate ferry from (New) York Island (Manhattan) to Hallett's Cove, near the northwestern edge of Long Island. This militia force was strengthened by three hundred Continental army troops from Lord Stirling's brigade.

Colonel Heard was ordered to scour Newtown and the rest of Queens County, take possession of Loyalist firearms, gunpowder and swords and arrest the prominent Tories. The officers rode horses and the soldiers marched through from the hamlet of Hallett's Cove to Middletown (now eastern Astoria) to the town seat of Newtown (now Elmhurst), on existing colonial farm roads; some of these road patterns are in use today. This force pressed inland to Long Island points farther east.

The military authority of Colonel Heard's Patriot militia made Tory resistance impossible. The protests of the Newtown disaffected could not prevent their arrest and removal to Philadelphia. Local Tory Nathaniel Moore "was one of four Newtowners arrested and taken before the Second Continental Congress in Philadelphia for aiding in the smuggling and stockpiling of arms to be used against the supporters of the United Colonies."[30]

Colonel Nathaniel Heard of the New Jersey militia. He rode into Hallett's Cove via the Hell Gate ferry in January 1776 to scour Queens County to arrest Tories. *Courtesy Woodbridge Township Historic Preservation Commission, General Nathaniel Heard marker.*

Nineteen dedicated Queens County Tories were arrested and examined by the Continental Congress, which turned them over to the New York Provincial Congress, which paroled them back to their Queens County homes.

Transgressions of troop discipline did occur. To be fair, when one party, force or army commands a town, there are bound to be ill-affected inhabitants who are on the minority side of the conflict. If Loyalists were not seized and imprisoned, as in the case of Newtown, Queens, some may have been treated roughly, been verbally abused or had money extracted from them. In order to curry favor with the ruling force, a subjugated person may pay for good treatment by providing goods, monies and information to those in charge. In many cases, in accordance with the madness of war, a fine line separated the disciplined soldier from the marauder. "Before the British soldiers occupied the area, poorly disciplined Continental militiamen frequently harassed local Tories and took their property."[31]

Colonel Heard's Patriot force confiscated nearly one thousand muskets and a small number of Long Island Loyalist militia colors. In all, 641 people, whether voluntarily or coerced, swore allegiance to the Continental Congress. Regarding Colonel Heard's three hundred Continental troops from Stirling's brigade, attached to his own six-hundred-strong New Jersey militia, it has been said that "the party of Continental troops behaved in so disorderly a manner that he was obliged to dismiss them."[32] One of Colonel Heard's officers offered a counterstatement—or, in his words, the reason for sending the Continental troops home was that "Col. Heard sent the battalion home last Tuesday, as he thought the militia sufficient."[33] A reader can only ponder what the freshly loosed and unruly Continental soldiers of Stirling's contingent could have wrought on Hallett's Cove and the Hell Gate ferry on their way back to New York Island. Soldiers with no enemy in sight will sometimes lose their focus and forget they are to always conduct themselves in a disciplined manner. Easier said than done. The officer went on to commend the colonel by saying Colonel Heard "is indefatigable, treats the inhabitants with civility and the utmost humanity."[34] The disarmed Loyalists of Queens County in January 1776 were "the disaffected." New York Tories who disobeyed the call of the Continental Congress were dispossessed of their land and belongings in the lead-up to August 1776.

A song of national importance was sung derisively on local Queens County soil. Here is a "Fragment of an old Song, intended to ridicule Col. Heard." This poem, sung to the tune of "Yankee Doodle" (you may sing it), reported:

> Col. Heard has come to town, In all his pride and glory;
> And when he dies he'll go to H—l [Hell] For robbing of the Tory.

The poem/song continued,

> Col. Heard has come to town, A thinking for to plunder;
> Before he's done, he had to run—He heard the cannon thunder.[35]

These types of songs fully intended to ridicule the opposition, whether it be Whig or Tory. The songs were known to stretch or even misrepresent the truth in order to suit the whims, rhymes and agendas of the writers. Poetic and pointed political whimsy quickly gave way to the fact that war was coming.

John Polhemus (1738, also 1743–1834) was from New Jersey and had extensive family from Kings and Queens Counties, New York. He was the son of Hendrick Polhemus, who came from Long Island and later settled in New Jersey. In 1770, Polhemus married Susannah Hart, a daughter of John Hart from New Jersey, a signer of the Declaration of Independence. Promoted to major, Polhemus is noteworthy because of his activities in January 1776 in Newtown, Queens. He may have been familiar with the local lands because some of his Polhemus relatives lived on properties north of Hallett's Point along the East River. Major Polhemus crossed the East River to Hallett's Cove and Queens County with Colonel Nathaniel Heard and the New Jersey militia in January 1776.

At the outbreak of the Revolution, when affairs, even to the most sanguine, wore a gloomy aspect, John Polhemus, then young and in the vigor of life and in good circumstances, deeply impressed with the importance of the crisis and the necessity of prompt action on the part of every true patriot, was among the foremost at the summons of his country to come forward and offer his services and his means.[36]

Remnants of the ancient Polhemus dock on the East River can scarcely be seen, destroyed during the dredging, excavations and construction of a deeper ship channel. Many of yesteryear's local Revolutionary stories are forever capped by the natural and unnatural detritus of the following decades and centuries.

Dispatched to New York by General Washington, Continental army lieutenant general Charles Lee reported on February 19, 1776. Lee and the available militia in New York had blocked the enemy from coming to invade New York via Hell Gate. The fort at Horn's Hook (Gracie Point), facing Hallett's Point and Hallett's Cove, was substantially fortified. One source shows fortifications and possible cannon batteries on Hallett's Point on Long Island as early as February 1776. American maps up to August 1776 do not show Patriot defensive works at Hell Gate. Also, on February 19, 1776, at their Hallett's Cove house, Joseph and Elizabeth Hallett brought their sixth child, Maria, into the world—born into a world which would soon know war.

The twisting bottleneck at Hell Gate could trap single-file British naval ships and subject them to close and destructive cannon bombardment. Likewise, a British warship could bring swift damage to a stationary land fort.

Continental army lieutenant general Charles Lee ordered Lieutenant Colonel Isaac Sears, per a letter of March 5, 1776, from Lee, that he secure the persons in Queens County who were "professed foes to American liberty" and "irreclaimable enemies to their country." Those likely to "turn openly against us in arms, in conjunction with the enemy, or covertly to furnish them with intelligence, and carry on a correspondence to the ruin of their country"[37] must be apprehended and removed to Connecticut. Sears's mission was to secure the remaining Tories in Queens County and to put the county and towns in a state of defense.

It is hard to put 1776 words—strong words describing the lead-up to war—into 2023 speech. The quoted phrases, speeches and tomes do their best to describe their current situation being that war was on its way. Of interest to Lieutenant Colonel Sears's expedition into Queens County, he wrote, on March 7, 1776, to General Lee:

Yesterday I arrived at Newtown, with a captain's company, and tendered the oath to four of the greater tories, which they swallowed as hard as if it were a 4 lb. shot they were trying to get down....I can assure your honor, there are a set of villains in this county, the better half of whom are waiting for support, and intend to take up arms. Nothing else will do but removing the ringleaders to a place of security.[38]

A four-pound shot is a small cannonball. The disaffected Loyalists were known to be hiding their best weapons and surrendering old hunting guns and ancient swords. Hostilities were imminent, even at this early March 1776 date. Sides were being taken. Something big was on the horizon. The Patriots were in charge of the town of Newtown, for now. March 17, 1776, saw the British evacuate Boston. The siege of Boston and its harbor by the American army sent the redcoats packing and very angrily so. The freshly defeated and unseated British, plus evacuated Loyalist citizens, sailed out of Boston Harbor and went to Halifax, Nova Scotia, British Canada, to repair and to plan. Although the Newtown, Queens locals were forced to take a stand for or against rebellion, actions up at Boston rerouted the revolution to the next theater of war.

New York City was the key to the whole continent. This colonial maritime center and mercantile city was the next target for capture by the British army. Long Island was key to invading New York City. The future Long Island City, strategically situated, would play a role in that invasion.

To divide the colonies at the Hudson River was the British plan. To split New England from New York and the mid-Atlantic states, Virginia and the South, was the goal. Commander in Chief William Howe and his brother Admiral Richard Howe were preparing to set loose their war machine to

Committee-Chamber, New-York, April 13th 1776.

THE following Persons of this City and County, are recommended by the General Committee of the same, as Persons worthy to serve in the ensuing Provincial Congress.

By Order of the Committee,

GARRET ABEEL, Deputy Chairman.

John Jay,	William Denning,	Evert Bancker,
Philip Livingston,	Joseph Hallet,	Thomas Randall,
John Alsop,	Abraham Brasher,	Isaac Roosevelt,
Francis Lewis,	John V. Cortland,	John Broome,
Jacobus Van Zandt,	John M. Scott,	Samuel Prince,
Comfort Sands,	James Beekman,	Peter P. Van Zandt,
Isaac Stoutenburgh,	Capt. Ant. Rutgers,	James Alner.

This April 13, 1776 document shows the names of prominent local leaders, Patriots or officeholders. John Alsop, Francis Lewis and Joseph Hallet(t) were eminent. *Public domain. Library of Congress.*

44

squash a rebellion on the North American continent. The British were planning. The British were coming.

An interesting document from April 13, 1776 (facing page), reveals that in the committee chamber meeting in New York, forty-three names were presented: "that it be recommended to the different Counties, to choose deputies, to meet deputies from all the Counties in the Province, in General Congress in this City."[39] Contained are the names of local Newtown men such as John Alsop and Joseph Hallett, who were recommended for the New York Provincial Congress, as they were men who would become major actors on the national and international stage. We will hear from the likes of Francis Lewis, Philip Livingston, John M. (Morin) Scott and John Jay in due time.

General George Washington arrived in New York City from Boston on April 13, 1776, and established his headquarters in the city on lower New York Island.

1776 was a critical year in the struggle for New York. John Alsop began the year at Philadelphia, in a session of Congress. He made several trips between there and New York, acting as an agent of congress through his business to acquire supplies, and particularly powder for the Continental Army.[40]

This circa 1905 photo displays a day gone by: a dirt road, a Dutch farmhouse and a hilly expanse. The only perceivable modern amenities are a fire hydrant and a lamppost near the road. Recorded as the Van Zandt–

The Van Zandt House, extant in 1776, was in the later-named Blissville, in Long Island City's southeastern section. Entirely built upon, the Revolutionary past here is long gone. *QBPL.*

Debevoise House, it later was known as the Old Debevoise House. The document from April 13, 1776, had signatories such as Jacobus Van Zandt and Peter P. Van Zandt. As the Van Zandts were local men of means and property, the old Dutch family's home made it onto the 1852 James Riker map, between the Dutch Kills creek and Calvary Cemetery.[41]

General George Washington, circa May 1776, as painted by Charles Willson Peale. The great general's portrait must grace a page of this American Revolutionary War book. *Public domain. Charles Willson Peale.*

The portrait at right by Charles Willson Peale (1741–1827) was painted just before the convening of the Second Continental Congress. The soon-to-be-tested General Washington is wearing the commander in chief's light blue sash he received in June 1775 when he was commissioned commanding general of the Continental army. In mid-April 1776, General Washington was in New York City.

It is unlikely that General George Washington was ever in Hallett's Cove, Dutch Kills or western Newtown in Queens County in 1776. Brooklyn (Kings County) and Manhattan (New York County) possess "George Washington was here" sites in abundance, where General Washington actually set foot, rode on his horse or slept. As for western Queens County, as far as has been discovered, George Washington was not here in 1776. There is zero proof that "George Washington slept here."

The commander in chief would have wanted to set his eyes on the storied and treacherous Hell Gate. This narrow chokepoint of the East River tidal strait was the nautical back door to New York City. American defense of this strategic city meant controlling its harbor, its two great rivers and its myriad waterways. General Washington may have ridden with his officers, scouts and guards along Long Island's East River coast as far north as Hell Gate and Lawrence Point.

Informed speculation concludes that soon after George Washington's arrival in New York, he would have gone to Long Island to survey the defenses that General Charles Lee was sent to build.

After surveying the lay of the land, General Washington may have even stopped for refreshment for officers, troops and horses at any of the local farmhouses or homesteads. For example, about a half mile south

Brigadier General Nathanael Greene was sent to Long Island by General Washington in April 1776 to reconnoiter and fortify the defensive positions in western Kings and Queens. *Coin from the Mystic Stamp Company. Julio Fernandez photo.*

of the mouth of Sunswick Creek was the Colonel Jacob Blackwell house. Blackwell, a veteran of the French and Indian War, was a prominent Whig and revolutionary and would have welcomed General Washington into his home with open arms.

Without a navy, the American position was untenable. The independence of the United Colonies was being debated in the Continental Congress. Long Island, New York, was where the first great clash for liberty versus empire would take place.

Brigadier General Nathanael Greene arrived at New York in April 1776 with General Washington and the Continental army. General Greene would survey and strengthen the defensive positions on Long Island from Gravesend to the Hell Gate. The ultra-important mission of land reconnaissance and surveying undoubtedly brought General Greene and his mapping units to the furthest reaches of Newtown and western Queens County, perhaps as far northeast as Flushing. Conjecture suggests that General Greene was the highest-ranking Continental army officer to set foot in western Newtown, the future Long Island City. Lieutenant General Charles Lee did outrank Brigadier General Greene yet probably never made it to Queens County. He sent subordinate officers to Newtown for deeper reconnaissance and missions to subdue Loyalists.

An election on April 16, 1776, chose deputies to represent Queens County in the Provincial Congress. Chosen from western Newtown were Jacob Blackwell and "Jona[than]" Lawrence. Others refused their own election, one due to "extreme weakness of his constitution" and another to the fact that he was "so little acquainted with such business"—yet he would "remain your hearty friend in the American cause."[42]

On April 29, 1776, Brigadier General Nathanael Greene was ordered by General Washington to take command of Continental troops, local militias and the fortifications that they were building on western Long Island. General Greene made it to Hell Gate by land, via Hell Gate Neck, the site of Hallett's Point, strategically overlooking the narrow water passage. Without a navy, this point was indefensible. The British could bring more firepower via the saltwater East River than the Americans could bring via land.

> *Near the end of April, Putnam sent energetic General Nathanael Greene across the East River to fortify Long Island and the bucolic burg of Brooklyn with its thousand inhabitants, mainly of Dutch ancestry, and their black slaves. Greene studied and inspected the roads, trails, landmarks, and knolls from Hellgate to Gravesend.*[43]

General Greene was here to do what he had to do as a military leader with an island and a city to defend. Could it be done? If this war was to be won by the spade, the Americans were trying their best to fight for New York. The Americans were digging in. The British were regrouping. The British were coming.

Of importance to the scheme of things revolutionary in western Newtown, every family name in the following paragraph played a role in the Revolution in Newtown and elsewhere.

James Way, was, if we may trust the Assessment Roll of 1776, the richest man in Newtown. He was nearly twice as rich as Simon Remsen or Thomas Lawrence, who were rated nearly twice as high as either Richard Alsop, William Sackett, William Lawrence or Hendrick Suydam.[44]

There was and is a Way's Reef in the Hell Gate close to Pot Cove. If these men of means were Loyalists, they, no doubt, contributed much of their fortunes to the British cause in order to hold their lands and homes. After signing an oath of loyalty to the Crown, Richard Alsop, a silent Patriot, was a perfect example of this. The other Patriots listed above fled before capture.

Below is a splendid example of the Continental currency, a "seven dollars" bill printed in Philadelphia on May 9, 1776. Although not issued in New York, bills of this type were widely circulated in the United Colonies. The round seal shows a storm at sea with the motto *serenabit*, Latin for "it will clear up."

A series of Continental bills had different designs and motivational mottos. Of note, printed on the bill is "the United Colonies." As the American Revolution moved into 1776, the form of currency known as

May 9, 1776 Continental currency. This is an actual bill, not a replica, signed by Ben Jacobs and T. Leech. *R. Melnick collection. Julio Fernandez photo.*

the Continental was, in many cases, worthless. The phrase "not worth a continental" referred to this currency that, due to rapid depreciation, had little value. Specie, which was money in the form of coins rather than notes, was more reliable, yet coinage was heavy and difficult to use in larger transactions. A bill type of currency was necessary yet very susceptible to the economic pressures that an internationally unrecognized breakaway nation might face. British counterfeiting would also bring down the Continental's value. Other Continental currency bills stated, ever so plainly, "'Tis Death to counterfeit." The image on the previous page is of actual 1776 currency, not a replica.

The Queens County militia, as per a document of May 10, 1776, encompassed troops from all sections, to include the town of Newtown, which was divided into two "Beats," North Beat and South Beat. More importantly to our study, the North Beat officers were:

> *Capt. Jona. Lawrence, 1ˢᵗ Lieut. Wm. Sackett, 2ⁿᵈ Lieut. Wm. Lawrence, Ensign Jesse Warner. Capt. Rich. Lawrence, 1ˢᵗ Lieut. Daniel Lawrence, 2ⁿᵈ Lieut. Samuel Riker, Cornet Jona. Coe, Quarter Master Peter Rapelye, Capt. Abm. Riker, July, 1776. In the unit of Light Horse, Aug. 21, '76. Capt. Dan. Lawrence, in place of Richard Lawrence, resigned from infirmity.; 1ˢᵗ Lieut. Saml Riker, 2ⁿᵈ Lieut. Jona. Lawrence, Cornet Thos. Betts.*[45]

Some families saw fathers, brothers and cousins in the same units. The North Beat officers were representatives of the main families in western Newtown, western Queens County, Long Island. The Lawrence, Sackett and Riker families provided brave men to the Queens County militia. One man, Peter Rapelye, was one of a very few Rapelyes from this area to not be Loyalists. Some of these Patriots experienced the worst that war had to offer.

The Rapalje Family Burial Ground was a cemetery formerly located on 20ᵗʰ Street between 20ᵗʰ and 21ˢᵗ Avenues. The former private cemetery is now a grassy lawn at 20–61 20ᵗʰ Street. The photograph marked "10-26-27" (1927) on the facing page reveals only two standing stones and a roughly trod on, poorly maintained cemetery. The end of this family burial ground was almost near. An older image from circa 1900 shows the Jacob Rapalje Family Burial Ground to have five headstones in a well-tended-to, small cemetery. Both old photos show a large glacial erratic boulder behind the cemetery. According to the Greater Astoria Historical Society,

The Rapalje Cemetery in 1927 had two standing brownstone gravestones, one for Sarah Rapalje, the wife of George Brinckerhoff, a Patriot during the Revolutionary War. *QBPL.*

This cemetery was behind the Polhemus House on Shore Boulevard, earlier the Rapalye family home. As late as 1904, there were eight stones of the Brinckerhoff, Rapalye, and Sheffield families with dates from 1776 to 1830. Two burials, Jacob Rapalye and his wife, Sarah [actually, it was his wife, Catrina Lott], *died within six weeks of each other during the turbulent year of 1776. Both tombstones were inscribed in Dutch.*[46]

More Dutch-to-English information revealed that Jacob Rapalje died on May 18, 1776, at age sixty-two. Sarah Rapalje, the wife of Patriot George Brinckerhoff, was the daughter of Jacob and Catrina. The year 1776 proved to be an awful one for these Rapaljes. Jacob Rapalje died just as the war was coming. Catrina Lott, the wife (*vrow*) of Jacob Rapalje, would not or could not endure without her husband. She died on July 7, 1776, in her fifty-fifth year. She passed merely two days before the Declaration of Independence was to be read in nearby Newtown and throughout Queens County. Adversity consumed the Rapaljes as the tragedies of war and occupation came for their surviving family members. Catrina was free from the shackles of this earth; her family and town were soon to be made captive. Patriot George Brinckerhoff (1739–1802), buried close by, outlived his wife, Sarah, who died in 1787 at the young age of thirty-two. Of the greatest importance to our landmark year of 1776 is that historian Arthur White, in translating the engravings of these ancient tombstones, helped save our local history so that authors can pass this information on to future generations. Solid information and research from the 1919 Queens cemetery survey reported ten burials and two remaining headstones. "Rapalje" had four different spellings in our local historical record.

The headstones and cemetery designation are long gone, yet the bodies are most likely in situ. In two major histories of the many local Queens and Long Island City private burial grounds, the author has found no record that states that the bodies here were ever removed and reinterred elsewhere. Such is the fate of a colonial family cemetery founded in 1776. In situ forever. Near clandestinely and most respectfully, the architects and builders of the Marine Terrace housing units (opened 1949) at the site elected not to build on the family plot. The *H* footprint of the building at this spot was modified to respect the remains of the deceased once laid to rest by Christian burial. An old property map at the Greater Astoria Historical Society revealed the exact outline of the former cemetery.

JUNE 1776

Colonel Jeromus Remsen, with a home on Old Bowery Road (now in northern Astoria), was the commander of half of the Queens County militia in 1775–76. There is an extant Remsen family burial ground in Forest Hills that holds the graves of the good colonel and his cousins, all Revolutionary War officers. Although well out of the Long Island City purview, the Remsens are very worthy of mention. Old Astoria Village once had a Remsen Street, now 12th Street, and a handsome antebellum Remsen house, torn down in 2005.

Traveling from Philadelphia, on his return to New York on June 6, 1776, General Washington again resided at the Mortier house.

> *After General Washington visited Congress in late May,* [until June 5, John] *Alsop returned with him to New York in early June.* [Alsop] *added efforts to find housing for 8,000 Continental Army troops to his earlier and continuing work on the supply problems.*[47]

General Washington was not to leave the secure confines of New York City until he had to depart for Long Island in late August. After inspecting the Long Island fortifications, the commander in chief went back to his familiar lodgings and headquarters on York Island every night. The author has found zero information proving that George Washington stayed a night in Newtown, Queens, or in the future Long Island City in 1776.

A Revolutionary War–era flintlock musket trigger mechanism. This is a replica 1762 British "Brown Bess" musket, which a reenactor allowed the author to fire. Huzzah! *R. Melnick photo.*

The weapons of the Revolutionary War are too numerous to list here. Pictured above is a Land Pattern flintlock musket, a muzzle-loading, smoothbore musket known to Brits and Patriots alike as the Brown Bess. This splendid death machine is a replica of a 1762 Grice Company–manufactured Brown Bess musket. Notice the engraved "G.R." and royal crown under the gunpowder pan. "G.R." stands for George Rex, Latin for King George. See the large flint secured in the clamp; when the trigger is pulled, the flint strikes and ignites the gunpowder in the pan, igniting the powder in the gun barrel, which fires the musket ball at its target. These were the most widely used weapons of the Revolutionary War. The approximate weight was ten and a half pounds, and the musket's total length was about 58.5 inches, nearly five feet of one-shot deadly force. The Brown Bess could affix a 17-inch bayonet, more feared than a musket or cannonball.

On June 7, 1776, the important Virginia Resolutions were put forth as delegate Richard Henry Lee "introduced a resolution in the Second

Continental Congress proposing independence for the colonies. The Lee resolution contained three parts: a declaration of independence, a call to form foreign alliances, and 'a plan for confederation.'"[48] With the declaring of independence not any longer just an idea, these determined members of congress realized that the reasons for separation from Great Britain must be clarified and codified. The Continental Congress formed, on June 11, 1776, a Committee of Five to draft a Declaration of Independence from Great Britain. Robert R. Livingston from New York was chosen for this committee along with Roger Sherman and the big three of the Continental Congress: Benjamin Franklin, John Adams and the declaration's primary author, Thomas Jefferson. Many delegates thought that the Lee resolution was a hasty yet necessary impetus for forcing delegates to consider independence over reconciliation. "Because many members of the Congress believed action such as Lee proposed to be premature or wanted instructions from their colonies before voting, approval was deferred to July 2."[49]

Colonel Nathaniel Heard of the New Jersey militia, who arrested Tories in Newtown, Queens County, in January 1776, arrested New Jersey's royal governor, William Franklin, on June 17, 1776. William was the illegitimate son of American Founding Father and major signer of the Declaration of Independence Benjamin Franklin.

Of interest to the goings-on nearby in Kings County, on June 18, 1776, a letter, per Brigadier General Nathanael Greene's orders, delivered correspondence to "Camp Long Island, N.Y." This simple fact proves that the area they were preparing to defend was called Long Island and not just Brooklyn, a small town at that time, strategically situated yet nondescript. Conversely, General George Washington, in a letter to Brigadier General Greene, on June 24, 1776, referred to Long Island as "Nassau Island."[50]

CASUS BELLI IS LATIN for the act or situation provoking or justifying war. The case for war. The reason for war. Perhaps stronger than the actions at Lexington and Concord or on Breed's Hill outside of Boston, the casus belli for these turbulent times of early summer 1776 was the Declaration of Independence. How dare they, said the British. This we must do, said the new Americans. If we must fight, and we are in preparation to do so, here are the reasons. A new age of man awaits.

In the image opposite, the Committee of Five, assigned to write a declaration, presents the Declaration of Independence to the Continental Congress. This scene is often misrepresented as the approval of the

The June 28, 1776 *Presentation of the Declaration of Independence to Congress*, is often mistaken for the approval of the Declaration on July 4. *Public domain. John Trumbull painting.*

declaration on July 4 or the signing on August 2, 1776. In this famous John Trumbull painting, standing in front of a seated John Hancock at the desk is the Committee of Five. They are, left to right, Adams, Sherman, Livingston, Jefferson and Franklin.

Other New Yorkers in the painting are Francis Lewis, William Floyd, Lewis Morris and Philip Livingston. The second person to the right behind Benjamin Franklin is New York delegate and Queens County resident Francis Lewis. On the back of the United States two-dollar bill, a new bill issued in 1976, the image is entitled "Declaration of Independence, 1776." Although one of many, Queens County resident Francis Lewis is forever enshrined on American currency.

The following day, June 29, 1776, at Turtle Gut Inlet, New Jersey, two Continental navy ships, the 6-gun brigantine *Nancy* and the 14-gun frigate *Lexington*, fought HM sloop *Kingfisher* and the HMS *Orpheus*.

The formidable 32-gun frigate HMS *Orpheus* would soon be in the East River.

HEALTH AND DISEASE

Examples of disease affecting the local participants in the Revolution and its war are as follows.

Joseph Hallett's father, Joseph II, died of smallpox in 1731. There was smallpox at the Jacob Blackwell house in western Newtown, along the East River, in December 1774. A footnote from a December 10, 1774 document reads, "This Committee did not meet till December 29, (owing to the small-pox in Colonel Blackwell's family,)."[51]

Malaria, dysentery, typhus and other scourges of the time ravaged camps. Camp fevers and terribly unsanitary conditions hobbled the army. Citizens, many as afflicted as the soldiery, suffered these sicknesses during war. British sanitary conditions were markedly better due to instituted health regulations for a professional army. Due to the close-quarters nature of military barracks and encampments, disease spread rapidly across troops of all ranks. Washington's army caught dysentery from contaminated water on York Island, and smallpox on Long Island left nearly 20 percent of his troops too sick to fight.

Chapter 4

July 1776

rancis Lewis, born in 1713, and his unsettling and storied life are very much worth mention. He, his wife, Elizabeth Annesley Lewis, and their family lived on an estate in Whitestone, Queens County, in the adjacent town of Flushing. Though they were outside of the Long Island City purview by a mile of water and two miles of land, we must note the truly patriotic lives of both man and wife. In 1765, the Stamp Act crisis arose, and Lewis became very active in politics during the lead-up to the Revolutionary War. Francis Lewis traveled through Newtown from Flushing to cross the East River to York Island or head south into Kings County. The honorable Mr. Lewis knew and probably visited the prominent local citizens. All the Newtown Patriots knew of the prestige that Francis Lewis possessed.

July 1776 is a month that will forever be known for the historic events that took place in Philadelphia, Pennsylvania. The concerns of the British subjects in Newtown and all the thirteen British colonies were being addressed in the most severe manner. There was still hope that a reconciliation might occur. Decision time was now.

On July 2, 1776, the Continental Congress passed a resolution saying that "these United Colonies are, and of right ought to be free and independent States."[52] As the Continental Congress was deciding on the merits and consequences of a declaration of independence, George Washington was thinking about how his new army would perform against one of the

Francis Lewis, of Whitestone, Queens County, on Long Island, was one of the four signers of the Declaration of Independence from the Province of New York. *Public domain.*

strongest armies of the time. The king's army, the Royal Navy and German auxiliaries were on their way to do the king's bidding. A prescient General Washington wrote, "The fate of unborn millions will now depend, under God, on the courage and conduct of this army."[53]

Relevant to the historic date of July 2, 1776, is the following important list of the men who elected not to or could not sign the declaration. To put one's signature on this document was to commit treason against the king and Great Britain. Not only was signing a great offense to the king, but the king's forces were also en route to America to extinguish these revolutionary ideas and actions. For a moment, consider their positions and put yourself in their places. Would you sign?

Eight men present on July 2nd never signed the Declaration, the New York delegation abstained from voting on July 2nd, and four delegates—John Alsop, George Clinton, Robert R. Livingston, and Henry Wisner—never signed the Declaration of Independence. Remember, Robert R. Livingston was a member of the Committee of Five, and yet not a signer.[54]

The signings did not happen on July 2 or on July 4, 1776. The document had to be finalized and printed, copies dispersed. Congress then reconvened, and the historic parchment was signed.

As per one of four brass plaques at the square base of the Minerva statue on Battle Hill atop the Green-Wood Cemetery, the highest point in Brooklyn, the plaque reads,

Declaration of Independence / July 4, 1776
The wisest document, ever written, of human rights and liberties, basic ethics, civic religion and democratic government. All these are expressed in this one essential paragraph "We hold these truths to be self-evident that all men are created equal, that they are endowed by their creator with certain unalienable rights, that among these are life, liberty and the pursuit of happiness. That to secure these rights, governments are instituted among men, deriving their just powers from the consent of the governed. EQUALITY-LIBERTY-HUMAN RIGHTS.[55]

The great American document, the Declaration of Independence. Presented to the British were the many reasons for the American rebellion against King George III. *Public domain.*

The revolutionary signers who passed through Newtown and western Queens County were Francis Lewis and William Floyd. There was reliable ferry service from Hallett's Cove across the East River to upper New York Island at Horn's Hook. Every vessel was subject to the tides, currents and forces of the East River. Local persons of consequence such as Joseph Hallett, Jacob Blackwell, John Alsop, Jeromus Remsen or even Nicholas Fish more than likely did have their prominent Founding Father friends to their Newtown homes. The above men were friends with John Morin Scott, Alexander Hamilton and Francis Lewis. Did Jacob Blackwell victual or provision the American generals and officers reconnoitering the area? Here, conjecture trumps verifiable fact. Did Mrs. Blackwell make lunch for General Greene?

JULY 4, 1776

On July 4, 1776, the Second Continental Congress in Philadelphia approved the Declaration of Independence. This is the date written at the top of the hallowed parchment. Congress ordered the historic document to be printed and distributed to each of the thirteen provinces, or colonies, now states.

The vote "was not unanimous. New York's delegates abstained from voting in favor of independence on July 2nd, based on outdated instructions."[56]

A single nay vote would have defeated the motion to approve the declaration. The vote passed; the motion carried with twelve yeas, one abstention (New York) and zero nays. In political and ideological contrast, British commander in chief General William Howe was at his Staten Island, New York headquarters on that July 4, 1776.

Just powers derived from the consent of the governed would be years off.

This day in world history, July 4, 1776, belonged to the Americans.

THE FIRST PUBLIC READING of the Declaration of Independence took place on July 8, 1776, in Philadelphia, the city where it was written. In New York on the following day, July 9, 1776, the declaration was read aloud to General George Washington's troops and to citizens, all still de facto British subjects. The townspeople heard the liberty-inspiring words that would soon bring war to their good city.

The New York Provincial Congress met at the courthouse in Westchester County on Tuesday, July 9, 1776. Remember that New York abstained from the approval vote on July 4. The vote was not unanimous. The illegal New York Provincial Congress, presided over by General Nathaniel Woodhull, on reading the Declaration, reported that

> *the reasons assigned by the Continental Congress for declaring the United Colonies free and independent States, were cogent and conclusive; and that, "while we lament the cruel necessity, we approve the same; and will, at the risk of our lives and fortunes, join with the other colonies in supporting it."*[57]

Henry Onderdonk Jr.'s 1846 book *Revolutionary Incidents of Queens County* states that the declaration "was read at the head of each company in Queens county, and at the head of each brigade of the army stationed at New-York." The editor notes here that "many officers and leading men now quit the American cause."[58] General Woodhull would soon be serving the new United States of America in Queens and Kings Counties in the lead-up to battle.

The Declaration of Independence was read in various places in Queens County on July 9, 1776. Queens militia and the Newtown beats, unless otherwise assigned, did, in fact, hear the declaration read aloud. "Copies of the declaration were received at Newtown and read at the head of each company."⁵⁹ The British were massing their armed forces on Staten Island and their Royal Navy in New York Bay. The British were coming.

Of the utmost importance, on July 9, 1776, the Declaration of Independence was adopted by the New York Convention. New York became the last "province" to adopt the declaration. The measure was decided. The existence of the sovereign nation of the United States of America was unanimously declared.

Good feelings generated by declaring independence from Britain would very soon turn to angst and dread, knowing that the British army was coming. Involving the local Newtown militia and those who espoused such a break from Great Britain, the following actions took place. "The convention ordered the militia of Queens county, with the troop of horse, to be called out, and all diligence to be used to prevent the stock from falling into the hands of the enemy."⁶⁰

A famous event, also on July 9, 1776, was the toppling of King George III's statue at the Bowling Green, at the southern end of Broadway in New York City. After the reading of the declaration to the people, many adjourned to the King George III statue and helped with or witnessed its felling.

There was no turning back. The Continental Congress and the Continental army were now traitors against the king of Great Britain. The revolution was on, the cause of liberty was just and the British were coming. Decisions had to be made. Sides had to be taken. At stake was living under the yoke of British rule or living freely under a new republican government. Both sides, at opposite ends of the spectrum, king and empire versus republicanism and a new nation, boasted of their merits.

On July 12, 1776, the HMS *Phoenix* (44 guns) and HMS *Rose* (20 guns) sailed up the Hudson River from Upper New York Bay. It was a show of British naval force against the American-held New York City and an act of defiance to see what mettle the Americans had when cannons were being fired at them. These British warships would be in the East River and in the Long Island City area of study in a short time.

July 13, 1776, left us with this information: "The deputies from Queens say the militia are destitute of ammunition. Congress orders 10,000 cartridges of different sizes, filled with powder and ball, and 1000 flints, to be delivered to Capt. Jona. Lawrence, and to be charged to the county."⁶¹ By July 15, news had reached the Continental Congress in Philadelphia that on July 9, 1776, the New York Convention adopted the Declaration of Independence. At the end of that week, on July 19, Congress resolved to begin the declaration with "the unanimous Declaration of the thirteen united States of America"—and, most importantly, that this unique and visionary document would be signed by every member of Congress.[62]

The primary focus of this book is to discuss and honor the good men and women with ties to the lands of the future Long Island City. People who lived locally or had reason to visit or to merely pass through were sought for study.

The following circumstance is like no other in the matter of making the final decision to vote yea or nay for American independence. "I am compelled," Newtown resident John Alsop stated in his July 16, 1776 resignation letter, "to declare that it [the Declaration] is against my judgment and inclination…as you have. I presume. By that declaration closed the door of reconciliation, I must beg leave to resign my seat."[63] The Continental Congressman John Alsop was unique in one respect, to his discredit. "Alsop was the only Congressman to resign specifically because of the adoption of the Declaration of Independence."[64] John Alsop, in good conscience, could not sign the Declaration of Independence. He resigned from the Continental Congress because he had hoped for a reconciliation with Great Britain. It is easy to pass judgment on a man who had much to lose and, with great risk, much to gain. John Alsop was one signature from being immortalized as a signer of the Declaration of Independence. James Duane and John Jay of New York and Pennsylvanians John Dickinson and Robert Morris elected not to sign, as they "were opposed to the timing, if not the policy of independence."[65]

On July 22, 1776, a British Royal Navy fleet had arrived at Sandy Hook, New Jersey, just outside of New York Harbor, and "the disaffected from Kings and Queens took refuge on board the fleet, and supplied him [General Howe] with all the information he desired."[66]

It was now time to rid these new shores of the old order. The Queens County militias were helping to present to the world a new way of thinking, a new form of governance. Newtown North and South Beats carried their own flags, marching behind the ensigns of the largest military unit. There are no records of what the Newtown militia flags looked like or their pedigree or lineage, unlike the famous "Liberty" flag of Suffolk County's Huntington militia.

Of pertinent interest to this war of words, on July 26, 1776, the sheriff of Queens County, Thomas Willets, was arrested and sent to Congress for the crime of posting in every Queens County town the Declaration of Sir William and Lord Richard Howe. Historian Henry Onderdonk Jr. states that the declaration granted "a free and general pardon to all those who, in the tumult and disorder of the times, may have deviated from their just allegiance, and are willing, by a speedy return to their duty, to reap the benefits of the royal favor."[67]

ON JULY 28, 1776, "Sargent and Hutchinson arrive at Horn's Hook, New York" as per History.com. "Colonel Paul Dudley Sargent with the 16th Continental Regiment and Colonel Israel Hutchinson with his 27th Continental Regiment, both from Massachusetts, as well as several British ships, arrive at Horn's Hook, New York, on this day in 1776."[68] This author is confident that the British navy did not have any warships up to Horns Hook and Hell Gate as early as July 1776. Any armed warship going up the East River would have been fired on by American cannon batteries on York Island and Long Island. The narrower East River allowed for more accurate artillery from land. The British were still massing and, up to that point, would not have had any warships or frigates in the East River.

> *Horn's Hook was first intended to house nine guns as a Patriot battery to defend Manhattan in February 1776. The battery, or fort, stood near the modern-day intersection of 89th Street and East End Avenue, opposite Ward's Island and Hell's Gate. After gathering at Horn's Hook, the Massachusetts regiments went on to Long Island* [to prepare for the great battle ahead].[69]

"Thompson's Battery…was the name given to the work thrown up at Horn's Hook by Colonel Drake's Westchester minute-men soon after Lee's arrival. It mounted eight pieces."[70] Thompson's Battery was erected as early as February or March 1776. That is when General Charles Lee was in charge of beginning to build the fortifications, redoubts and barricades necessary to defend New York. General Lee was then sent south by General Washington to Charleston, South Carolina, to help fortify that city and harbor. Thompson's Battery would later be named Sargent's Battery. Interestingly, the author could find no references to any American fortifications on the Queens County shoreline to defend the Hell Gate. There were no American guns on Long Island at Hell Gate. The American cannon at Horn's Hook (Thompson's Battery) alone defended the back door to New York City and its great, strategic, deep-water harbor. The Johnston map of 1878 shows the units of "Sargeant" and "Chester" at Horn's Hook in 1776. The American fort at Horn's Hook was strategically important. These cannons would soon fire.

Chapter 5

AUGUST 1776

From August 1 to 26, 1776, events unfolded as two armies moved closer to battle. The kettle of revolutionary fervor was near boiling.

AUGUST 2, 1776

At the bottom right of the Declaration of Independence, second column from the right, the four New Yorkers signed: "W[illia]m Floyd, Phil[ip] Livingston, Fran.[cis] Lewis, Lewis Morris." Three New Yorkers signed the parchment in Philadelphia on August 2, 1776; Morris signed the following month. The author mentions Francis Lewis with great zeal since he was the nearest signer of the Declaration of Independence to Hallett's Cove and to the town of Newtown. Lewis's homestead in Whitestone is well outside of this book's Long Island City purview yet expressly noteworthy.

> *Like the other New York signers, Francis Lewis was condemned by the British authorities, and a price was put on his head. They thirsted for revenge upon a man who had dared to affix his signature to a document that proclaimed the independence of America.*[71]

John Hancock, the president of the Continental Congress, signed the declaration on August 2, 1776, as did forty-nine of the delegates. "Seven delegates were absent from the Continental Congress that day, some of which signed the parchment at later dates."[72] And, of course, some delegates who approved the declaration on July 4, 1776, could not or did not sign. Floyd,

Livingston, Lewis and Morris signed away their fortunes and livelihoods for the cause of freedom. Their families were treated roughly, and British harshness caused them hardship for the rest of their lives.

During the buildup of British military forces and materiel, on August 4, 1776, junior officer Lieutenant Rawdon, who had shown exemplary valor at Bunker Hill in June 1775, dined with his superior officers Lieutenant General Henry Clinton, Admiral Richard Lord Howe, Lieutenant General Charles Earl Cornwallis and others. This dinner most likely took place on Staten Island, where the British headquarters were during the buildup of land and sea forces. All the above high-ranking British soldiers would be in western Newtown, the future Long Island City, in a short time.

On August 10, 1776, about half of the Kings and Queens Counties militiamen were ordered to march immediately to Brooklyn. "The levies from Kings and Queens counties were to be formed into one regiment under command of Col. Jeromus Remsen, Lieut. Col. Nicholas Covenhoven [probably Couwenhoven, or Kouwenhoven], Major Richard Thorne, and continue in service till September 1."[73] The Couwenhoven family owned a prominent home on Old Bowery Road, as did Colonel Remsen, in northwestern Newtown, now northern Astoria.

Also on August 10, 1776, King George III, the British Parliament and all of London, England, learned of American independence. A copy of the declaration, printed on July 8 or 9, was sent immediately across the Atlantic Ocean to arrive in London one month later. The heads of all signers now had prices placed on them.

This August 13, 1776 facsimile Continental currency ten-dollar bill reads, "NEW-YORK. THIS BILL shall pass current in all Payments in this State, for TEN SPANISH MILLED DOLLARS, or the Value thereof in Gold or

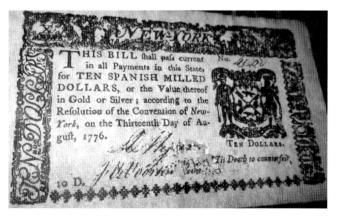

Continental currency issued by the Province of New York. This was most likely the last printing of American currency in New York City until after 1783. *Replica bill, GAHS collection. R. Melnick photo.*

Silver; according to the Resolution of the Convention of New-York, on the Thirteenth Day of August, 1776." This impressive attempt at a uniform continental currency here is signed by two men. This ten-dollar bill, its serial number illegible, has a "10 D" in the bottom left corner. Under the seal of the city of New York reads, in most straightforward wording, "'Tis Death to counterfeit." The New York–minted bill is of the utmost importance to our study as it very likely passed through the hands of a New Yorker merely one month before their city's governance would violently change hands. Queens County and the town of Newtown would soon suffer from this abrupt turnover. Liberty and tyranny were the currencies that would change hands.

A VERY IMPORTANT NOTE: These naval actions did not take place in the East River or in waters near western Queens County, later Long Island City. The painting below is used to illustrate how both the HMS *Phoenix* (44 guns) and the HMS *Rose* (20 guns) looked in 1776 and to confirm their importance to the British conquest and control of New York. Painter Dominic Serres shows the HMS *Phoenix* on the left, under attack by an American fireship on the Hudson River on August 16, 1776. It and the HMS *Rose* (middle) were often utilized in tandem, and both ships survived this engagement relatively unscathed. Sir James Wallace (1731–1803) captained the HMS *Rose*. These warships would press on to further serve the Royal Navy in local East River waters and beyond.

This image is important because both of these British warships, the HMS *Phoenix* and the HMS *Rose*, would be in the East River in September 1776. *Public domain. Dominic Serres.*

ON THE NIGHT OF August 21, 1776, a heavy rainstorm struck New York and Long Island with the utmost ferocity. David McCullough writes about the major chroniclers of that moment and of the war. They described the storm as being full of omens and unleashed fury: "a night so violent seemed filled with portent."[74] One writer suggested that the massive number of armaments in the area held the storm by electrical attraction and that the storm actually drew energy from the metals and the anger. The British were coming to Long Island the next day. War was coming. The town of Newtown and western Queens County would soon feel the thunder of marching boots. An army of men would soon tread heavily on Long Island City soil.

If it was military action the rebels wanted, the British would bring war to their Long Island shores. British armed forces sailed into New York Harbor in July and August 1776, landing on Staten Island to mass and prepare for war. The British crossed the Narrows on August 22, 1776, and amphibiously landed at Gravesend Bay, Kings County, Long Island. Bringing battle to New York were "30,000 troops, 10,000 sailors, 300 supply ships, 30 battleships, 1,200 cannons, the largest seaborne attack ever attempted by England until the 20th century."[75] Important to the Newtown, Queens County narrative, on August 22, "the British advance guard, under Sir Henry Clinton, with the Hessian chasseurs and grenadiers, commanded by Colonel von Donop, crossed the Narrows to Long Island."[76] The massive landing culminated on August 25. The British and their Hessian allies were very much on their way. They were within sight of the American lines on the Brooklyn Heights. British lieutenant general Clinton, Hessian colonel von Donop and their well-trained forces would be in western Queens County in due time. Both would set foot and tread heavily on Long Island City soil. They came to prosecute the war against the damned rebels. Some of Europe's best soldiers were set forth on these Long Island shores to bring them battle. And it is battle that they brought.

This color mezzotint image of the Honorable William Howe (1729–1814) depicts the commander in chief in November 1777. General William Howe became the commander in chief of all British armed forces in North America in October 1775. After occupying and eventually evacuating Boston in April 1776, Howe recovered, rested, plotted and planned at Halifax, Nova Scotia, British Canada. Many books have listed General Howe as Sir William Howe at the Battle of Long Island, yet he was not awarded Knight of the Bath, an old bestowment of knighthood in Great Britain, until 1777. The Knight of the Bath medallion is on his left breast.

Above: "The HON.(ORA)BLE S.(I)R W.(ILLIA)M HOWE." Commander-in-chief of "his Majesty's Forces" in America, General Howe achieved victory on Long Island in 1776. *Public domain.*

Opposite: This proclamation was put forth by General William Howe on August 23, 1776. Your decision must be made very soon. *Public domain. New-York Historical Society exhibit, October 2016. R. Melnick photo.*

An interesting book at the Greater Astoria Historical Society contains clippings or extracts from Newtown, Queens town meeting minutes, proof of binding sales and civic decisions that were made. Prominent Newtown family names prior to and at the start of the August 1776 armed hostilities on Long Island are featured. Jacobus Lent, John Berrien Riker, Ruth Riker, Abraham Riker, Samuel Moore III, Joseph Hallett, Daniel Rapelye, Hendrick Brinkerhoof and Richard Alsop are among those mentioned. ("Brinkerhoof" is spelled erroneously; this is most likely Brinckerhoff, also spelled Brinkerhoff.) Last names that appear on numerous and successive documents of the period are Moore, Riker, Hallett, Waters, Sackett, Lawrence, Betts, Furman, Burroughs, Morrell, Suydam, Warner, Way and Remsen; all of these families played roles in the Revolution. Based on the entries in the collection, the author speculates that the book of extracts was compiled circa 1884.

After his first overnight on a soon-to-be inhospitable Long Island, General William Howe, from his New Utrecht, Kings County headquarters, put forth this August 23, 1776 proclamation. Howe offered the Loyalists of Long Island permits, protections and amnesty for any rebellious transgressions if they delivered themselves to headquarters and stated their loyalty to the king. This proclamation made its way into Queens County and to all Newtown prior to the beginning of the clash of arms. These were the proclamations that Dr. John Berrien Riker tore down before the oncoming battle. Patriots and their sympathizers were able to tear down the new British proclamations for only a few days. The dragoons were coming. The British regulars were coming.

On August 24, 1776, half of the western regiment of Suffolk County was ordered by Congress to march into the western part of Queens, with the officers and the whole of the Queens militia and its troop of horse, to

A PROCLAMATION.

By His Excellency the Honorable WILLIAM HOWE, General and
Commander in Chief of all His Majesty's Forces, within the Colonies
lying on the Atlantic Ocean, from Nova-Scotia, to West-Florida, in-
clusive, &c. &c. &c.

WHEREAS it is reprefented, that many of the loyal Inhabitants of
this Ifland have been compelled by the Leaders in Rebellion, to
take up Arms againft His Majesty's Government: Notice is hereby given
to all Perfons fo forced into Rebellion, that on delivering themfelves up at
the HEAD QUARTERS of the Army, they will be received as faithful Subjects; have Permits to return peaceably to their refpective Dwellings, and meet with full Protection for their Perfons and Property.

All thofe who chufe to take up Arms for the Reftoration of Order
and good Government within this Ifland, fhall be difpofed of in the beft
Manner, and have every Encouragement that can be expected.

GIVEN under my HAND, at Head Quarters on Long Island,
this 23d Day of Auguft, 1776.   WILLIAM HOWE.

By His Excellency's Command.

Robert Mackenzie, Secretary.

"use all diligence to prevent the stock falling into the hands of the enemy."[77]
This was a major undertaking, as it would be a grand strike, very strategic in
nature, for the invading British army to gain control of hundreds of head of
cattle on which to feed their troops and to smoke and salt meat for later use
in this war. General Nathaniel Woodhull, as of August 25, 1776, was under
congressional orders to remove all horned cattle, sheep and horses to points
well east of Newtown. To keep these vital supplies out of British hands,
General Woodhull and his force were ordered to destroy grain as necessary
and, if "he be compelled to retreat," to "dismantle the mills by carrying
away the upper stone."[78]

The East River

"Picture yourself in a boat on a river," with currents and swirls and seven-knot tides. Somebody call to the old Hell Gate pilot; I see the rocks with my own eyes.[79]

The East River is a saltwater tidal strait sixteen miles (fourteen nautical miles) long that flows from Governors Island in Upper New York Bay north and east to the Long Island Sound. This tidal strait floods and ebbs twice a day, every day, bringing in the Atlantic Ocean tide, first from New York Bay and, later in the cycle, from the Long Island Sound. Hudson River water, via the Harlem River, also contributes tidal volume to the Hell Gate, well named and historically well respected. A tidal strait, by definition, connects two larger bodies of water and is often treacherous to water navigation due to tidal surges, currents, eddies and other factors. Many maps and charts of the East River denote the flood tide, or tidal flow, from south to north and the tidal ebb flowing south back into New York Harbor.

The East River has many old and ancient names of navigation points. Some, if taken out of context, could be construed as distasteful and derogatory by 2023 standards. National Oceanic and Atmospheric Administration (NOAA) charts reveal the local East River place and waterway names: "Dutch Kills, Newtown Creek, Hunters Point, Gibbs Pt, Hallets Cove, Horns Hook, Rhinelander Reef, Hallets Pt, Hell Gate, Pot Cove, Ways Reef, Negro Pt, Middle Ground, Lawrence Pt, Rikers Island Channel, Steinway Creek, Rikers Island, Bowery Bay."[80] Most of these names were in use in 1776 and will be mentioned going forward.

Hellegat / Hell Gate

The Dutch named this waterway Hellegat, meaning "bright or beautiful passage." The name was later anglicized to Hell Gate, an appropriate term, suggesting sailors take care near the gate to hell. Hell Gate is a very important pinch point in the East River. Here is where the not-straight strait, with rocks and reefs and currents abounding, tosses its watery mix. Varying and contrary winds also factored into whether Hell Gate was to be successfully navigated. By August 1776, British warships had not yet ventured into Hell Gate.

Hell Gate was a difficult water route since Native American days; here is a 1671 explanation:

> *About ten Miles from New York is a Place call'd Hell-Gate, which being a narrow passage, there runneth a violent Stream both upon Flood and Ebb, and in the middle lie some Rocky Islands, which the Current sets so violently upon, that it threatens present Shipwrack; and upon the flood is a large whirlwind, which continually sends forth a hideous roaring, enough to affright any Stranger from passing farther, and to wait for some Charon to conduct him through, yet to those that are well acquainted, little or no danger. It is a place of great Defence against any Enemy coming in that way.*[81]

The historic and treacherous Hell Gate is over 100 feet deep just off Horn's Hook, now Gracie Point. Older navigation charts had it deeper than 100 feet in five different places; the deepest section was a 170-foot-deep crevasse just off the Astoria coast near the present-day Ralph DeMarco Park. At some points, rocks and reefs were very near or at the surface and could ruin your boat.

A brisk ride upriver on a rapid six- to seven-knot flood tide plus a commanding wind could steer a ship of sail into Hell Gate before the crew realized it was upon them—or they upon it. Quick decisions requiring nerve and navigational prowess were to be demanded in a moment. Today, disregard the warnings on the current NOAA navigation chart no. 12339 and the tides, currents and winds will disregard you and your vessel. In Revolutionary times, the constantly stirring ocean tides would wreak havoc with boats of oar and ships of sail. The untamed Hell Gate would play a very important role in how the British would attack and attempt to control New York in 1776. Hell Gate was known to mangle ships and send many a good boat to the bottom, sunk, and not a few good sailors to the bottom, dead. The East River–faring British colonists knew full well the dangerous and strategic elements that Hell Gate presented. The British Royal Navy, in a short time, would have to attempt to traverse Hell Gate.

THE AUTHOR, HAVING EARNED river credentials, or "river cred," has kayaked on the East River and through Hell Gate at full flood and full ebb tides. As when riding a true river, a paddler or rower needs to stabilize his or her boat to control it from getting turned around or upset by the swirling eddies, whirlpools and tidal push reverberating off a seawall or bulkhead. The paddler and kayak must withstand and work with the large wakes created by fast-moving private and party boats and large commercial tankers, tugboats and tug-pulled barges. One cannot paddle or row against the opposing tides unless one is a seasoned and sturdy boater. The favorable tides will whisk any rowed boat or wind-powered vessel along at the river's speed, sometimes carrying a vessel to wherever the river may take it. A paddled boat is merely a speck on the East River. The river itself carries driftwood and man-made litter and detritus. Many vessels, concerned with their own safety, can easily injure or kill an unsafe or unlucky paddler. It's called Hell Gate for a reason. This treacherous waterway will always illuminate the highest of the ocean mariner's truths: respect the sea.

IMPORTANT TO REVOLUTIONARY WAR events on the East River, Newtown Creek created three miles of the border separating Queens and Kings Counties. From the creek's mouth across the East River to Kip's Bay, 34th Street in Manhattan is nearly one mile. The distance from Hallets Point, Queens, to Horns Hook, Manhattan, is approximately four hundred yards. Scaly Rock(s), off Astoria Park, to Negro Bluff on Wards Island, the narrowest part of the river, is only three hundred yards. Hell Gate would have strategic repercussions in the military exertions of 1776 and afterward.

On August 26, 1776, the enemy's ships HMS *Niger*, HMS *Brune* and HMS *Halifax* (a schooner) sailed around Montauk Point and entered the 110-mile Long Island Sound. These ships were on their way to the waters north of the future Astoria, patrolling near Riker's Island, Lawrence Point and the north entrance to Hell Gate.

Lieutenant Robert Troup was a schoolmate of and New York "Hearts of Oak" militia member with Alexander Hamilton and Nicholas Fish. Troup was in Lieutenant Colonel John Lasher's battalion of New York militia. Lieutenant Troup's mounted patrol of five horsemen was captured near the Jamaica Pass early on August 27 by advance British dragoons. This secured the pass that would allow ten thousand British troops to quietly pass through within hours. Lieutenant Troup was taken prisoner at three o'clock in the morning on August 27. There was zero doubt that the British were coming, yet the Americans did not know from where and when. The Americans' chance to alert the defenders against the British flanking movement and assault was foiled. Lieutenant Troup was soon to be confined in the notorious British prison ship *Jersey* in Wallabout Bay, in the East River.

THE BATTLE OF LONG ISLAND, AUGUST 27, 1776

The Lord is my light and my salvation;
whom should I fear?
The Lord is my life's refuge;
of whom should I be afraid?
When evildoers come at me to devour my flesh,
my foes and enemies themselves stumble and fall.
Though an army encamp against me,
my heart will not fear;
though war be waged upon me, even then will I trust.[82]

One can wonder: If both sides prayed to the same Christian God, which side was favored by Providence?

GEORGE WASHINGTON'S CONTINENTAL ARMY CHAIN OF COMMAND, AUGUST 27, 1776

The American Continental army, under Commander in Chief General George Washington, was ready for action on August 27, 1776, the day of the great Battle of Long Island. No local Newtown or Queens County officers were Washington's aides-de-camp or higher-ranking officers.

The author has elected to write about American officers with links to western Queens County only. This list of the chain of command is vast, encompassing hundreds of men. Local western Queens County men who fought in the battle:

> Brigadier General John Morin Scott's brigade major was Nicholas Fish, a prominent resident of New York, with properties in Newtown, Queens County, New York.
> Colonel Paul Dudley Sargent would play a role at Hell Gate July to September 1776.
> Division commander Major General Nathanael Greene had under him Brigadier General Nathaniel Heard of New Jersey, who brought his New Jersey militia to Hallett's Cove, Newtown, and deep into Queens County back in January 1776.
> One leader of American troops that was also in Greene's division was Brigadier General Oliver Wolcott, who led the Connecticut

militia. Oliver Wolcott was a signer of the Declaration of Independence. Oliver's grandson Frederick Henry Wolcott Sr. (1808–1883) later lived in the freshly minted Astoria.

Brigadier General Nathaniel Woodhull led the Long Island militia, and he commanded local resident Brigade Major Jonathan Lawrence. Colonel Jeronimus (also Jeromus) Remsen led a militia contingent of two hundred and was in charge of part of the Queens County militia. Woodhull, Lawrence and Remsen would all try to serve their country and their cause well. On the sturdy earth of Long Island soon would spill the blood of good men beginning the long fight for liberty.

August 27, 1776: Terms

The Battle of Long Island is sometimes called, incorrectly, the Battle of Brooklyn or the Battle of Brooklyn Heights. The borough of Brooklyn was, in 1776, Kings County; the smaller town of Brooklyn and its heights would host this battle. British general William Howe, in his September 3, 1776 letter and battle account to Lord Germain in London, referred to the battle as the "Battle of Long Island."[83] The Green-Wood Cemetery refers to its annual late August commemorative events as the "Battle of Brooklyn." Semantics aside, battle was fought on this island, Long Island. The island's capture was a stepping stone for an attempt at the grand military and commercial prize, the town of thirty thousand people: New York City.

In the opposite image, the Green-Wood Cemetery reenactors and historical portrayers stand in one rank for all to review. General George Washington commands at left; second from the left is a militia officer (notice the sword and no musket) and three troops, either Continentals or militia. Men and women portray the soldiers. The soldier on the far right is a troop from the First Rhode Island Regiment, a unit that had numerous free Black soldiers. These reenactors know their units, weapons and crafts extremely well and answer many questions lobbed like mortars into their camp. This Rhode Islander is provisioned with a musket, a (gun) powder horn and, on his belt, a sheathed long knife. While the three center soldiers wear tricorn or brimmed hats, the red-capped fellow is wearing a hat similar to the historical Phrygian cap or liberty cap, which symbolized freedom and was on several flags at the time. The Phrygian cap is on the

Battle of Long Island reenactors at the Green-Wood Cemetery in Brooklyn, on western Long Island. Education so that we may better appreciate our good land. *General Washington reenactor Michael Grillo, the Green-Wood Cemetery "Battle of Brooklyn" reenactment. R. Melnick photo.*

modern New York State flag, adopted in 1778. To arms, my good men. To liberty!

The British Brown Bess musket was the dominant musket in 1776. The French had not given the Americans much weapons and materiel yet, so early in the rebellion. It was unlikely that secretly acquired muskets from the French would have been given to any assorted rebellious colonists. The local militias hardly had a chance to get newer muskets. Some militia units, however, were outfitted with uniforms and weapons by wealthy citizens or local militia officers of a high station and holding positions of trust. A noteworthy observation is the realness of the reenactors, especially the horse troops and aides. These men and women value their craft and always wish to convey the historical truth to those who wish to learn.

Queens County militia and men from Newtown were present at the Battle of Long Island. To what extent they were used is hard to ascertain. A number of them were killed and captured during the disastrous first armed

An American troop loading his Brown Bess musket. During this mock battle, General Washington (*in right distance*) did not lose one "Brave Fellow." *The Green-Wood Cemetery reenactment. R. Melnick photo.*

encounter between well-trained British troops and the green Continentals. It was time to defend these newly declared United States of America.

A fine example (opposite, top) of uniformed Continental soldiers, as opposed to lesser equipped and accoutered local militia.

The Delaware Regiment, along with Marylanders, specifically the "Maryland 400," battled the British at the Continental army's left flank, allowing the Americans to escape the disastrous Long Island defeat. These actions took place in Kings County, not in Queens, yet some Queens County militia fought here.

British grenadiers, depicted by reenactors in the bottom opposite image, demonstrated movements, tactics and marksmanship techniques on the green in lower the Green-Wood Cemetery in Brooklyn. These men pretend to fire musket balls at Continentals and militia defending this chain of high Long Island hills. Combat took place here on August 27, 1776, in the Battle of Long Island. On the high and imposing Grenadier hats, flanking the royal lion and the crown, read the letters *G* and *R*, standing for the Latin "George

This painting of the August 27, 1776 Battle of Long Island shows the Delaware Regiment firing a volley of musket balls at the redcoat British enemy. *Public domain. Domenick D'Andrea.*

Now, gentlemen, we have ourselves a war. These reenactors at the Green-Wood Cemetery depict the professional and feared British grenadiers firing a musket volley. *The Green-Wood Cemetery reenactment. R. Melnick photo.*

Colonel Johann Rall's Hessian grenadiers and field jaegers (hunters) spent time in western Newtown. They encamped in the area that later became northern Astoria. *Public domain. Painting by Jean Leffel.*

Rex," as in their sovereign, King George III. These grenadiers would soon be in western Queens.

The drawing of Hessian soldiers shown above provided a caption, "Privates of the Grenadier Regiment von Rall of Hesse-Cassel, Infantry Regiment von Sprecht of Brunswick, and Officer of the Field Jager Corps of Hesse-Cassel 1776–1781."[84]

Rall's Regiment of Grenadiers formed part of the first division of troops from Hesse-Cassel and Waldeck under Lieutenant General von Heister. This regiment first saw action at Long Island on August 27, 1776.

A diary, published in a magazine at Frankfort-on-the-Main (Frankfurt am Main, on the Main River), Hessen, in the following year, gave a graphic account of this operation and of those that followed. Important Hessian officers are mentioned here. Regarding the attack:

> *August 27….About ten o'clock we were all put under arms (the colonel having then spoken with General von Heister), and about eleven we were all in order of battle. On our left and right the English advanced on the flanks, and destroyed those that we drove back. On the left wing, where I commanded the advanced guards (thirty chasseurs and twenty grenadiers), stood Colonel Block, with his battalion. Behind me I had Captain Mallet with one company, as a reserve. In the centre Captain von Wrede attacked, and had the battalion von Minnigerode behind him. On the right Captain Lory pressed on, supported by the three remaining companies of Linsig's battalion.*[85]

This account of the battle is meaningful because Hessian lieutenant general Leopold von Heister (also de Heister) and Colonels Block, Minnigerode and "Linsig" (Linsingen) would let their presence be known in western Newtown, the future Long Island City, within days. The Hessian grenadiers and jaegers, commanded by officers wearing green coats, all spent time encamping in the future northern Astoria in 1776, at, east of and north of Astoria Park. These units were under such famous professional officers as Colonel Johann von Rall, Colonel Carl von Donop and Lieutenant General von Heister.

Colonel von Rall's military career is worth mentioning, as he did actually set foot and encamp in northern Astoria in September and October 1776. Colonel Carl von Donop was here in western Newtown also. Colonel von Rall's days were numbered. Lieutenant General von Heister stayed for three weeks at the William Lawrence house along Newtown Road in September–October 1776. Colonel von Donop and General von Heister would not fare well in 1777.

The British would outflank the Americans near Bedford during the battle. Other British and Hessian troops would engage the Continentals at their front while ten thousand flanking British collapsed the American left. Many Continental army and militia troops were captured or killed during this battle, forcing General Washington to call for all remaining generals to consider the abandonment of Long Island. "Colonel Smith's regiment of Suffolk and Queens County militia was engaged in sentry and guard duty, a part of the time in advanced positions, during the engagement since known as the Battle of Long Island."[86]

Jeromus Remsen, "born November 22nd 1735, was a man of unusual abilities, and deserves honorable notice in the history of his native town. He did service in the French war and stood conspicuous among the Whigs of Newtown at the opening of the Revolution."[87] Colonel Jeromus Remsen owned a house on Old Bowery Road (now 20th Road) and was present at the Battle of Long Island. Queens County and Newtown militia, under Colonel Remsen, took part in this battle, most not at all ready for battle. Were the North Beat Newtowners shot outright? Killed by the Hessian bayonets? Forced to surrender and thrown into the soon-to-be-fetid British prison ships or sugar houses? One local man, Captain Richard Lawrence (1725–1781), married to Amy Berrien, a relative of Dr. John Berrien Riker, was made captive and may have died in a sugar house prison. The fates of some of the Queens County troops will never be known; some names are forever lost to history. We can only honor their sacrifice.

The Newtown militia presumably lost their flag, their unit colors, not to mention the loss of brave men. The author speculates that those captured colors traveled to Queens County with the victorious Hessians. These very Hessian grenadiers would encamp in the hills of far western Newtown.

In the blur of combat on August 27, of note is the fact that Continental army major general William Alexander, Lord Stirling, directing the American retreat, surrendered to General de Heister of the Hessians as the defeat closed in. Surrender to British troops and officers would have meant rougher treatment and possible death at their hands. Remember the American generals already fallen, like General Warren at Bunker Hill and General Montgomery at Quebec. General Stirling was, after all, a traitor and a "Damned Rebel." General de Heister's headquarters would soon be, in September 1776, where Steinway Street and Newtown Road now meet.

The route was complete, the pincer movement incomplete. George Washington's army of nine thousand men was pinned back between the fortified Brooklyn Heights and the East River. The Continental army's position was untenable.

Enter Colonel Benjamin Tallmadge II (1754–1835) of Suffolk County, a colonel in command of the Second Light Dragoons, Continental army, and the future leader of George Washington's elite Culper Spy Ring. Benjamin's brother William Tallmadge (1752–1776) was a Continental army lieutenant who was captured at the Battle of Long Island and put in the prison ship *Jersey*, the most notorious British prison ship in Wallabout Bay. His bones are among the many in a mass grave at the Prison Ships Martyrs Monument at Fort Greene Park in Brooklyn. Colonel Benjamin Tallmadge, a stalwart and

This painting of the Battle of Long Island by Alonzo Chappel depicts the battle in the distance and the hasty retreat by the Americans across Gowanus Creek. *Public domain.*

true Patriot, would have future family links to Hallett's Cove and western Queens County.

Let us now retreat. We will fight them again on another day. General Lord Stirling and the Maryland troops attacked the British at the Battle of Long Island on August 27, 1776. Alonzo Chappel's 1858 painting (above) depicts the retreating Continental army heading into the Gowanus Creek to get across and back to the American fortifications surrounding Brooklyn Heights. A water crossing by equipment- and musket-laden soldiers could not have been as daunting as the sight of pursuing British and Hessian soldiers, bayonets fixed, looking to end a revolution on the first day of battle. Lord Stirling, in leading this attack against the British, bought time for hundreds of other American troops to retreat and escape from the disastrous battle. Continentals died trying to cross the creek, and this hasty retreat across the Gowanus Creek was painted by Chappel onto the canvas of American history.

The British light dragoon, a fast-moving soldier on horseback, was armed with a sword, a short musket and a single-shot pistol or two. "The British light horse was a mobile cavalry unit of any size, usually a company of men mounted on horseback ready to ride directly at you and ruin your day. These horsemen were often the scouting units and first to contact with an enemy. British outriders swept through western Queens County after subduing Newtown Village, the town seat of Newtown. The dragoons rode to the Long Island City shoreline from Newtown Creek to Lawrence Point and secured the town. The British army followed, completed the conquest and occupied. The dragoons were famous for capturing the poorly guarded Jamaica Pass, a minor strategic point, prior to the Battle of Long Island, allowing for ten thousand British soldiers to outflank the Americans on the hills near Bedford. Notice the skull and crossbones on the headgear pictured,

Right: The British dragoon was a feared horseman. The dragoons, or mounted infantry, rode into Newtown to subdue fleeing rebels and to confiscate their property. *The Green-Wood Cemetery reenactment. R. Melnick photo.*

Below: Lieutenant General Charles Earl Cornwallis (*center*), with a dragoon on the right and a local scout on the left. Because it was August, General Cornwallis had the wherewithal to rehydrate. *General Cornwallis reenactor Hugh Francis, the Green-Wood Cemetery reenactment. R. Melnick photo.*

Opposite: "Map of the Progress of his MAJESTY'S ARMIES in NEW YORK" references the extent of British operations to reconquer its temporarily lost colony, New York. *Public domain.* London Gazette, *1776.*

from the 17th Dragoons, whose horsemen rode amok throughout Newtown, doing the king's work of capture, conquest and perpetuating empire.

There are certain skills required to be a reenactor, especially one on horseback, as they take care that their uniforms, weapons and accessories are precise and true to historical accuracy. Pictured in the role of Lieutenant General Cornwallis is reenactor Hugh Francis. He is accompanied by a scout and a dragoon. At this particular event, the author witnessed a woman depicting a redcoat British officer being accidentally dismounted from her horse. The beast was frightened by the boom of a nearby cannon demonstration. Luckily, she was uninjured, yet she was momentarily hung up by her hand tangled in the horse's reins. The horse might have run if not for another uniformed redcoat rider grabbing the reins and securing it. This brought an unexpected realism and a reminder that the mere reenactment of war can be hazardous.

The Battle of Long Island was the first battle between Great Britain and its rebellious colonies after the American Declaration of Independence, the Americans' first battle as a Continental army. They were no longer quasi-united colonies. They were a new nation about to fight their first battle as a new nation. It was no longer a rebellion but a war between two sovereign powers—at least in the Americans' eyes. To the British king and colonial powers, it was rebellion and sedition and treason. Those out of favor with the king and those not offered the protection of British military power must pay for their treachery.

This 1776 overview map, below, of the entire region depicts the lower Province of New York and part of New Jersey. Lest we lose sight of our topic

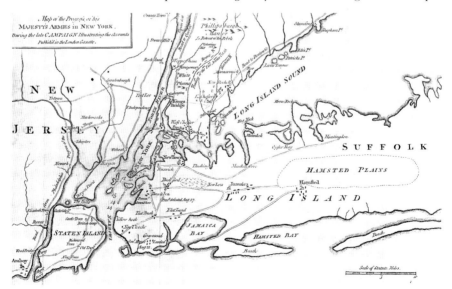

of study—Astoria, Long Island City and the western Queens County area—this map will get us there. The British outriders quickly advanced north from Brooklyn to Bedford to Newtown, Queens County. Note New York Island (Manhattan), the East River, the Hell Gate, "2 Brothers" (Islands), a misspelled "Buswick" (Bushwick) and exactly how western Queens County fits into the entire scheme of military operations in New York in 1776. Note also "New Town" in northwestern Long Island.

During the lead-up to the Battle of Long Island in late August 1776, Major General Nathanael Greene suffered a severe fever, possibly from malaria. General Greene missed all the action of August 27–30, 1776, and he nearly died. A reliable general absent from battle would have affected the command structure and battle scenario.

NICHOLAS FISH (1758–1833)

A major, brigade major and, later, a colonel in the Continental army, Nicholas Fish was born in New York City, New York Province, on August 28, 1758, into a wealthy family. He was the son of Jonathan Berrien Fish (1728–1779) and Elizabeth (née Sackett) Fish (died 1778). The Sacketts had properties and homes along the Bowery Bay Road area and family homes near Woodside Avenue, and some were buried in the Lawrence Cemetery in Astoria.

Future Continental army general John Morin Scott taught and read law to Nicholas Fish at King's College, where Fish became active in the Sons of Liberty. "In 1775, he formed a lifelong friendship with Alexander Hamilton, who was a fellow member of a drill corps and a debating society."[88] Fish, Hamilton and Robert Troup served together in the "Hearts of Oak" New York militia, later a provincial artillery unit, starting in 1775.

The Fish family was very prominent in Newtown, with landholdings on Flushing Bay, east of our Long Island City purview but very important still. There was a Fish's Point and a Fish's tidal gristmill on the future Jackson Creek. This topographical point is now forever buried under the terminals, tarmacs and runways of the modern-age La Guardia Airport—history capped. Fish was appointed Colonel Scott's brigade major and an aide-de-camp on August 9, 1776. Colonel Scott was soon to be commissioned a brigadier general. On August 21, 1776, Nicholas Fish was appointed major in the Second New York Regiment. August 27, 1776, found Major Fish in Brooklyn fighting in the Battle of Long Island with the Continental army.

The local Fish family provided other Patriots to the cause of liberty. Captain Samuel Fish died on August 17, 1776, missing by ten days, on this island, the first battle of a great war and missing by only two weeks the hardships of armed occupation. His family would have to endure such a hard, prolonged circumstance. Major Nicholas Fish had two brothers who served during the Revolutionary War, Richard and Jonathan. "Captain Richard Fish, sailing a merchant ship, was captured by the British. Captain Fish died a prisoner of war. Jonathan Fish died in 1779, leaving a son."[89] A John Fish was tortured by the British in 1776, and this may be an account:

> *In 1776, marauders from Westchester tortured Fish with hot irons to discover the hiding place of his hoard, but without success. Even Fish himself finally forgot where the gold was hidden and the pot was only discovered by strangers years afterward.*[90]

Exactly which Fish was tortured is unclear. John Fish, a Patriot, if he was forced to swear an oath of allegiance to the occupying British, would have been considered a Loyalist by any Patriot marauding from across the river. One source has the British as the marauders and torturers. Speculation suggests that the marauders may have been Patriot raiders or whale boatmen from across the upper East River in Westchester (now part of the Bronx). They would raid Loyalist homes, estates and farms in Queens County and, if they could, abduct prominent Loyalists to use as collateral for a prisoner exchange. If it was known that John Fish was related to Major Fish, he most likely would have been kidnapped for ransom or imprisoned. Also, it is unlikely but not impossible that any Patriot whaleboatmen could have crossed the East River, occupied and heavily patrolled by the British Royal Navy.

At strategic Narrow Passage, along the future Woodside Avenue, there was a large and conspicuous "Great Chestnut Tree" just south of the heavily guarded pass. This giant tree was written about in colonial and Revolutionary times and was an area landmark along the road from Newtown to Hallett's Cove. The tree is on the 1852 James Riker Jr. map and was mentioned in his important book *The Annals of Newtown*.

By August 27, 1776, a fateful day in the lives of everyone in Kings and western Queens Counties, General Woodhull, having completed only part of his mission of cattle removal, was "within six miles of the British camp, and their light horse had been within two miles of him."[91]

Depicted on the following page is a British officer on his steed at the Battle of Long Island. Sometimes an officer would have to dismount to

A British officer reenactor barked orders to nearby foot soldiers. These reenactors take great pride in their strict attention to historical detail. The British were Newtown bound. *The Green-Wood Cemetery reenactment. R. Melnick photo.*

lead and fight on foot. Entries to Henry Onderdonk's chronological events book mention Queens and other Long Island locals of note: Mr. (John Sloss) Hobart and Colonel Smith, both from Suffolk County, and Mr. Van Wyck, Major Lawrence and Colonel Remsen, from Queens. Local places of note were mentioned, such as Hoorn's Hook and Flushing. Onderdonk informs the reader that "it is not known precisely what duties the Queens county militia performed at Brooklyn, other than throwing up fortifications and standing guard at the outposts and ferries.…The Kings and Queens county militia guarded alternate days at the Flatbush pass."[92]

As for the battle, approximately 20,000 British troops, with 10,000 soldiers and sailors in support, met with about 11,000 American troops on the Long Island battlefield. The casualties and losses, were, for the Brits, 64 killed, 293 wounded and 31 missing. The Hessians had only 2 killed and 26 wounded, yet they inflicted memorable damage on some American infantry. Conversely, the defeated Americans suffered 300 killed, 800 wounded and over 1,000 captured.[93] The public was regaled with stories of victory as celebratory maps of the battle were printed and sold in Great Britain. A few of these maps were copied hastily and with blatant errors, readily available to misinform today, yet many are excellent and accurate historical maps. The author will mention certain major battles of the Revolutionary War, each battle as noteworthy as any in New York in 1776. The details of each event not within the scope of this book will purposely be abridged.

AFTER THE BATTLE OF LONG ISLAND AND INTO NEWTOWN, QUEENS COUNTY, LATE AUGUST 1776

The capture of Newtown, Queens County, occurred from August 28–29 to September 3, 1776. After the August 27 defeat at the Battle of Long Island, the British and Hessians swept into Long Island City from the southeast. American soldiers, local militiamen and Whig sympathizers were sought for capture. Businesses, farms and homes were confiscated by British troops in Dominie's Hook (Hunter's Point), Dutch Kills, Hallett's Cove, Hell Gate Neck and Bowery Bay. This incursion enabled British and Hessian regiments to occupy every home throughout western Queens. Once Long Island was abandoned by the Americans, all of Kings and Queens Counties were open to the predations of the angry British conquest.

It should be remembered that the August 27 Battle of Long Island was the greatest military defeat that men from Queens County had ever endured. The troops who were shot, overrun and bayoneted in the British and Hessian onslaught did not get their due in the historical reports of the battle. Most Americans who perished, one may dare to speculate, fought until death; some were killed while surrendering. Many Americans did not die gloriously, though their cause was just. Most Americans marched toward battle; others ran from it. The decision, as always, was made in a moment. Some soldiers that were lucky enough to flee the disastrous defeat tried to regroup.

> *Dr. Riker informs Maj. Lawrence that a number of scattering troops had posted themselves on the ridge of hills between Newtown and Jamaica: that they had been in many houses: had taken victuals and drink, but had not plundered, as he understood.*[94]

In 1776, both these men lived in western Newtown, in what is now northern Astoria. A rebel doctor and a Patriot officer had to flee their homes and leave their families. The Rikers and Lawrences were at the front of the men seeking liberty.

Of the greatest interest to our local story, on August 28, 1776, the American brigadier general Nathaniel Woodhull, the highest-ranking officer on Long Island not at the August 27 battle, was captured by British outriders. General Woodhull led a detachment of Long Island militia ordered to remove cattle from all of Newtown and Jamaica and herd them to the east, to the Hempstead Plains, away from the oncoming British army. From Suffolk County on eastern Long Island, General Woodhull, a veteran of the French and Indian War, was married to the sister of William Floyd of Suffolk County, a New York signer of the Declaration of Independence. A member of the New York Provincial Congress, he was elected its president in August 1775. Woodhull had been made a brigadier general of the Suffolk and Queens County militia by October 1775.

General Woodhull, with Queens County militia members including Richard Bragaw, George Brinckerhoff and Robert Moore, was ordered to drive off the cattle. "While the party were scouring Newtown and vicinity for cattle the British troops cut off his communications with the camp and he and several of the citizens of Newtown were taken prisoners."[95] Very importantly to the narrative of the place, Bragaw, Brinckerhoff and Moore were established and respected Newtown residents. Bragaw had homes along Dutch Kills Road (now 39th Avenue); Brinckerhoff, a strong Patriot, was a neighbor; and Major Robert Moore, of the local Moore clan, will be discussed later.

Major Jonathan Lawrence served as a major in a brigade of militia from Queens and Suffolk Counties. The British landing in Brooklyn hastened military action on Long Island. The Newtown militia was there, near the battle. The British army would be coming in large numbers to western Queens in a very short time. Major Lawrence served under General Nathaniel Woodhull on Long Island in August 1776 in an attempt to remove all livestock from Kings and Queens Counties. Major Lawrence was dispatched to New York Island by General Woodhull to gain assistance from George Washington in these cattle removal operations. Meanwhile, on August 28, 1776, General Woodhull was captured.

Of importance to western Newtown is the lead-up to the general's capture involving Major Robert Moore.

They stopped at Mrs. Cebra's, and inquired for Col. Robinson. The Colonel had gone off with Gen. Woodhull, but Robert Moore, of Newtown, (who had stopped in the house to keep the women company during the violent thunder shower,) came to the door. Mistaking him for the Colonel, they nearly cut off his hand with a sabre blow. On finding their prey had escaped, they hastened on eastward.[96]

Another report stated that Major Moore nearly had two fingers severed by the saber blow. The three Newtowners were captured and hastened to a prison ship, most likely the notorious *Jersey*. The rebel prisoners were urged to enlist in the British forces to save their skins from hopeless imprisonment. Luckily for them, they were able to bribe a friend in the British government and were released.

General Woodhull was captured in Queens County, east of Jamaica, now Hollis. His British captors, "a detachment of the 17th Light Dragoons entered the village amid thunder, lightning, and a violent rain, in pursuit of Gen. Woodhull's party, who were driving off stock."[97] General Woodhull was ordered to say, "God save the king." In his final act of defiance, Woodhull replied, "God save us all." Thus commenced his being hacked by British swords. One witness to the hardships endured by General Woodhull was Lieutenant Robert Troup, a friend of both Alexander Hamilton and Nicholas Fish. Troup wrote about this horrific event in his later years. The mortally wounded General Woodhull's prospects were not good.

It is puzzling to local and Revolutionary War historians that a battle-wise officer such as Woodhull was not given a brigade of Continental troops or Long Island militia for battle and not for cattle removal. Perhaps he and his men knew the area best, and a local general of high esteem would have garnered respect and trust from the local Whigs and, perhaps, some Tories. General Washington and his staff thought that General Woodhull was the best man for this difficult mission.

HENRY ONDERDONK JR. GOES further to reveal where some of the local Newtown Whigs or Patriot officers fled to escape the oncoming British outriders and army. Locals included the Lawrences, and the Remsens from southern Newtown. "The Rev. Simon Horton escaped to Connecticut; D. Lawrence lived seven years at Milford; Major Remsen remained in Jersey till January, 1777; Richard Lawrence was put in the sugar house."[98] Confusion ruled the days following the battle for the defenseless Newtown Whigs and their families. Their prospects were gloomy. The choices were capture and interrogation or leaving their homes, farms and possessions. Major Robert Moore's link to our area of study, Long Island City, is not only his local residence in one of the Moore houses in the vicinity but also that the major was buried with Colonel Jacob Blackwell in the former Blackwell Cemetery west of the current 37th Avenue and Vernon Boulevard.

On the night of August 28, 1776, British general William Howe moved his headquarters, in accordance with the movement of battle operations, from New Utrecht to Bedford, Long Island. His counterpart, General Washington, quite sleepless, was deeply involved with getting his army off Long Island. This headquarters allowed General Howe and his officers to consider plans to pursue and capture the well-entrenched Americans.

August 29, 1776

The territory now embraced within the limits of the city [Long Island City] *was the scene of stormy events during the Revolutionary war.*[99]

On the morning of August 29, 1776 the British light dragoons from Jamaica scoured Newtown, "and while it was yet early," wrote Riker, in his Annals of Newtown [1852], "guided by one George Rapelye, a loyalist, came along the poor bowery and halted at Jacobus Lent's to get some bread. Brandishing their naked swords they declared that they were in pursuit of that d—d rebel, Dr. Riker."[100]

The 1776 Jacobus Lent house is now the extant and historic Lent-Riker-Smith house featured later in this book. Dr. John Berrien Riker was a physician who would make a major contribution to the cause of America in future months. He had been riding throughout the town of Newtown trying to get the inhabitants not to fall victim to the enticements of General Howe's proclamations. Dr. Riker had been tearing down the most recent proclamation, issued on August 23. At this critical juncture, the good doctor feared that the offer of British protection might cloud the minds of those inclined to join or assist the American forces.

A British army under General James Robertson was ordered to march from Brooklyn through the countryside to Newtown, Queens County. The course marched in Newtown was from present-day Elmhurst to Woodside, along the future Woodside Avenue and through the Narrow Passage. Marching northwest, they hoofed the colonial road now called Newtown Road. The road brought them through Middletown (now southeastern Astoria), then along 30th Avenue, to Newtown Avenue and Main Avenue to Hallett's Cove, Hell Gate Ferry and the East River.

THE BRITISH THOUGHT AMERICAN lieutenant General Charles Lee and his army were to cross from Manhattan Island to Hallett's Cove and the river coast to flank the conquering redcoats. He did not find the enemy on western Long Island. General Robertson then "took up his quarters at William Lawrence's place (known later as Whitfield's and Halsey's) and encamped his army of 10,000 in tents on the hill and in Hallet's lot. At that time nearly the whole English army was within a few miles of there."[101] This William Lawrence house was near the intersection of the future 30th Avenue and Steinway Street, at Newtown Road. This major colonial road was crossed by the ridgeline that became a British military boundary line, the modern Steinway Street.

Queens County was taken, subdued, occupied and fortified. Any American fortifications or redoubts on the western shoreline of Long Island were now British fortifications. Western Queens County was quite securely British, yet the forward British pickets and artillery were correctly fearful of American cannon fire from York Island.

The capture of General Woodhull the previous day allowed the British forces to secure most of the cattle that the local militia were trying to keep out of the enemy's hands—and stomachs. Driving a huge herd of cattle into Newtown Village, some British soldiers committed hostile acts against the populace. "Their behavior caused Gen. Robertson to write an apology to the people of Newtown Village, although pillaging and looting of local homes continued for seven years of the British occupation."[102]

Triumphantly, on British conquest of Newtown, the Tories took pleasure in informing on their Whig neighbors, most of whom were exiled or imprisoned. The recently defeated Whigs and Patriots had their property confiscated and their homes despoiled and occupied. The residents of Queens County, whether ardent Tories or subjugated Whigs, were coerced by the ruling British military to sign a petition so that they might be restored to royal favor. Now that these citizens were under the dominion of Great Britain in every respect, the conquered people were quick to sign this petition.

Sometimes finding unique, or found only once, information is worthy of an asterisked mention. The author has tried to arrange these events and people accurately and systematically for others to learn from. A changing demographic, a fading breed of patriotic American and a passing generation have prompted the author into literary action, to save the idea of ardently and earnestly recounting our Revolutionary War history.

"In September of 1776, after the Battle of Long Island, part of Washington's Army fled through Hallett's Cove," according to an old calendar listing the historical dates of Long Island City.[103] This information is hardly substantiated. Any of a small number of troops could have fled back to their families and spirited their lives to anywhere but here. It is possible that Colonel Jacob Blackwell housed American troops for a night. Western Long Island was quickly becoming unsafe for any rebel. York Island was to be safe, for a short while. New Jersey, Connecticut and Westchester County in New York were the only options to evade the wave of British troops that was fast on its way. It was in late August 1776 that all local Patriots would have had to flee. By September 1776, any Patriot combatant or Whig sympathizer in Newtown would have been captured. After the near envelopment in Kings County, some militia could have been caught north and west of the British pincer movement. They could not come closer to engage and would have been overwhelmed; their only way to preserve themselves was to retreat. If one were a provincial in rebellion, it was best to evacuate western Queens County fast. If a Patriot remained, they were treated intolerably by their Tory and Loyalist neighbors and suffered humiliation and unfairness, yet they were alive.

Life in an occupied land is barely more tolerable than a glorious death by sword or musket ball or cannonball or bayonet. Miserable about their prospects of again serving the cause of liberty, the Patriots were trapped in the heart of British military, intellectual and commercial operations in North America. They were now Loyalists, not by design but by a very real necessity. Liberty was no longer an option. Death was possible if one's loyalty to the Crown faltered. Acquiescence and toil kept one alive.

General Howe's hesitancy, it has been postulated since that 1776 day, allowed the Americans to survive. A swift and decisive action by the British and Hessians to drive the Continental army from their fortifications and into the East River may have forced an unconditional surrender. The capture or death of American general George Washington would have, in all likelihood, ended the rebellion. General Howe's failure to advance his armies and close the trap to surround the rebels allowed them another day to stay and fight or to retreat. This one more day proved crucial in the American War of Independence, which could have been summarily snuffed out on August 28, 1776—an unrealized day of glory for the British king, army and navy.

By August 28, one full day after the Battle of Long Island in Kings County, Newtown in Queens County was in the throes of capture and submission. These never-quite-Patriot lands were soon to be again entirely British.

JOHN ALSOP IN 1776

Patriot John Alsop served New York Province as a Continental Congressman from 1774 to 1776. He rode with General Washington from Philadelphia to New York in June 1776.

> *In that last year* [of his service, 1776,] *he served as a Congressional agent tasked with securing food, material, gunpowder, housing and other critical supplies for the Continental Army, even after his house in Queens, New York was captured and occupied by British forces.*[104]

John's brother, Richard Alsop (no. 1) (circa 1726–1776), was in the early provincial legislature and owned the Alsop mansion in Newtown along Newtown Creek. Richard died in 1776 and is buried in the Alsop family cemetery. Another Richard Alsop (no. 2) lived in subjugation on this very farm. Alsop Cemetery burials of consequence during the Revolutionary War were Elizabeth Alsop, 1776; Hannah Alsop, 1777; and Thomas Alsop, 1779. John Alsop, hoping for British reconciliation and having declined to sign the Declaration of Independence, escaped to Middletown, Connecticut, and did not contribute much to the revolutionary effort. His daughter, Mary Alsop, born in 1769, achieved her own fame by marrying a future founding framer.

JOSEPH HALLETT

After the Battle of Long Island, Joseph Hallett and other prominent Long Island men were forced to leave their homes and properties. To flee the oncoming British dragoons and the following army, Joseph Hallett escaped to the relative safety of New York City. Many Patriots and Whigs literally ran for their lives, leaving their families in their homes to face the punishments that a highly perturbed and motivated British army could inflict. The capture of treasonous "damned rebels" was first and foremost, even before the total conquest of Newtown. Joseph Hallett, a strong Patriot, quartered American soldiers in his New York City home. The American Continental army and state militias were near to escaping from Long Island and were battered and war-weary. Their continued stay on this York Island was about to be cut short. The Halletts' Hallett's Cove home, at this time, was just being captured by the advancing British army, just days away from full control of western Queens County.

Women

Women of western Newtown, who were made mention of in period literature, are included and inserted in the chronological sequence of this book.

Ruth Lawrence

The day after the great battle, on the night of August 28–29, 1776, "the British light horse, searching for rebels, entered the Lawrence house and demanded food. Mrs. Lawrence and her sister-in-law, the wife of Capt. Abraham Riker, fed them and then fled with the Lawrence children to the East River. Guided by a slave, they crossed to Ward's Island and at daylight found a boat to take them to Harlem. They did not see their homes for the next seven years."[105] The British light horse were the 17th Dragoons, captained by Samuel Birch. A faithful family slave rowed the boat that helped Mrs. Lawrence and Mrs. Riker escape. It is surprising that these two women, wives of prominent Newtown Patriots, were not taken into custody, as was the fate of other local Whig women, including Elizabeth Lewis, wife of signer Francis Lewis. Their decision to flee was wise. The light horse were looking for rebel males. The ladies might have been captured and confined by the British army, which was soon to follow.

On August 29, 1776, at the Lent house at the Poor Bowery in northern Newtown, now the Lent-Riker-Smith house:

> *The females at Mr. Lent's were terrified at the ferocious appearance of the light horse, and, observing the greediness with which they broke and ate the dry bread, Balche, a colored woman, innocently inquired of her mistress whether they would not eat* them. *They dashed off toward Hell Gate, but the doctor had escaped in a boat to Barn Island and thus eluded the demons in human form.*[106]

The escaped doctor was the notorious Dr. John Berrien Riker, a vehement Patriot.

After the Battle of Long Island, British invaders-turned-marauders sought food and plunder. No residence was safe, especially those of the Whigs. Patriot women left behind in their homes were subject to all types of indignities. While their men had the option to escape, the women and children often could not leave. "The days that tried men's also tried women's souls."[107]

Elizabeth Hallett

The wife of patriot Joseph Hallett, Elizabeth, was captured by the British and taken prisoner, along with her children and other patriot wives, to New Jersey. "The house they were in was eventually set afire and they were only saved by a mob of British soldiers who rioted. The next day these women were returned to New York City."[108] Elizabeth lived there and remained under guard until she was reunited with Joseph after the war.

Onderdonk lists some of the Queens County militia payrolls in his 1846 book *Revolutionary Incidents of Queens County*, although there are no Newtown North Beat statistics listed. North Beat documents may have been captured and destroyed by the victorious British, or maybe they reside deep within a British or Hessian archive somewhere in Europe. Yet some local western Newtown names appear, suggesting that the units may have been consolidated for whatever purpose was necessary. From the Queens County militiamen, upward of forty-four troops were detached to General Woodhull's unsuccessful mission to move all livestock to the east and away from the oncoming British.

One of the most famous retreats in the annals of world military history, General George Washington's nighttime retreat from Long Island was nothing short of a miracle. *Public domain. Library of Congress.*

After the news of the American defeat in Kings County, some of the demoralized soldiers abandoned their mission and went home to save their families and themselves. To remain was assured capture. To flee was prudent and would enable a soldier to move to a safe area to regroup and further serve the just cause of liberty, as many did. The names of local importance were Sergeant William Penfold and Privates James Hallet III, Samuel Blackwell, Nathaniel Hallet, Peter Bragaw, Jeromus Rapelye, Luke Remsen (from the South Beat), James Morrell and Edmund Penfold, all of whose families had property and dwellings within the future Long Island City.

General George Washington's Continental army and militias had their literal backs against the wall, that wall being made of water, the formidable East River. From their positions on the Brooklyn Heights, Continental troops were told to discreetly abandon their dug-in positions and to join the clandestine evacuation at the Brooklyn ferry point. Some units were left behind to make noise and tend to the campfires to perpetuate the illusion that the American high ground was still fully occupied. Come nightfall on August 29, 1776, there commenced an attempt at a great retreat of Washington's army off Long Island.

AUGUST 29–30, 1776: THE AMERICAN EVACUATION OF LONG ISLAND.

When you go through deep waters, I will be with you. When you go through rivers of difficulty, you will not drown.
—Isaiah 43:2, NLT[109]

The British Royal Navy could not yet venture into the East River to cut off the American retreat due to ill winds and questionable deliberate British military delays. If the Continentals had gotten trapped between the British and Hessians on land and the Royal Navy on the East River, the revolution may have ended right there. The nights of August 27, 28 and 29 saw General George Washington behind his lines in Kings County. The general needed to hazard a daring and desperate retrograde water operation to get his nine-thousand-man army to the relative safety of New York City. The one-mile-wide East River presented an obstacle of the highest order.

Major, not colonel, Nicholas Fish played a role in the August 29, 1776 evacuation of Long Island across the East River to Manhattan. One article about the retreat was titled "Mob of Soldiers Were Crazed with Fear":

On the East River banks, baggage, ammunition, and artillery disembarked first for New York. The ranks, although ordered not to speak or even cough, began reacting to the threat of British ships looming out of the darkness between them and safety. Colonel Israel Hand saw "frightful disorder" growing at the ferry, with "the mob of soldiers, maddened by fear… crowding the declivity from Sands Street to the water." Colonel Fish, one of Washington's aides, lifted a stone above his head and threatened to sink an overloaded boat and its unruly, panicking soldiers unless order was restored. Some groups tried climbing over the shoulders and heads of those in front, but other regiments were not infected with contagious panic and disembarked in disciplined order.[110]

The acclaimed American historian Patrick O'Donnell, in his book *The Indispensables* (2021), attributes the above "lifted a stone above his head" episode to none other than General George Washington himself. According to O'Donnell, to quell the panic and continue with a quiet and orderly water retreat, the irate commander said, "I will sink this boat to Hell if there's not order."[111] Contrary winds, heavy fog and, perhaps, divine Providence allowed the Continental army and militia units to escape to fight another day.

With so much military activity in Kings and Queens Counties on August 30, 1776, many local Tories and former Whigs were enlisted to aid in the martial maneuvers of the king's army. A conquering army on your land and in your town has overwhelming demands. "Wm. Warne, from Long Island, reports to Congress that 'Suffolk county sent three hundred wagons to transport Howe's baggage and cannon towards Newtown or Hell-Gate, and that Justice Kissam was administering oaths of allegiance.'"[112] Western Queens County had to be subdued, surveyed and mapped to facilitate efficient and deliberate troop movement and the difficult conveyance of cannon, wagons, equipment, horses and baggage. The British were massing in Queens County for an assault on New York. The lands of the future Long Island City were teeming with battle-seeking Britons and Germans.

It is important to point out errors in the historical narrative. Quasi-facts and mistruths may lead one to believe errors to be truth. On August 30, 1776, regarding the Patriot Jacob Blackwell house along the East River: the Jacob Blackwell "mansion has been called the Washington House, as it is said that Washington, on his retreat after the Battle of Long Island, passed a night there," stated the *Brooklyn Eagle* in 1900.[113] Unless stated in a source not found by the author, General George Washington's retreat off Long Island to New York (Manhattan) Island on August 30, 1776, did not happen from this Blackwell house or from Queens County. The overwhelming majority of the Continental army troops evacuated Long Island from the Brookland or Brooklyn Ferry across the tidal East River to southern New York Island. Some local Queens and Suffolk County militia could have escaped behind the British army's near-encirclement and fled to their homes. Their goals were to save their families, some scant possessions and themselves. In Queens, the British were hot on the trail of retreating rebels.

There is no doubt that the generals and officers had the greatest difficulty in the near chaos of evacuation. Panic strikes hard when trying to flee a nearby and impending doom. Not only did American officers have to control the fear-stricken troops, but rumor also played a role in exacerbating the urgency to get off Long Island. The British army and navy were very close by. Time was running out. Daylight and the enemy were on their way. Order prevailed, as their lives depended on order, stealth, efficiency and stamina. Dear God, don't let us die here. Get us across this rough East River. On the night of August 29–30, 1776, Major Benjamin Tallmadge, who did not yet know that his brother, William, had been taken captive by the British during the battle, wrote of the historic and hasty American retreat. Being one of the last Patriot officers, after nine thousand troops, to evacuate Long Island, Major Tallmadge wrote, "In the history of warfare I do not recall a more fortunate retreat."[114] Most military leaders would not want to be remembered for a battle defeat and a pell-mell retreat. Shame and dishonor readily attach themselves to defeated generals. This was one of the greatest retrograde operations in military history, and American historian Richard M. Ketcham wrote that he "will be the first to acknowledge that this retreat should hold a high place among military transactions."[115]

Up the East River at the northern end of the narrow Hell Gate, beyond Lawrence Point on northwest Long Island, the East River widens. Some early maps called this the upper section of the East River or the Long Island Sound itself. From the Long Island Sound westward into the East River is the back door to New York Harbor. Only the treacherous Hell Gate hindered a strong enemy navy from attacking New York. In late August 1776, British warships were closing in on western Newtown waters. The British warships HMS *Halifax*, *Niger* and *Brune* were on their way to the waters around Riker's Island and Lawrence Point via the Long Island Sound.

From August 30 to September 8, 1776, the majority of British troops had to encamp inland on western Long Island due to American cannon batteries on Manhattan. The king's men near Hallett's Cove had to fear

Thompson's Battery of nine guns at Horn's Hook, now Gracie Point. A wayward American shot from Horn's Hook could send an iron cannonball not only 450 yards to Hallett's Point but also up to 1,200 yards inland, some further. Maps from 1776 reveal some high ground, a low bluff no more than forty feet above sea level at Horn's Hook. At Astoria, the highest ground where the British artillery batteries stood was but a small, fortified hill near the western edge. The topography at this site was totally flattened by nineteenth-century development.

In late August 1776, when John Alsop's home in western Newtown was captured by the British, Alsop was said to have kept working from Manhattan. The former Continental Congressman did not sign the Declaration, yet he was still considered a friend of liberty and was allowed to remain within the American lines. As history would have it, John Alsop's stay in New York City was soon to come to an end.

Flags of 1776

The flag that flew over Newtown and all of Queens County in 1776 was the British Union Jack, the flag of Great Britain. Lesser flags and ensigns may have been flown by Loyalists or Patriots, depending on their leanings. Those local men holding a predilection toward liberty were most likely to raise the Grand Union flag for the United Colonies or a local Newtown militia flag. All other ensigns and flags raised by rebels in Queens County were torn down to make way for the Union Jack. After the August 29–30, 1776 conquest of Queens County, British national and regimental flags were raised. Patriotic fervor in western Queens was squashed. If a Patriot did not flee, he was captured. No other flags dared fly in this heavily occupied land we would later call Long Island City. A new American flag would not be seen in these parts for years to come.

On the British conquest of all western Queens County, zealous Royalists were convinced to join the Crown's local militia forces. "In Newtown the following new officers were chosen in the northern beat: George Rapelye, captain."[116] George Rapelye was an ardent Tory, helping the British occupiers and informing on all persons with suppressed Whig proclivities. This Rapelye was one of many area Tories strongly British in sentiment and, knowing their place in the hierarchy of military rule, highly motivated by monetary and societal gain. Other Loyalists turned militiamen were "Daniel Rapelye, lieutenant; Jeromus Rapelye, ensign. The south beat was commanded by: Captain Dow Van Duyn. The officers of the light horse were: Cornelius Rapelye, captain; Daniel Rapelye, lieutenant; Daniel Lent, cornet."[117] Interestingly, not only were the Rapelyes ardent Tories, but Daniel Lent, from a Whig family, also served in the king's forces, irrespective of his true political leanings.

Queens County, especially at its farthest western points, the future Long Island City, had to be conquered and occupied. The British knew that Long Island, once theirs, was a tenable springboard to a major assault on New York Island.

The situation on the ground was this: a found-out rebel was doomed to arrest and imprisonment, at worst, and, at best, to loyalty oaths, subjugation, ridicule and never ever being considered a true British subject. Colonial Tories, though truly loyal to King George III, were never to be part of the British aristocracy and military officer corps. Merit and valor would often not be enough to enter the upper hierarchy of British leaders and officers.

From on the Brooklyn Heights, the last Continental army troops left the forward positions perhaps as late as sunup and after the heavy fog lifted on August 30, 1776. The last American troops had left Long Island with General George Washington in the last boat. As for Long Island, the Americans were gone. One river, the strong tidal East River, separated two different ideologies and two great armies. They would meet again. The night of August 30, 1776, witnessed a temporarily relieved and highly fatigued General Washington. Every troop under his command needed to collapse into the sleep of exhaustion. Washington's army, his American army, his Continental army, was safe. For now.

August 31, 1776

With the British conquest of Newtown in full force, British troops not only secured the land and property for their king but also marauded and pillaged the houses and farms. This was the raw and rampant power of empire. These discrediting undertakings appalled the British commander. Hearts and minds are not won this way.

> *Newtown, L.I., Aug. 31, 1776. Maj. Gen. Robertson, responsible for the actions of those he commands, takes upon himself the responsibility of satisfying the people of the village for the depredations committed last evening by part of the 1st brigade, who came for water. He hopes for the*

future his troops will abstain from a crime which disgraces even victory, and defeats the King's intention to protect and reclaim his American subjects.[118]

Colonel Jeromus Remsen, of White Pot, now Forest Hills, commanded half of the Queens County militia. Colonel Remsen mentioned troops wishing to return to Queens and Suffolk Counties on Long Island to rescue their families and effects. He had a family home on Old Bowery Road, freshly occupied by the British. Major General William Heath wrote to General Washington of his Queens troops' situation. "Aug: 31st 1776. Since Enclosing—Col. Remsen's Regiment are here, they say their Time of Engagement is up this Day many of them are desirous, to go over and if possible save their Families & Effects, Should be glad to know your Excellency's Pleasure in this respect—They say they mean to return, I cannot answer for them."[119] The options for a Whig retreat from Newtown were (1) eastwards beyond Queens County, (2) to York (Manhattan) Island or (3) to the mainland. On the main was Westchester County and Upstate New York, with Connecticut to the east and New Jersey across the Hudson River to the west. Many local Patriots retreated to these places before recommencing their war efforts in various capacities.

GENERAL WILLIAM HOWE HEADQUARTERS

British outriders and the following army conquered and secured western Newtown. On August 31, 1776, General William Howe stayed for one night at "Hell Gate, Long Island August 31, 1776."[120] It is not readily known to the author where exactly General Howe headquartered, as the location of Hell Gate is vague. It must have been either at a Lawrence home at Hallett's Cove or the more prominent Lawrence house two miles inland. In 1776, the Lawrences also had a home later owned by the Woolseys, today the site of the Queens tower of the Robert F. Kennedy (Triborough) Bridge, overlooking the Hell Gate. It was wise that, after that one night, General Howe and his officers moved inland, away from the coastline, to ponder their next move.

British grenadiers maneuvered across the wooded rolling hills and farms, en route to occupying all of western Newtown, in 1776, as shown in a mural originally from 1939, shown on the following page. These skilled soldiers trod heavily on the rugged hills above and east of Hallett's Cove, the creek valley and high hills of Dutch Kills and the hills, marshlands and tidal islands

This is a section of the 1939 Vincent Aderente mural depicting the history of Long Island City. Three British grenadiers patrol the conquered Newtown countryside. *Courtesy Quinn Funeral Home, Astoria, New York. Building closed December 2018. R. Melnick photo.*

at Bowery Bay. The original mural was thirty by ten feet; this section from a smaller copy, half its size, recalls a major chapter in Long Island City's important past: the Revolutionary War.

The British authorities put a price on the heads of all four New York signers of the Declaration of Independence. Francis Lewis was the only signer of the Declaration to hail from Queens County. Although his Whitestone home was outside the purview of this book, Francis Lewis was of great importance to the county, the state and the country. In late August 1776, Francis Lewis's home was fired on by the HMS *Niger*, and his property and effects were destroyed. Obviously, this was a retaliatory strike against the treasonous Lewis, who was away dealing with congressional matters in Philadelphia. Lewis would most assuredly have been arrested on the spot or hanged as a traitor from the nearest tree on his own estate. The enemy jailed his wife, Elizabeth Annesley Lewis, whose trials and tribulations were worthy of mention.

A few sources mention the British ships patrolling and anchoring in the eastern (upper) portion of the East River. The HMS *Niger* (32 guns), HMS *Brune* (32) and HMS *Halifax* (6), a schooner, were protecting the northern entrance to Hell Gate, the lower East River and New York City. These medium-sized frigates, and support brigantines and schooners, had yet to pass through the Hell Gate. Bold attempts at her passage were necessary and imminent. War dictated such things.

Lieutenant Colonel Samuel Birch (1735–1811) led his 17th Regiment of (Light) Dragoons, a fast-moving cavalry unit, into northwestern Queens. Birch fought in the major battles of Bunker Hill and Long Island and, later, at Fort Washington and Monmouth. This fierce horse commander had free reign throughout western Queens and made encampments in the northern Astoria area. On the 1776 Charles Blaskowitz map on page 172, just south of "Bowry Pt.," which is actually Lawrence Point, was, below the unnamed Berrien's Island, a place called "Birch Pt." The colonel was here, with his dragoons, imposing the king's will and law on all his subjects.

THE EPISCOPAL CHRISTIAN CHURCH was spared by the invading and occupying British due to its being aligned with the Church of England. Episcopalian was the denomination of British leaders and military officers and the only faith recognized by the king of England. Other Christian Protestant denominations, such as the Presbyterians, had their churches vandalized and dishonored as being the churches that helped incite rebellion. The

Revolutionary War was sometimes referred to as the "Presbyterian War," and that church garnered the greatest disdain from the ruling British and their supporting Tories. The two branches prayed to the same Christian God yet served different masters, either the Crown or the rebellion.

It is well known that throughout history, when confronted with an enemy force marching up your road, a fateful choice must be made. In order to remain alive and not imprisoned or dead, one has to change their stripes—or hide their stripes. Perhaps, and most likely, the area Newtown Presbyterians had to convert to the Episcopal faith or suffer the consequences—a religious oath of loyalty to the British Anglican Church, if you will.

> *Owing to the circumstances described earlier, the Tory inhabitants of Newtown were the majority and, just as soon as the British had shown their supremacy at the beginning of the War, these Tories turned violently against their Whig neighbors and spied upon them, refused to buy and sell trade items, did damages to their lands and farms, and, in one instance Dr. Moore led a group of young Tories to cut off the steeple of the Presbyterian Church in Elmhurst, because that group of people said that they stood for Independence.*[121]

> *Do not gloat over me, my enemy! Though I have fallen, I will rise. Though I sit in darkness, the LORD will be my light.*
> *—Micah 7:8*[122]

Chapter 6

ANCIENT HOUSES IN LONG ISLAND CITY, QUEENS COUNTY

There is something about these ancient habitations that commands respect, especially from those who possess love of country and admiration for its early struggles, and the sturdy, courageous men who once resided here.[123]

On the Americans abandoning Long Island, the King's army moved from Bedford, leaving Heister with two brigades of Hessians on the Heights, one brigade of British at Bedford, and took five positions in the neighborhood of Newtown, Bushwick, Hell-Gate, and Flushing.[124]

Patriot houses, homesteads and farms were the earliest targets of the conquering troops. Whig homes in western Queens were used for billeting British officers, and some were used to house horse troops and foot soldiers. Loyalist homes were also billets for officers and troops, yet the terms of occupation for the Loyalists was less harsh. The ancient colonial homes in the future Long Island City, many pictured in this chapter, were all extant in 1776, the primary year of revolutionary activity in this locality. Each of the featured old houses had an event or British and Hessian troop occupation associated with the home and its residents.

The Alsop House was built circa 1655 by Thomas Wandell, who died at the house in 1691 and was an uncle of Richard Alsop, the first Richard Alsop. Richard's sons and grandsons continued to occupy the formidable homestead and farm. One Thomas Alsop married Catherine Brinckerhoff, the daughter of George, a fervent Revolutionary Patriot who lived along the Dutch Kills Road. The Alsop farm was in the not-yet-named Laurel

The Alsop Mansion, circa 1655, served as the temporary headquarters of Lieutenant General Charles Cornwallis, and Hessian colonel Carl von Donop. *QBPL. Courtesy* Once Upon a Time, *LIC Savings Bank booklet, 1951.*

Hill section of Newtown. Just south of the home was a ferry crossing the Newtown Creek, made very busy by the occupying British. The ferryboat ran here at the southern terminus of the strategic colonial road that ran from Newtown Creek to points north to Bowery Bay. Alsop's house "was one hundred feet long, and the first floor was divided into four rooms, with a hallway eighteen feet wide."[125]

Fresh water was a precious commodity on a long and relatively narrow island surrounded by the salt water of the Atlantic Ocean, New York Bay, the East River and the Long Island Sound. There was fresh water at "the well on the Alsop property, which was sunk at the time the mansion was built, [and] still [as of 1880] supplies water to many families in the neighborhood."[126] As in ancient times, the proximity of a freshwater well was of supreme importance to quench the thirsts of family and nearby friends, livestock and farm crops. During the Revolutionary War, the thirsty British and Hessian soldiery required fresh water to exist and to operate a grand military occupation.

From the Alsop house, it was a hill's climb to the small family cemetery plot to the northwest. The first interment in the Protestant Alsop burial ground was in 1718. Today, the Alsop Family Burial Ground lies entirely within the First, or Old Calvary, Cemetery (the first of four large sections), as per an agreement between the Alsop property executors and the Roman

The Alsop Family Burial Ground, a Protestant cemetery, lay entirely within the boundaries of the 1848, First or Old Calvary Cemetery, a large Catholic burying place. *QBPL.*

Catholic Church diocese in New York City. It opened to Catholic interments in 1848. The Alsop house stood nobly just across the road and down the hill until 1879. The Alsop family history, the burial ground and the surrounding giant cemetery present excellent stories and unique scenic vistas. The views verify the high ground as formerly sparse yet fertile and militarily strategic. This vantage point kept an eye on Newtown Creek and the southwestern edge of the town of Newtown. The British army and its highest-ranking officers were at the Alsop house.

A note with the Queens Borough Public Library (QBPL) photograph (shown on the following page): "End wall bulging out and bracing in place to keep the wall from collapsing. / demolished early 20th cent. / Stone wall and posts disappeared by mid-1925."[127] Confusion enters the discussion regarding this ancient Moore homestead. Not only is there uncertainty as to the actual house name, but there are also two different and conflicting road names that muddy the path. This grand stone house was on Old Bowery Road, although the road was called "Bowery Bay Rd." on this QBPL image. Bowery Bay Road was a strategic military defense, patrol and supply road between Newtown Creek to the south and Bowery Bay to the north.

This ancient and demolished house, the old Captain Samuel Moore house, was along Old Bowery Road, currently in the Steinway section of northern Astoria. It is not the old home of Nathaniel Moore, formerly near

The Captain Samuel Moore House was actually on Old Bowery Road, not to be confused with the nearby and well-traveled Bowery Bay Road. *QBPL.*

the extant Moore-Jackson Cemetery on the colonial Bowery Bay Road. There are two different houses, and there is veracity in each claim. Upward of ten different photographs present two houses. Definitive identifiers are a sturdy stone wall with five-foot-high stone pillars, house chimneys, certain tree patterns and shadows cast, which are noteworthy as they can be used for comparison purposes in other photographs. One Greater Astoria Historical Society (GAHS) photograph's caption reads, "Moore Homestead, Shore Rd., Steinway." By modern location points, the house would have been on the north side of 20th Road, part of the former Old Bowery Road, at 45th Street, the former Titus Street.

The Lieutenant General Henry Clinton headquarters, in September 1776, was to be at the Nathaniel Moore house, on Bowery Bay Road, not at the pictured house. The Moore-Jackson Cemetery, as of 2023, uses this image on its informational signage as being the Nathaniel Moore homesite. The extant colonial cemetery has been there since 1733. A Samuel Moore was the Newtown town clerk during the British occupation. During the tumultuous year of 1776, until he was forced to escape, Colonel Jeromus Remsen owned this Captain Samuel Moore house.

The Lent-Riker-Smith house as photographed in 1923 by Eugene Armbruster, a man famous for his prolific photography of Queens County and New York City. *QBPL.*

The stone pillars and gate pictured in the foreground are from a long-gone Riker home and property, home to Jacobus Rapelye in 1776. Across this portion of Bowery Bay Road is the surviving Lent-Riker-Smith house. The Lent house was built on "the lands allotted to the Dutch Reformed Church by the Crown as an '*armen bouwerie*' or poor farm, to be used for the support of the indigent; from this comes the later name for the area, Bowery Bay."[128] In 1729, the house was willed to Abraham Lent, and it belonged to Jacobus Lent in 1776. On August 27–28, 1776, "Dr. Riker, a family connection, took refuge here from the British after the battle of Long Island."[129]

The March 1923 photo on the top of the following page shows the still-rural character of the area, prior to the nearby Marine Air Terminal and bridge to the Riker's Island Jail being constructed. This view from behind the Lent-Riker-Smith house at the Bowery Bay's edge, near the family cemetery, shows the former Jacobus Rapelye house in the right distance. Notice the trolley tracks along 19th Avenue (the former Riker Avenue), headed from Steinway Street eastward to the soon-to-be-defunct North Beach amusement park. This road, which ran behind the Lent house and Riker Cemetery, is still there, now a lesser thoroughfare that was forced south at 81st Street.

This Eugene Armbruster photograph, facing southeast from 19th Avenue (formerly Riker Avenue), shows the Lent-Riker-Smith house and Riker Cemetery. *QBPL.*

The Riker Cemetery fence and walls enclose the family graves and headstones on the Lent-Riker-Smith house property. Participants of two rebellions rest here. *R. Melnick photo.*

"A short distance from the house is the Riker burying ground, where repose the remains of many members of this prolific, long lived and active family."[130] The Riker cemetery plot contains 131 interments, the oldest being rough-hewn fieldstone tablets rudely lettered and shaped, the earliest dating to 1744. Many prominent Newtown families, such as Fish, Brinckerhoff, Lawrence, Berrien, Remsen and others, married into the Riker family, some of whom are buried here. The Riker Cemetery gate on the Lent-Riker-Smith house grounds gives access to the old graves and the informative stones. The cemetery is meticulously cared for by house and property owner Marion Duckworth Smith. The "most illustrious occupant of this little burial ground is Dr. Berrien Riker, surgeon-general of the Revolutionary army and companion of Washington at Valley Forge, before whose grave annual services are conducted on Memorial Day. Three stones away is the memorial to Capt. Abraham Riker, who fought at Quebec and White Plains, and died at Valley Forge when only 38."[131]

This Revolutionary War veteran grave marker (below) announces to all that an original American here rests peacefully. Lest we forget. The weathered and dented medallion states, "Revolutionary War Veteran," encircling the letters "US" in a five-pointed star. The outer ornamentation is a circle of laurel branches, a known symbol of peace. The cemetery and property under the shade of tall trees at the "Poor Bowery" has a country feel, so close to urban roads, bus routes and a major national airport.

A U.S. Revolutionary War veteran grave marker in the Riker Cemetery. Dr. John Berrien Riker saved the life of a future American president at the 1776 Battle of Trenton. *R. Melnick photo.*

This splendid view of the house on the following page reveals paths, an ivy-covered wall, gabled windows, verdant grounds and Old Glory—the American flag—gracing the ancient structure. This historic and visually appealing house is located at 78-03 19th Road just east of the Astoria border at Hazen Street in East Elmhurst, Queens. With tall trees and cultivated gardens, the property recalls a time gone by. Most of, if not all, the old-growth forests in Queens County were destroyed during the British occupation. The great need for wood for cooking and fuel caused the large army to cut down the trees and brush. The flags that

A magnificent photograph of the present Lent-Riker-Smith house, facing east. This is an excellent example of dedicated historic preservation done correctly. *Courtesy Marion Duckworth Smith.*

must have flown at this home are many: the Dutch flag, the English flag, the British Union Jack and perhaps an American colonial militia flag. During the war, the British Union Jack flew again, and since the peace of 1783, the numerous American flags spangled with thirteen to fifty stars.

The house is the only ancient home remaining in western Queens County, very close to the future Long Island City, although the Lent-Riker-Smith house is just beyond our area of study. Strategically located in 1776, at the north end of Bowery Bay Road, it is such a noteworthy house, cemetery, grounds and story that it must be included here. It was merely a stone's throw from the future town line.

The powers that be didn't think it necessary to preserve any dwelling or site that commemorated a battle loss or the harsh British occupation. Sometimes defeat can be forgotten, when the defeated are long gone. The Battle of Long Island was an inglorious defeat for the Americans. There were other battles and days to celebrate. The importance of the Lent house is illustrated with the image above. "The spacious old house surrounded by many trees along the sea beach, with its classic library and numerous patriotic prints was in earlier days a sort of Liberty Hall, where distinguished guests were hospitably entertained."[132]

The quaint inside of the Lent-Riker-Smith house, revealing period furniture and a finely polished wooden plank floor. The home is magnificent. *Courtesy Marion Duckworth Smith.*

The home is an active residence, not only a landmarked house. The extant ancient houses of New York City often rely on some portion of an older house existing within a later home. Note the different owners of the house: for example, Rycken, Riker, Lent, Rapelje/Rapalye, Smith, etc. The historical record reveals the house's name based on when a given story was written, not on the occupant in 1776. Its strategic location on the waterfront enabled the home to play a vital role during the Revolutionary War. During the British occupation of Newtown (1776–1783), "the highway [Bowery Bay Road] became a military road and was constantly patrolled by British troops safeguarding the moving of supplies to the permanent troop encampments along 39th Ave. Woodside (old Dutch Kills Rd.)."[133] Modern references to colonial times still exist in nearby Lawrence Point and on Berrian Boulevard and, of course, Rikers Island, the good family name now forever sullied by the large and notorious New York City jail.

COLONEL JACOB BLACKWELL

The story of Jacob Blackwell (1717–1780) quite possibly depicts the strongest struggle of any Newtowner. The most controversial and outspoken Patriot in all of Newtown, Colonel Jacob Blackwell proudly promoted the cause of liberty. Serving the British cause as an officer in the French and Indian War, Colonel Blackwell was later a member of the New York Provincial Congress for three years, 1774–76. The Blackwell family had properties and homes on Long Island and on Blackwell's Island in the East River. Now Roosevelt Island, it was named Blackwell's Island from the 1680s until 1921. Colonel Jacob Blackwell's Long Island homestead stood from circa 1730 until 1901, along the road that became Vernon Avenue.

A circa 1890 photograph shows the Jacob Blackwell house front door, still at one with the house. The two became separate in 1901 when the house was demolished and, surprisingly, the door was saved as a Revolutionary War artifact. The large brass door knocker still exists, apart from the door, as part of the Franklin Delano Roosevelt archive in Hyde Park, New York. GAHS has excellent documentation of the grand history of the house, door and knocker.

Around August 30, 1776, British military power arrived at the Jacob Blackwell house. Colonel Blackwell, knowing full well that the British would come following the American defeat at the Battle of Long Island, had to flee. An outspoken and ardent Patriot, Colonel Blackwell had to escape the enemy onslaught of late August 1776. "When the British troops invaded Newtown, room was not left for patriots such as he, and he fled to Hopewell, New Jersey. His home at the foot of Webster Avenue (which we adjure the reader to see before it falls under the infirmities of age) was confiscated and marked with the Broad Arrow of the King of England."[134] Francis Lord Rawdon, a British officer of the highest caliber, and his staff, for a time, occupied the Jacob Blackwell house. We recall Lord Rawdon's bravery at Bunker Hill in June 1775.

The occupation was evidenced by the British "Arrow of Confiscation" that remained from the 1776 seizure of the Blackwell home. The circa 1730 house had a huge, eight-foot-high Dutch door, and from circa 1765, its light portals had flaunted the British glass manufacturing laws; it was later made famous by the king's broad arrow. A conquering British army officer hacked the broad arrow into Blackwell's front door, their method of confiscating rebel property. Some sources referred to the mark as the Crow's

An outstanding photograph in terms of the historicity of the Jacob Blackwell House. The door has been GAHS property since 2007; here, it is still attached to the house. *GAHS collection.*

Foot. Other confiscated houses, businesses and horses were marked with "G.R.," for the Latin "George Rex," meaning the property belonged to British king George III. Also confiscated was the former Blackwell tidal gristmill on Sunswick Creek at Hallett's Cove. During the war, it was Suydam's mill. The British had deep ire toward Blackwell and the rebels for flaunting their nonadherence to the laws placed on the colonists by the Crown, as specified in the punitive 1767 Townshend Acts. Wherever you are, rebel colonel, what was yours is now the king's.

The writing along the photograph's perimeter is that of the prolific Queens historian Vincent Seyfried. It reads, at the top: "Now with L.I. Historical Society Brooklyn." At the bottom: "Old Blackwell House Front Door." The Blackwell family burial ground was north of the house, and in

The Jacob Blackwell mansion, built circa 1730, hasn't aged well in this image, circa 1890. Colonel Blackwell's home was confiscated in 1776 and occupied by the British. *GAHS collection.*

1900, the bodies were disinterred and moved to the St. George's Episcopal Church cemetery on 14th Street (then Woolsey Street) in Old Astoria Village. There are a Blackwell plot and numerous other Blackwell headstones in the graveyard. The grand Blackwell home was torn down in 1901. Another prominent Revolutionary War officer and veteran buried in the old Blackwell Cemetery was Major Robert Moore.

The photo above depicts the rough later years of the circa 1730 Jacob Blackwell house. The stucco-type concrete wall covering has peeled away in parts, down to the ancient stacked stone that the house was built with. Some sources mentioned a possible earlier home built there, dating to as early as circa 1700, 1711 or 1692. The year 1730, according to GAHS, is most likely the year for the home's original construction. The house bore witness to both Patriot ideas and British plans. In this photo, circa 1890, there are three gentlemen looking at the camera from the front porch where the famous Jacob Blackwell house front door was. Note the period bowler hat on the middle fellow. The Vincent Seyfried writing informing the photograph reads, "Old Blackwell House N/S Webster Ave. Front Towards River." The

The Royal "Arrow of Confiscation" was hacked into the door of the Jacob Blackwell house along the East River. This home now belonged to the king. *Door, GAHS property. R. Melnick photo.*

"N/S" means on the north side of Webster Avenue, now 37th Avenue, which once went to the East River's edge and, in later years, to a steamboat dock.

In late August 1776, just after the battle, Colonel Jacob Blackwell fled to New Jersey, as the British invaded Newtown, Queens County. Escape or hang from a tree. The British dragoons are in our town. We must go…now!

The magnificent Blackwell house door languished perilously at the Brooklyn Museum until it was rescued through deacquisition to GAHS in 2007. This grand door had a new home at 35-20 Broadway, Astoria, at the corner of 36th Street (formerly named Blackwell Street), from 2007 until 2018. Fittingly, the door's reclaimant, the Greater Astoria Historical Society, was located in this building. The door, of little import to Brooklyn, had come full circle back home to Long Island City.

Red Ribbon of Loyalty

Loyalists and oath-signing Whigs, as a sign of subservience to the British military authorities, were forced to wear a red ribbon or a red cloth on their hat or shirt to indicate their allegiance to King George III. If a British officer rode by or soldiers came to their homes, citizens and residents had to show deference to the military. Respect was given by a tip of the cap and providing refreshment to the troops and horses, no questions asked. Only acquiescence and subservience would do. "The badge of loyalty was a red cockade, a red ribbon around the hat, (the longer it streamed down behind the more loyal,) or even a red flannel rag tucked under the hat-band."[135] British announcements on broadsides may have been as follows: "To all Newtown residents: Your home and farm and places of rest, and your neighbors' homes and farms are now and once again part of the British realm. Your local Officer in Charge is Major Willoughby of Lord Cornwallis's 33rd Regiment. Grievances and Inquiries may be submitted at the Brinckerhoff house on Dutch Kills Road."[136]

A red ribbon, the color of the redcoats, was the color of blood. More blood was sure to be shed to achieve one of two conflicting goals, either British or American victory. By dawn on August 30, 1776, the Whig evacuation of western Long Island had allowed for the long and harsh British occupation of Kings and Queens Counties. The future Long Island City was completely occupied by the armed forces of Great Britain.

The opposite photograph from QBPL lists this as the Lawrence-Leverich family burial place. Eugene Armbruster's photograph, facing southeast, is of the brick and iron north wall of the 1703 Lawrence Manor Cemetery, extant in northern Astoria, along the former Old Bowery Road, now 20th Road. The more famous Lawrence Cemetery in Flushing, Queens, has a rich history of its own. A third, smaller Lawrence family cemetery, according to Astoria Lawrence Cemetery caretaker James Sheehan, was near 37th Street and Ditmars Boulevard. The headstones are long gone, the site now in a backyard somewhere. Unfortunately, this author has found no corroborative information in books or on maps concerning this old, almost forgotten graveyard. James Sheehan, now in his nineties, is the sole person sharing these important facts. It is this author's duty to pass this information on.

A brass plaque, affixed in 1976 to the Lawrence Cemetery gate's stone pillar, informs, "Designated Landmark New York City." The plaque reads, "Lawrence Family Graveyard. In this private cemetery are buried members of one of America's most distinguished families....The roster of family notables includes Major Jonathan Lawrence, patriot, statesman, and soldier in the American Revolutionary War."[137]

The east stone column has an inscription that reads, "Lawrence Cemetery / Founded 1703." The opposite, west column reads, "Consecrated St. Lawrence." Other Lawrences served their colonial or American governments in the military and in civic capacities from Dutch colonial days (1630s–64) to the U.S. Civil War (1861–65). There are about thirty Lawrences in this burial ground and seventeen Sacketts, among other local families.

Plot 62 contains the remains of William Lawrence, who had a house at Hallett's Cove (Main Ave and Vernon Blvd in Astoria) that was used as a British Headquarters in Sept. 1776. Plot 74 contains Lt. Nathaniel

The sturdy brick wall and fencing that surrounds the 1703 Lawrence Cemetery, along the former Old Bowery Road, still stands, in parts. *QBPL.*

Lawrence, who left Princeton college to join the North Carolina line and was one of 70 troops captured by the British at Fort Lafayette on the Hudson River on June 1, 1779. Later rescued from captivity, after the war, he, in 1788 was at the N.Y. State convention to ratify the United States Constitution.[138]

Captain Richard Lawrence, captured after the Battle of Long Island, lies in an unmarked grave. He was imprisoned in a sugar house in New York City, most likely the notorious Rhinelander Sugar House, a large brick building that stood long enough to be photographed. Other Revolutionary and exiled Lawrences included Colonel Daniel, Thomas and Samuel.

Major Jonathan Lawrence (1737–1812) was born in Newtown, Queens County. His mother was Patience Sackett of the nearby prominent Sackett family. A New York City merchant, militia officer and politician, he was a delegate to the New York Provincial Congress representing Queens County. On the commencement of hostilities, Lawrence served as a major in a brigade of militia from Queens and Suffolk Counties. Major Lawrence served under General Nathaniel Woodhull on Long Island in August 1776 in an attempt to remove all livestock from Kings and Queens Counties. He was sent to New York Island to gain assistance from George Washington in these cattle removal operations, yet Washington, now on Long Island, had the Battle of Long Island to contend with. Lawrence was safe, yet General Woodhull was captured on August 28 near Jamaica, Queens.

Major Lawrence was saved by this unsuccessful mission. There was no help available to General Woodhull's cattle drive only one day after the great Battle of Long Island. Major Lawrence's Hell Gate home was sacked by the British as the family escaped by boat to safety across the East River. Lawrence was exiled while the British destroyed and dismantled his home. Lawrence fled to Duchess County soon afterward. In 1778, Major Lawrence served the cause of liberty in the Rhode Island campaign.

Major Lawrence returned to Newtown with his family after the war and later served in the New York State Constitutional Convention and was elected to the New York State Senate. "Of the eleven sons bequeathed by John and Patience Lawrence to the struggle for Independence, Major Jonathan Lawrence was the eighth. Merchant, Navigator, Financier, Soldier, Statesman, Patriot, he marked each sphere of Duty with rare ability and distinction."[139]

The leftmost marker reads, "Revolutionary Soldier. Major Jonathan Lawrence. 1775–1783. Placed by Major Jonathan Lawrence Charter D.A.R." This is a Daughters of the American Revolution grave marker.

"Veterans of Foreign Wars of the United States" encircles the seal of the United States of America with a cross and radiant sunbeams in the middle marker. The VFW emblem is the one-thousand-year-old Cross of Malta. In the forefront, the Sons of the American Revolution placed this fine grave marker. It shows a minuteman soldier with thirteen stars in the center of a cross and a circular laurel wreath and the year 1775. The VFW, the DAR and the SAR present fine examples of responsible and necessary grave site commemoration. In the land that Jonathan Lawrence loved and fought for, an American veteran's grave should never go unattended.

Three Revolutionary War grave site markers and medallions honor Major Jonathan Lawrence in his family's burial ground. Revolutionary graves throughout America have these. *R. Melnick photo.*

Here are some of the fascinating and extant Sackett gravestones in the Lawrence Cemetery; one older source calls it the Lawrence Manor Family Burial Ground. *R. Melnick photo.*

The Sackett family had a number of contributors to the cause of Liberty. On the left, the crumbling tombstone no longer reports who that person was but more when that person died. Of interest to our story is that this anonymous person was born in December of an unknown year around 1727. This unknown person "departed [this life?] April 28th, 1802, aged 74 years and 4 months." Earlier records of the graveyard have solved the above puzzle. A 1919 cemetery survey book revealed that grave and gravestone no. 3, considered then to be in "good" condition, read, "In Memory of WILLIAM SACKETT, born December 29, 1727 O.S., and departed this life April 28th, 1802, aged 74 years and 4 months."[140] Anna Sackett, center, was the wife of William. Below a mourning angel's head, the fragile brownstone gravestone reads, "Inscribed to perpetuate the remembrance of ANNA SACKETT, wife of William Sackett, who died the 11th April Anno Domini 1798, aged 66 years, 4 months & 21 days. She was her husband's fond companion, her children's tender & careful parent, & the friend & support to the needy. Reader! Art thou prepared to follow?"[141] The stone on the right is that of Nathaniel Lawrence Sackett (1765–1797), son of William and Anna Sackett. The scholarly and accurate cemetery surveys done in 1919 are invaluable resources that have saved these long-ago names from the oblivion of a crumbling and illegible tombstone. The Leverich family had burials in both the Lawrence and the Moore-Jackson Cemeteries.

A heavy granite millstone from the former Burger Jorissen tidal gristmill. In 1776, the Ryerson mill ground grain using the waters of Dutch Kills, a tidal tributary of Newtown Creek. *R. Melnick photo.*

James Sheehan has been the caretaker, historian, gardener and horticulturalist of this Lawrence Manor burial ground since the 1960s. He has provided this historian with great tours of this time-honored Patriot cemetery. Although Sheehan has repeatedly applied for support funding, he reports that the Tory Moore-Jackson Cemetery gets funding, but this Patriot cemetery, sadly, does not.

The Bolting Act of 1674 allowed New York City an exclusive monopoly to mill and export grain for the whole of the thirteen colonies. This created great wealth for those involved and facilitated the growth of New York City and its surrounding counties in the province. Milling and local tidal gristmills would play an important role in the governance and sustaining of this large colonial English and British province. The Revolutionary War would certainly stress these quaint, small tidal mills as providers of ground grain and flour to a large, long-term occupying army. The Dutch Kills mill was the first in this part of Long Island and was called Ryerson's Mill during the British occupation. The mill was used to its fullest capacity during the war. Of note is that there was a Ryerson's Tavern near the mill, which served

British troops, local Tories and Loyalists and perhaps even some Hessians during the brutal seven-year occupation.

The west Dutch Kills millstone is one of two millstones on display in Queens Plaza. The mill was powered by the waters of a creek called Dutch Kills, which is a tributary of Newtown Creek. The local creeks fed into the strongly tidal East River, tides compliments of the mighty Atlantic Ocean. The mill served western Queens County and points beyond until circa 1861, when the mill was destroyed for the coming of the Long Island Rail Road.

Dutch Kills Green park is in the eastern portion of the major transportation hub of Queens Plaza in Long Island City. Local historians were hoping that these large, four-foot-in-diameter and five-inch-thick granite millstones would date to the 1650s, making them two of Queens County's oldest artifacts. Just like replacing ruggedly used wooden parts in a mill over the years, the worn stones had to be changed, replaced one at a time or in tandem, if necessary. A worn millstone grinds grain inefficiently. Pictured below is the east millstone. These millstones most likely date back to circa

This east Dutch Kills millstone sits unprotected in the park. Unenlightened passersby may think it merely an oddly designed table to place their lunch, coffee or feet on. *R. Melnick photo.*

The Jackson Mill on Jackson Creek was on the former Sackhieknayah Creek, a tidal saltwater tributary of the East River near Fish's Point on Flushing Bay. *GAHS collection.*

1800, according to the Greater Astoria Historical Society (GAHS), and were the last generation of millstones to work in the gristmill. The stones ground grain for flour to feed thousands of British and Hessian troops and later, after the war, free Americans.

GAHS can provide much more info about the mill here, how it worked and its remnant millstones. Surprisingly, the Ryerson Mill on the Dutch Kills was not found by the author on any 1776-era map, perhaps due to its being inland and not very close to the East River coastline. GAHS has an excellent photograph, circa 1930, of a Dutch Kills millstone in the sidewalk in front of the nearby ancient Payntar residence. It was later moved to a small traffic island in front of the demolished Long Island City Savings Bank building very near its present location. The author had found no photographic or sketch images of the Ryerson Mill.

The original Dutch tidal gristmill above dated to the 1650s. Under the old names of Wessels Mill, Ludovic's Mill and Fish's Mill, it later became the Jackson Creek Mill near Fish's Point. The Jackson Creek Mill appears in the 1939 Vincent Aderente mural of the history of Long Island City, though outside of our Long Island City study's purview. The three main western Queens County tidal mills, Suydam's, Ryerson's and Fish's, were used to their fullest capacities to feed the occupying British and Hessian troops and the local citizens.

Chapter 7

SEPTEMBER 1776

SEPTEMBER 1, 1776

The East River now only separated these hostile legions of Britain and the army of Washington. Two such combatants were not calculated to remain inactive in such close juxtaposition.[142]

Within days of the American defeat at the Battle of Long Island, the British army had swept into western Queens to plan its next move, a major assault on New York Island. General Robertson encamped his ten-thousand-man army from the ridgeline that is now Steinway Street westward, safely inland. On Sunday, September 1, 1776, a British artillery battery was placed near Hallett's Cove, which fired on "Horn's Hook, on New York Island, and being returned in a spirited Manner an incessant firing was kept up on both sides the whole day, during which the [British] enemy threw above 100 shells, killing one of our men and wounding several."[143] These British cannons and mortars fired from the southwestern part of the Hallett peninsula at the American cannon battery at Horn's Hook, now Gracie Point, across the East River. Clearly better trained and equipped than their Continental army counterparts, the redcoats unleashed their cannonades at the Americans "for several days, but to little purpose, we having two men killed and four wounded. The Americans returned the fire, and some of the shot fell on Wm. Lawrence's land."[144] The British cannon fire brought "a spirited response from the sons of freedom, who now have well learned the smell of gunpowder."[145]

The British fanned out across western Newtown in search of an opposing force led by American general Charles Lee. Finding no army at Hell Gate, General Robertson was able to completely occupy Queens County by land. American air rights reached into British Newtown, via cannonball. This opportunity allowed the British cannon battery "to hold controversy" with the Continentals across the river.[146] Tempers were high; men on both sides were in harm's way. Command of the East River at Hell Gate was at stake. As of 2023, the westernmost buildings on the grounds of the Astoria Houses complex are the approximate location of the 1776 British cannon batteries.

General Howe stayed at the Samuel Renne house in Newtown, Queens County, from September 1 to 14, 1776. The British commander may have occasionally stayed at, as other sources have reported, the Moore family homestead in Newtown Village and the Brinckerhoff house in Dutch Kills. Wartime reality dictates that a commander's headquarters is wherever that officer is, not where he wishes to sleep that night or where his maps are. The Blaskowitz map below reveals in superb detail both sides of the Hell

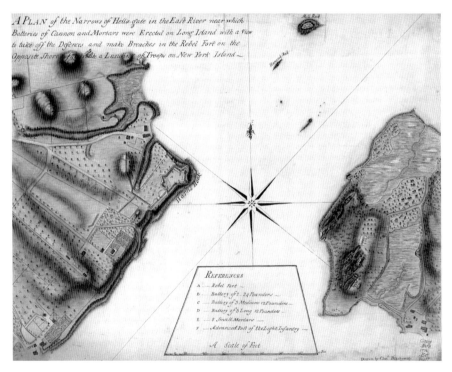

"A Plan of the Narrows of Hells-gate in the East River…" This 1776 Charles Blaskowitz map shows British artillery batteries near Hallett's Point opposite Horn's Hook. *Public domain. Library of Congress.*

Gate. The land mass on the right (east) is the Astoria peninsula. Notice the Hallett's Cove structures and the British cannon batteries facing toward Horn's Hook.

The British cannon bombardment from Queens County commenced to destroy the capabilities of the American nine-gun Horn's Hook battery on York Island. September 1 is also the date of the so-called Battle of Hallett's Cove.[147] Only one source, a Long Island City history calendar from 1980, has called this artillery exchange a battle. It was, indeed, an artillery battle with casualties and deaths on both sides. Though it is secondary in importance to the major battles, it was nonetheless a major maritime operation in September 1776 to bring Hell Gate under the control of the British Royal Navy. British operations to capture Kings County and western Queens County were nearly complete. Long Island was the largest and last stepping stone to attack New York City. Sadly, the importance that this Queens, New York portion of the Revolutionary War had on the entire outcome is unheralded and underrepresented. Nearly every aspect of warfare would pass through western Newtown. For now, the British plan was recover, maneuver, cross the East River and strike.

With a touch of irony, on this map, the rock to the south of Mill Rock in Hell Gate is named "Hancock Rock." This British cartographer's goal of accuracy led him to label Hancock Rock, yet it was named after the treasonous American Patriot John Hancock. If there was ever a reason for the British to change a local name, here it was.

The British Royal Artillery fired their guns at the Americans at Horn's Hook, who, from August 30 to September 8, 1776, were able to defend their turf and fire back from a mere four hundred yards away. Western Long Island was now British and armed to the teeth, snarling across the river at the weary, unsettled and regrouping Americans. The Americans still had fortifications and cannon batteries along the East River shoreline and high ground on Manhattan Island. Western Long Island was nearly under total British control. The mighty East River was next. British naval operations were now getting closer to Queens County as the Royal Navy was making its way up the East River.

The British cannon fire was real. The fast-moving iron cannonballs were very difficult to defend against were an enemy in any place without cover. No man, horse, tent, wooden cart or flimsy walls could stop a cannonball.

The Queens County citizens who were disaffected changed in early September 1776. Patriot sympathizers once had the upper hand. It was the Whigs in Newtown who were to become the disaffected. The choice

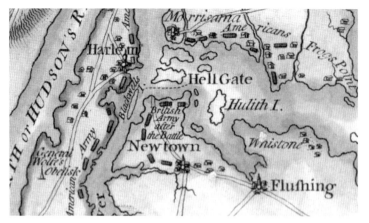

"The Seat of Action between the British and American Forces…" This map isolates the Newtown area showing the "British Army after the Battle." *Public domain. Major Holland map.*

was to either stay a professed Patriot and be arrested or sign an oath of allegiance to the British Crown. To endure a difficult life under British rule among passionate Loyalist neighbors was what was next—either that or to jail or a prison ship. A striking dilemma confronted many of the militiamen. "In order to live among their neighbors after the British triumph on Long Island, these men to all outward appearances, became Tory Sympathizers also, rather than go into exile, as did many who were patriots."[148]

On September 2, 1776, the HMS *Rose*, a 20-gun frigate, entered the East River. The following day, it ventured farther up the river and anchored off Blackwell's Island, now Roosevelt Island. To the north, the HMS *Niger* was patrolling in Whitestone Bay. Once the British Royal Navy made it up to Blackwell's Island, smaller naval vessels sailed and rowed into Newtown Creek to help supply the occupation of western Long Island.

British Army after the Battle reveals Newtown from Newtown Creek in the south to Blackwell's Island and the islands in and near the Hell Gate and the larger "Hulith I. [Island]," which was also then and is now Riker's Island. "Hallett's Cove played an important part in the American Revolution; it was a British artillery base. In September of 1776, after the battle of Long Island, part of Washington's Army fled through Hallett's Cove."[149] Queens County was nearly entirely subdued—as in conquered and occupied—by September 3, 1776. A defensive line of British troops stretched from Newtown Creek to Bowery Bay, a strategic line that allowed or rejected entry into western Queens County to points west such as Dutch Kills, Hallett's Cove and the East River.

This Long Island City historic dates calendar is the only source the author has found that reports American troops retreating to the north and east through western Queens County. The brilliant flanking movement exacted by Lieutenant General Henry Clinton and ten thousand British soldiers surrounded the Continental line from Red Hook to Wallabout Bay. Upon the post-battle retreat, nearly 99 percent of Continental army and militia troops had to escape or die—between the Brooklyn battlefields, over the Brooklyn Heights and to the ferry point at the East River.

Some troops may have been to the north and east, outside the British pincer movement at Bedford. There is no source to confirm that any large number of soldiers or "part of Washington's army" escaped from Brooklyn in Kings County to Hallett's Cove in western Queens County. Onderdonk writes, "The King being now in possession of Queens county, and his soldiers scattered over it, the leading Whigs having been thrown in prison, and the property of those who fled seized by the enemy, the remainder were constrained to join the Loyalists in petitioning the King's Commissioners that Queen's county might be restored to Royal favor."[150]

The excellent William Faden map below is titled *A Plan of New York Island, with Part of Long Island, Staten Island & East New Jersey, with a Particular*

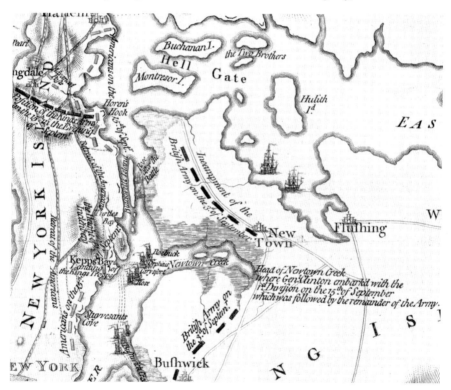

This William Faden map is rich with imagery, information and ship and troop locations. The frigate HMS *Rose*, of 20 guns, ventured into Hallett's Cove in September 1776. *Public domain.*

Description of the Engagement on the Woody Heights of Long Island between Flatbush and Brooklyn on the 27th of August, 1776.[151] The map's value lies in its reiteration of the British defensive line of September 3, 1776, and the completeness of the occupation of Newtown and western Queens. Focusing on the lands of the eleven-square-mile Long Island City, see the British Royal Navy ships to the left (west) of Newtown Creek, His Majesty's Ships *Roebuck, Orpheus, Carysfort* and *Rose* opposite "Kepps" (Kip's) Bay. The HMS *Phoenix* was also there, shown in the lower East River in a larger Faden map. To the right of Newtown Creek, under the town seat "New Town," map information reveals: "Head of Newtown Creek where Genl. Clinton embark'd with the 1st Division on the 15th. of September which was followed by the remainder of the Army."

At Hallett's Cove, see "Rose after the Battle," and the inland line of defense, "Incampment of the British Army on the 3.d of September." Notice the American positions on Manhattan Island, to the left (west). One error on this map is that Montresor Island and Buchanan Island are reversed. In 1776, today's Wards Island was Buchanan's Island and was more southerly and closer to Horen's (Horn's) Hook. The Hell Gate was half a mile long and a treacherous part of the East River. The true Hell Gate lay one water channel to the south. "Hulith Id" (Hulith's Island), was also called Riker's Island, yet the British cartographer is loath to give the rebel Riker family their due. The map also depicts British warships in the upper East River, via the Long Island Sound, in Flushing Bay.

By September 3, 1776, all western Queens was occupied territory, yet the western shore of Long Island was still within shot of American artillery on Manhattan. All revolutionary sympathizers and Whigs, if they did not flee, were captured. Harsh fates awaited seized rebels. Their Tory neighbors would gladly give them up. It was acquiescence or imprisonment. Even Loyalist residents were treated unfairly by the British military.

While George Washington's demoralized army fortified New York Island, the British forces planned their attack on New York, while predominantly encamped in Queens County. The conquerors of Kings and Queens Counties were massing their forces to attack the Americans. But where?

The 20-gun HMS *Rose* was one of the most important British Royal Navy ships to patrol the East River waters, those of the East Channel, Hallett's Cove and Hell Gate. More than one 1776-era map shows the HMS *Rose* in Hallett's Cove. It was the British warship that came closest to Long Island City in 1776, dropping anchor in Hallett's Cove in September 1776 under the command of Captain James Wallace. As a frigate and not a larger

This HMS *Rose* replica ship was built in 1970 in Lunenburg, Nova Scotia. The actual British HMS *Rose* plied our Long Island City East River waters near and in Hallett's Cove. *Image via DeviantArt.com.*

warship, the HMS *Rose*'s firepower was sufficient to protect the cove and its size small enough to sail the shallow East Channel and traverse the rock- and reef-laden Hell Gate. Larger British warships were yet to attempt to sail the full length of the treacherous Hell Gate. Larger vessels were advised by Hell Gate pilots not to attempt to pass through the gate.

Since this 1970 replica, to-scale vessel (shown above) is not a part of the British Royal Navy, it is officially the "HMS" *Rose*. "*Rose* is the largest active traditionally built wooden sailing ship in the world."[152] The actual 1757 HMS *Rose* was 108 feet in length and its width (beam) was 30 feet at the waterline. Of the utmost importance to its sailing in New York City waters was its draught, or draft. This is deepest part of the ship's hull into the water. The *Rose*'s draft was 9 feet, 7 inches.

This meant that to enter any waters shallower than ten feet was indeed a risky venture. In Hell Gate, at a lower tide, Pot Rock was said to be a mere eight feet from the surface, always ready to tear at the fragile wooden bottoms of 1776-era ships and boats. The HMS *Rose* was a full-rigged sailing

The HMS *Rose* with another vessel in the East Channel at Hallett's Cove and the British defensive line of September 3, 1776. Western Queens was nearly conquered. *Public domain.*

ship with a crew complement of 160 and an armament of twenty cannons that fired nine-pound cannonballs and other explosive or rigging-entangling ordnance. The HMS *Rose* served the British Royal Navy in these New York waters throughout 1776 until naval operations shifted from New York toward points farther south.

To bring this HMS *Rose* (1757) warship into the modern era, the only large boat one will see in Hallett's Cove in this day and age is the NYC (New York City) Ferry that stops, since 2017, at its docks on the south edge of the Astoria peninsula. The dock is mere yards from where the British artillery battery bombarded upper Manhattan in September 1776. For perspective's sake, the "small" 108-foot-long HMS *Rose* was larger than the NYC Ferry, at 86 feet long.[153] The next time you see the NYC Ferry in Hallett's Cove,

Astoria, try to visualize a fully armed twenty-gun British frigate, with masts and sails, in the same cove, ready to bring the war to you.

The fine sketch opposite reveals ships on the East River and the HMS *Rose* up at Hallett's Cove after the battle, the closest approach of battle-ready British Royal Navy vessels in waters off the Newtown coastline. The future Astoria peninsula, along with Hallett's Point, fully thrust into Hell Gate, was also called Hell Gate Neck. Here, the HMS *Rose* patrolled the East Channel of the East River and Hallett's Cove. From the September 3, 1776 conquest, the British troops at Hallett's Cove and along the coast were still within range of both effective and errant cannon fire from the American artillery battery at Horn's Hook. Being struck by a cannonball was not likely, but it was possible, causing soldiers and citizens alike to flinch at the sound of cannon fire from across the river. Carry on, men. Don't lose your head over it.

The caption written on the photograph below reads, "6-25-36. Gen. Howe (Renne) Hdqrs." General William Howe, commander in chief of all British forces in North America, headquartered at the Renne house from roughly September 1 until September 14, 1776. At the Renne house on September 3, 1776, General Howe wrote his account of the Battle of Long

Newtown's old Samuel Renne house on the former Hoffman Drive, now part of Queens Boulevard at 57th Avenue. General Howe commanded from here for two weeks. *QBPL.*

Island to Lord George Germaine in London. The September 3 document reveals the correct names and ranks of the many different officers at this exact date in 1776, just after the major military actions on Long Island occurred. Some lines of the document with direct links to the future Long Island City were: "Camp at Newtown, Long Island, Sep. 3, 1776…Gen. Howe; Lord Geo. Germaine; Col. Donop, Corps of Chasseurs and Hessian Grenadiers; Lieutenant General Clinton commanding the first division of troops; Lord Cornwallis; [and] Lieut. General de Heister."[154] All these officers and their battle units served the British forces in western Queens County in the earliest stages of the war, August to October 1776.

This house was on the south side at 89-16 Queens Boulevard, Elmhurst, and stood until 1937, when it was demolished. Notice in this 1936 photograph, in the second-floor, right-side window, a child is forever gazing at the photographer, Eugene Armbruster (1865–1943). In 2023, the extant Rock Church, formerly the 1928 Elmwood Theater with the wooden water tanks on the roof, stands to the left (east) of the long-gone Renne house.

Meanwhile, in September 1776, the Alsop house and the Richard Alsop marriage were proof of divided loyalties. "The Alsop house was the rendezvous of Cornwallis and Clinton, with their respective staffs, and the country round about was taken up with the army encampments, during the Revolutionary struggle. Richard Alsop himself was devoted to the cause of independence, while his wife was an ardent Tory" who fully supported the king's cause.[155]

The strategically located old Alsop Mansion along Newtown Creek was made the headquarters of Lieutenant General Charles Cornwallis, the commander of the British reserve, and Major General John Vaughan. On the grounds and surrounding areas were Colonel Carl von Donop's Hessian grenadiers and chasseurs, some of whom were encamped in northwestern Queens, overlooking the Hell Gate. These British and Hessian officers would play major roles in their continued battles to dislodge George Washington's rebels from New York. At the Alsop House, "two round windows, resembling port holes, were cut in the ends of the building in 1776 by Lord Cornwallis for musket practice, and as lookouts to guard against surprise."[156]

General Grant and Lord Percy were in the camp at the Newtown village as of September 4, 1776. By September 5, 1776, Lieutenant General Henry Clinton was quartered at Nathaniel Moore's on Bowery Bay Road, later the Samuel B. Townsend house, as seen on the 1852 Riker map. Regarding the ancient Nathaniel Moore house, "The center of all the camps in Newtown, was the now decayed mansion of the Moore family, which was

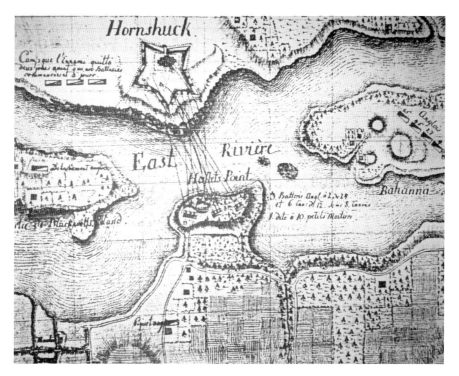

A very detailed 1776 French map of the British artillery and troop positions at Hallett's Cove, Hallett's Point, the surrounding lands and the islands in the strategic Hell Gate. *Public domain. Anonymous.*

the headquarters of General Sir Henry Clinton."[157] The Loyalists assisted the generals in every way, while at the Nathaniel Moore house, Lieutenant General Clinton "planned the capture of Manhattan."[158] The Nathaniel Moore house "on the Bowery Bay road, is fast yielding to decay; desolation surrounds the house, once of such fine proportions that even for this age it would be an ostentatious country seat."[159] The Moore family was one of the oldest in Queens County. Their lineage stretched back to military service with William the Conqueror in AD 1066. "Sir Henry Clinton established his headquarters on these premises after the battle of Long Island."[160]

This anonymous 1776 French-language map revealed Hell Gate and the lands and islands in this section of the East River. This significant close-up shows far western Queens County, including British and Hessian troop locations on Long Island and on the surrounding islands. The prominent lines of artillery fire across the East River are enhanced by cannon battery information and "*Anglois*" (English) and "*l'ennami*" (the enemy) locations. Of note, in the lower left portion of the map, to the left (south) of "*Piquet anglois*" (English pickets), is the French word "*Moulin.*" This identifies the Suydam tidal gristmill, on Sunswick Creek at Hallett's Cove. These military maps reveal the September 1776 cannonade across the "*East Riviere*"; our focus is the Long Island side of the equation. Army positions on "Blackwell's" (Roosevelt) and "*Bahanna*" (more correctly Buchanan's, now Wards) Islands are clearly marked. Note the main American (rebel) artillery fortification at "*Hornshuck,*" Horn's Hook (Gracie Point) on New York Island.

In September 1776, the first two weeks of conquest and occupation brought a terribly unsustainable number of soldiers into one area, mostly Newtown, Queens, and parts of nearby Kings County. Ten thousand invading troops would put a real strain on the land, dwellings, resources and psyches of the conquered inhabitants.

An expanded image of the previous French map (below) shows the arrows in the East River denoting the flood and ebb tides of this strong and treacherous tidal strait. The Jerome Carre translation is focused

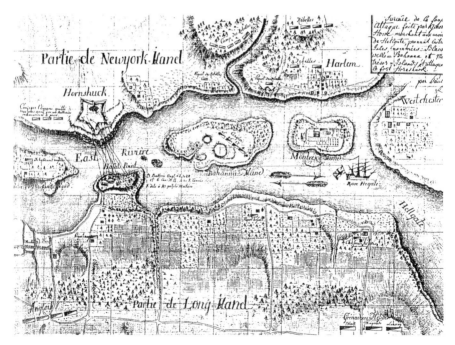

An excellent 1776 French map disclosing much exciting detail about the Astoria coastal area from Hallett's Cove to Lawrence Point. See the "Rose *Fregate*" in the "*Hellgate.*" *Public domain. Anonymous.*

solely on Long Island, as his full translation of the map, to include all American positions on "Newyork Island," would be a chapter in itself. From left to right, south to north: "*Partie de Long Island*" (part of Long Island) and "*Piquet anglois*" (English pickets). Pickets were advanced troops sent forward to secure an area, yet in harm's way from enemy artillery fire. With the American battery at Horn's Hook firing at their British positions on Long Island, the forward British and Hessian troops were, in fact, in harm's way.

> Chemin a Newtown: Road to Newtown, from Hallett's Cove eastward, on roads that are today Main Avenue, Newtown Avenue, 30th Avenue, Newtown Road, Woodside Avenue and Broadway, into the center of British military operations in the town of Newtown.
>
> Piquet hessois: Hessian pickets. At the site of the western end of the path that became Ditmars Boulevard. Houses along the coast were most likely the Penfolds, Polhemus and Rapalye homes.
>
> Chasseurs Hessois: Hessian fighters; *chasseurs* in French translates into "hunters" in English. The German equivalent is *jaegers*. The Hessian Feldjaeger Corps were assigned to Colonel von Donop and were positioned in northwestern Queens at this time.
>
> Grenadiers Hessois: Hessian grenadiers. See lower right section of map. The grenadier battalions were named after their officers, who were lieutenant colonels. On this map, see Lieutenant Colonels Block, Min(ne)gerode and Linsing(en). The correct names of these three Hessian officers were Bloch, von Minnigerode and von Linsingen. These three battalions were under the command of Colonel von Donop, who, for seventeen days, had his headquarters at the Richard Alsop house, along Newtown Creek. In the Hell Gate above, to the west, off Long Island, north of Bahanna and Montresor Islands, see the "Rose Fregate."

The Hessian State Archives map in Marburg, Germany, shown on the following page, is slightly less detailed than the previous map. See the unnamed British Royal Naval vessel in the river, along with the British and Hessian troop positions in western Queens County. "Hessisches Staatsarchiv Marburg" is the watermark printed on the map. Less information is provided, but the existing info is taken nearly verbatim

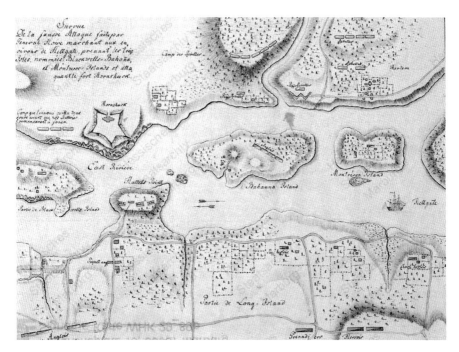

This 1776 French map is very similar to the previous map, yet the writing style differs. "Grenadiers Hessois," or Hessian grenadiers, and British troops occupy the coast and hills of Astoria. *Hessisches Staatsarchiv Marburg, Germany*.

from the previous map, yet the handwriting is different, suggesting a map rewritten by a different hand.

The British Royal Navy approached closer and closer to Newtown, Queens. Hell Gate was thus far impassable by the larger British ships. On September 5, 1776, the HMS *Halifax* was off the coast of Hunt's Point in the Bronx, then southern Westchester County. That same day, the HMS *Rose* challenged American artillery on York Island as it plied the East River. The HMS *Niger*, on September 6, was still off the coast of Whitestone, visible from Bowery Bay. As mentioned earlier, the HMS *Niger* was the British warship most likely to have bombarded signer of the Declaration of Independence Francis Lewis's homestead in Whitestone. Meanwhile, the HMS *Phoenix*, HMS *Roebuck*, HMS *Orpheus* and HMS *Carysfort* entered the East River. They probed American coastal defenses and drew fire from enemy guns. To draw the enemy's cannon fire, as with musket fire, while inherently dangerous, enabled British gunners to identify and commence fire on the American positions. Such is warfare.

This old postcard, below, from circa 1900, reads, "Gosman Farm House, Middleberg Ave., L.I. City 200 yrs. old. recently destroyed." "Middleburg" is the correct spelling. The homestead was built around 1700 by the Bragaw family, ancient Dutch settlers to the area. John Bragaw owned the house in 1755. His son, Andrew (1755–1828), a Tory like his father, owned it next. John died here in 1782. The house, later the Bragaw-Gosman house, was on the Dutch Kills Road, now 39th Avenue, east of 45th Street, on the north side of the street. The Gosman home was close to the current railroad embankment just inside the Sunnyside Yards.

During the hard days of 1776 and beyond, "the British Army established camps all along the Dutch Kills Road. The campground for British Army General Charles Cornwallis and his 33rd Regiment of Foot occupied the farm of John Bragaw, which was adjacent to Teunis Brinckerhoff's property. The soldiers baked bread in the ovens of the Bragaw's and Brinckerhoff's homes, stored wares in their large barns, and etched their names in their window panes."[161]

The ancient Bragaw, later Gosman, House is correctly placed on the erroneously spelled Middleburg Avenue. Note the boy standing for eternity in the house doorway. *QBPL.*

Generals Clinton, Cornwallis, Sir Hildebrand Oakes and many other occupying British officers met, consulted and even entertained at the John Bragaw house. In an activity not exclusive to the Bragaw house, soldiers left behind etched names to be viewed long after the British troops had gone back home. One such remnant was "a sash containing a pane of glass on which is written the name of Finlay McKay, an officer of the Scotch Fusilier Guards, quartered at the Bragaw Homestead at Dutch Kills during the Revolution in 1776."[162] One source revealed that Finlay McKay "cut his name on a pane of glass in the old Brinckerhoff house in 1776, and it remains there to this day," according to the March 28, 1889 *Brooklyn Eagle*.[163] In terms of hidden family fortunes, "several historians believe that it was during this time that Teunis Brinckerhoff buried an earthenware pot filled with gold and silver coins next to his barn. The British soldiers often committed acts of petty thievery, so it was common practice for the residents to bury their money to save it. Teunis passed away a year after the war ended, but apparently never had time to let any of his heirs know about the buried treasure under the barn."[164] Old maps show the John Bragaw farms under new names. These name changes have created conflicting ideas as to the exact former locations of each farmhouse. The 1852 Riker map shows the former Brinckerhoff house as belonging to "H. Kneeland."

Middleburg Avenue had previously been called Dutch Kills Road, Road to Dutch Kills and Middleburg Road. The current 39th Avenue runs west to east from 43rd Street in Sunnyside, to Woodside Avenue in Woodside, Queens.

William Gosman had the house in 1852. The western Dutch Kills Road disappeared due to the massive construction of the Sunnyside Rail Yards, along with the historic ancient home, taken down in 1903. Gosman Street, since the 1920s, is 48th Street in Sunnyside, from Queens Boulevard to the edge of Astoria at Northern Boulevard. The Bragaws had more than one home in the area. In a human link to the Revolutionary War, one postcard in the Greater Astoria Historical Society's collection with the same image was sent from Dutch Kills, Long Island, and postmarked in Norwalk, Connecticut, on August 28, 1908. The postcard had writing on it as it traveled through the U.S. Mail, and it may have been sent by a Gosman family member. It read: "Picture taken 10 years after any of the family lived in it."[165]

The Bourgon Bragaw house, home to a Patriot, was sacked by the Hessians in late August 1776. The Bragaw house was near the Ryerson

VIEW of THE OLD PAYNTAR MANSION near the BRIDGE PLAZA erected by Isaac Bragaw 165 years ago.

The ancient Payntar house belonged to the Bragaw family during the Revolution. The Ryerson mill here ground local grain for the occupying British and Hessians. *QBPL.*

mill and the Ryerson Tavern, which, undoubtedly, served not quite the finest alcoholic drink to the thirsty British military occupiers. The Ryerson mill used Dutch Kills creek tidal waters to grind grain for the British soldiery and area residents. The commentary under the photograph above reads: "View of the Old Payntar Mansion near the Bridge Plaza erected by Isaac Bragaw 165 years ago." This photo, circa 1910, gives the house an approximate construction year of 1745. Bridge Plaza was the original name for the area and grand transit hub now called Queens Plaza. The house existed until November 1912, formerly at the western bank of the Dutch Kills creek. This is near where Dutch Kills Road met the Ridge Road, important narrow highways of old. Other Dutch families at Dutch Kills during these Revolutionary times were Debevoise (also DeBevoise), Van Alst and Van Dam. Bourgon Bragaw sided with the Patriots. His brother was John Bragaw, mentioned earlier, a Tory.

The Jacobus Riker farmhouse along Bowery Bay Road was nearly opposite the old Wilson Avenue, now 25th Avenue. The house was plundered by the British in 1776. *QBPL.*

These Old Astoria Village homes were not 1776-era houses but stood on foundations that had once held homes dating back to before the Revolutionary period. *R. Melnick photo.*

William Payntar was born in 1731 and married Hester Skillman in 1764. Payntars intermarried with area families, including Bragaw, Brinckerhoff, Debevoise, Rapalye, Skillman, Van Pelt and Wyckoff, many of which played important roles locally during the Revolutionary War.

The Patriot Jacobus Rapalje Riker's house was sacked by the British in 1776. Later in the occupation, "Hessian troops encamped nearby used the great oven to bake their bread."[166] British army officers billeted in every house in Newtown. If they were lucky, sergeants or rank-and-file troops had a solid roof overhead and dry ground or floorboards below them, especially during the harsh winters. This is one of a few Riker farmhouses in this part of Newtown; the small center part of the house was built in 1717 along Bowery Bay Road. Jacobus Riker died in 1809 and is buried with his wife at the Riker Cemetery, nearly a mile to the north. The house was south of present-day Astoria Boulevard, and the site was destroyed by the construction of the New York Connecting Railroad and the Brooklyn-Queens Expressway.

Revolutionary War–era houses once stood on these foundations. A William Lawrence house, occupied by British leaders, was yards away. Here, in 2016, the houses still had their residents: the final residents in a doomed residence, the last household in a condemned house. These two homes, of three in this immediate vicinity, represented the flavor of the old village, quickly being usurped and demolished by big development. Wherever a one- or two-family home and property stood, now stands a taller, multi-apartment building, on the verge of completely wiping out Old Astoria Village. A very short time after this photo was taken, the vines of yesteryear were roughly shorn from the pale-yellow house and a large, boxed X was spray-painted on it. This dreaded symbol, from the house's perspective, tolled the sad bell of imminent destruction. The former 9-24 Main Avenue was soon to be demolished, as in torn down, razed, destroyed, from extant to extinct, as in no more. The old houses, gone by 2018, were witness to many years, but now the site is forever silenced. As for the fifty-foot-tall giant green tree between the two houses? Gone. Gone like it was never there.

The Penfold family owned the house depicted on the following page during the Revolutionary times of 1776. Built by William Penfold along Shore Road in 1719, it was one of the earliest homes in this area. In the distant left is the former Berrian-Rapelje house on Shore Road, built in 1740. The two houses were north of the modern Astoria Park.

The Penfold house, built in 1719, was not the home of Dow Ditmars until after the Revolution. The distant 1740 Berrian-Rapelje house saw Revolutionary activity. *GAHS collection.*

JACOB RAPELJE AND HIS wife, Catrina, both passed away just before war arrived in 1776. They were buried in their nearby Rapelje family burial ground, now extinct. Of note, in the historical record, there have been four different spellings of "Rapelje."

During the war, "in the house of Jacob Rapelye, on the Shore Road, Dominie Froeligh, of the Dutch church, at Jamaica, found refuge from Tory wrath, having 'prayed the Almighty to strike the fleets of the invaders with his bolts and sink their soldiers into the seas.'"[167] Continuing the saga of the good minister, "fortunately, his host was a skillful boatman or else the patriotic refugee would never have placed, as he did next day, the swirling currents of the Hell Gate between him and his pursuers."[168] The above Rapelje house was later a Polhemus house, located on the east side of the Boulevard (Shore Road), at the corner of 21st Avenue, at 20-57 Shore Road.

Of important note for the local history are some ancient, 1776-era houses in our area of study, without photographs. The William Lawrence house once stood at the southeast corner of modern-day Steinway Street and 30th (Grand) Avenue. "In the Revolution it belonged to William Lawrence, a strong patriot. Here, Maj. Gen. Robertson took up quarters on August 30,

1776, and encamped 10,000 British soldiers north of the house. Two weeks later he withdrew, crossing to Westchester, and Gen. DeHeister's Hessians succeeded them. Many [cannon] balls from the American battery at Hoorn's Hook fell on the heights back of the house."[169] The Lawrence-Suydam-Whitfield-Halsey house was at the southeast corner of Vernon Avenue and Main Street. A new house was built by William Lawrence in 1770, and he was living in the house in 1776 when the victorious British arrived. During the late summer of 1776, "British Generals Heister and Clark put up here for a few days during the passage of the British Army through Astoria."[170] Noteworthy is that William Lawrence had two homes mentioned above. It is possible that the British and, later, the Hessian officers utilized both homes.

The Baylies Mansion at 26-07 12th Street in Old Astoria Village, built circa 1840, still stands. The first owner, and possible builder, Joseph Craig, later sold the home to a Dr. Hersey Baylies in the 1850s, thus adding to the home's lineage and Astoria's link to the Revolutionary War. "First of the line was Dr. Gustavus Baylies, born in Uxbridge, Mass. in 1761; he served two enlistments in the Revolutionary Army."[171] The Woolsey house grounds were from 23rd Avenue to between 24th and 25th Avenue. Part of Astoria Park is now on the site. The property was Lawrence land from 1768, and they built a manor house where a Lawrence lived up to the Revolutionary War. In 1777, the Woolseys came into possession of the house, and this may have been made possible by the evacuation of the house and property by Jonathan Lawrence, a rebel, who had to flee or be captured. On the front cover of the 1951 "Long Island City Savings Bank 75th Anniversary" brochure is shown: "Stone tavern built by Jacob Rapalye, circa 1737. This may have been the Polhemus stone house and later, the Trowbridge house. This house stood on the Shore Road north of Wolcott Avenue, now 21st Avenue. Its lawn stretched to the East River. Torn down to make way for the Astoria Housing Development."[172] The Polhemus house and dock had, early on, Patriot leanings and activities. Later, the waterfront house was occupied by the British and its private

Lieutenant General Henry Clinton was second-in-command of British forces under General William Howe until 1778. Their incompatibility proved detrimental to their mutual cause of Empire. *Public domain. John Smart painting, circa 1777.*

dock on the East River heavily used, most notably by departing Hessians on October 12, 1776.

Lieutenant General Henry Clinton (1738–1795) made his first wartime appearance in Newtown, Queens County, around August 30, 1776. General William Howe's second-in-command from 1775 until May 1778, Henry Clinton served the British forces admirably, though not without controversy, throughout the entire war.

While not nearly as inglorious and ill-fated as the Battle of Long Island was, fought in Kings County, western Queens County suffered a rapid subjugation and a harsh occupation starting in late August 1776. On or near September 3, 1776, western Queens County was secured. British troops in Newtown would only be within American cannon range for another few days. Lieutenant General Clinton established his headquarters at the Nathaniel Moore house on Bowery Bay Road. This is where Clinton quartered and plotted the capture of New York Island, planned for September 13, a significant date in British military history. "In this building he wrote his orders to the commanders to debouch their troops from the many camps which covered this section, and converge to Newtown Creek, there to embark in boats for the capture of New York city….Adjoining Clinton's headquarters, on the Bowery Bay road, is the Moore burying ground."[173]

Lieutenant General Clinton, General Howe's immediate subordinate, knew the western Long Island area well from his youth in New York and used it to British advantage. In early September 1776, all the local Long Island City–area homes, and those in Newtown, would become billets for British and Hessian officers. The British army was here. This was a prime example of the free reign of the British military in "their" Newtown.

The caption written in white ink on the opposite image was: "Brinckerhoff-Schuyler House, Middleburg Rd. Built by Teunis Brinckerhoff—1721." The original photo, circa 1900, was used in a Vincent Seyfried book, and the photo credit went to "Wil A. Holst Sr."[174] This typical Dutch farmhouse site is now inside the Sunnyside Rail Yards. The Brinckerhoff house was situated between 39th Street and 39th Place, on the north side of the street, and its fate was decided around 1903 as a profound engineering operation was to obliterate everything in its path. Here, colonial and wartime Queens County history surrendered to progress. The house owner, George Brinckerhoff, was a strong Patriot before and during the war and was in exile while British officers confiscated and lived in his home. His lands were often, if not permanently, encamped on by British and Hessian troops. "During the War for Independence, British General Sir William Howe used the house as

This house has been recorded as being under various family names. The 1721 George Brinckerhoff house was occupied by the British for seven years. *GAHS collection.*

his headquarters, and gave orders to his officers from the front stoop each morning."[175] Any home that a commanding general occupied at any given time would have qualified as a "headquarters," although the designation was fluid. The Brinckerhoffs married into other prominent local Revolutionary families, such as Lawrence, Fish and Alsop.

In a copy of an old New York picture book page, found in the GAHS archive, the Brinckerhoff house photo caption read: "Gen. Howe's Headquarters On Middleburg Avenue. Torn Down For Fire Wood By Residents Of Sunnyside." There was no info in the caption about exactly which old Dutch house it was, only that General Howe had been there. With New York as the home base of British military activity in North America, General Howe undoubtedly traveled throughout the local British dominion and more than likely stayed at local homes.

SLAVERY

More than twenty-five thousand slaves and free Blacks fought for the opposing armies, espousing both causes, whether by or against their own free will. At

147

the onset of British control of New York City and the surrounding counties, Black slaves escaped to the safety of the British lines, as the British offered freedom to the slaves after their service to the Crown. They were called slaves, Black servants, property, indentured servants, chattel, Negroes and other names. The African people were brought here by Dutch, British and, later, American ships. They were in bondage, enslaved, in servitude, under total subjugation, in captivity. Locked in dehumanizing chains, they came across the Atlantic Ocean in slave ships as cargo. By war's end in 1781, there were over ten thousand Blacks in New York, a major enclave of free Blacks in North America.

Truth be told, the foul institution of enslaving Black Africans, or any other people, by English colonists and, later, American plantation, farm and business owners in the South and North, will always be reprehensible. To some people, this may disqualify George Washington and other Founding Fathers from the pantheon of great leaders in world history. We must not place our 2023 sensibilities and prejudices into the nineteenth or eighteenth centuries. Most of humankind has evolved beyond even considering enslaving any one people to advance the wealth and progress of another. In this modern age of political correctness, statue toppling and cancel culture, George Washington should be held in the highest esteem. He was both a brilliant and flawed man of his eighteenth-century times. Yes, it was a gross contradiction to set one group of men free and not allow another the same freedoms. It is my hope that his ownership of slaves on his large Virginia plantation doesn't overshadow his monumental contributions to the founding of the United States of America. George Washington was a man to be studied and learned from, and it would be correct to emulate his intelligence, courage and forbearance.

What work, if not everything, did slaves do? Many individual slaves developed tangible skill sets that made them valuable not only to their masters but also to the community, whether they were builders, stonecutters, carpenters, farmers, sailors, cooks or general servants. Female slaves were proficient, if not skilled, in the innumerable facets of home living and family care. Both enslaved men and women would work the crops, fields and woodlands, as the seasons dictated; some were relegated to easier work in and around the home.

Incidents involving local slaves appear readily in the records and scholarship of the Revolutionary period and afterward, a number of which will be mentioned in these pages. There was a female slave, Balche, a Riker-Lent house slave in August 1776. Also in August 1776, a servant girl admired

THE REVOLUTION COMES TO QUEENS

her mistress Mrs. Lewis's defiant actions while the British Royal Navy bombarded the house in Whitestone. Fronce and Sam were slaves at the Rapelye house on Bowery Bay Road. Silas Jupiter was a slave of the Hallett family, who fought in numerous Continental army engagements and was at Valley Forge in the winter of 1778. Swan, a Hunt family slave, was a "Black Jack," a Black river pilot involved in the perilous voyage of the HMS *Hussar* when it attempted to sail through Hell Gate in November 1780.

Many slaves lost faith in and respect for their masters when they were subservient to British military power and coercion. Loyalists and conquered Patriot sympathizers had to defer to British military authority at all times. Harsh treatment and various punishments awaited these British subjects if they were disobedient or uncooperative. Temporary obfuscation of British ends could result in arrest or some type of physical harm and monetary extraction. A saber blow or a musket butt to the body would help to assure compliance.

A very noteworthy man regarding slavery here in Newtown and Queens County and in the Province of New York was British lieutenant colonel Samuel Birch. Along with his meritorious service leading the 17th Dragoons, he helped free and shelter thousands of slaves from the various areas in the North that he operated in. Many of the enslaved Africans became Black Loyalists, numbering three thousand, and are mentioned or annotated in the *Book of Negroes,* created by the later brigadier general Samuel Birch. The great majority were later evacuated to Nova Scotia, Canada, as free men and women.

The abolition of the reprehensible institution of slavery had to wait. The creation of the American nation had to happen first. Problems could not be solved without functional, good government. We hold these truths to be self-evident, that all men are created equal.

COMBATANTS

As with the British army in 1776 and today in 2023, with a few differences, the American army officer rank structure is thus: second lieutenant, (first) lieutenant, captain, major, lieutenant colonel and colonel. Then the general rank structure: brigadier (general) (*), major general (**), lieutenant general (***) and general (****). (Asterisks denote number of general's stars.) All are referred to as "general," yet there is a distinct rank and chain of command. For example, for expediency's sake, Lieutenant

General Clinton or Major General Greene were generals of a lower rank than their commanders-in-chief.

Ensigns (junior officers), sergeants, corporals and privates make up the noncommissioned officers (NCO) corps and enlisted ranks. In many cases in early military history, an ensign would carry the unit ensign, or flag. Ensigns would often be the next soldiers to be promoted to lieutenant. On the battlefield, promotion and command may be thrust on you. You're next. The captain is dead. You are in command. Now, take that hill.

British Troop Locations

A large number of British troops were barracked within the future Long Island City borders. Some troops stayed for a short period, like the British army when it passed through in August, September and October 1776. Other units were stationed permanently in western Queens County, serving large occupation encampments and winter quarters. Many British and Hessian troops returned, in some capacity, to Newtown during the non-campaigning months from, roughly, December to May. Winter battles in New York climates and northward can seldom be fought, let alone won. Remember Quebec. The British troops to occupy the future Long Island City were:

"In the camps along 39th Avenue, Dutch Kills, were the Royal Artillery and Lord Cornwallis' 33rd Regiment" and a troop of Grenadiers stretching from Woodside to Queens Plaza.[176] There was a great British encampment along the road that became Skillman Avenue from Queens Plaza east to Sunnyside and into Woodside, linked to the Dutch Kills Road encampments. The "Royal Highland Regiment was posted in Jackson Heights," with some troops westward to Woodside and Astoria.[177] This gives credence to a story later in the occupation in which two of the Cornelius Rapelye slaves, Fronce and Sam, had a rough encounter with two Scottish Highlanders.

The 37th Regiment of Foot, a light infantry unit led by Lieutenant Colonel Robert Abercromby, bivouacked at Hell Gate. The exact location of the encampment at Hell Gate is vague, as the entire area from Blackwell's (Roosevelt) Island north to Lawrence Point was the full stretch of Hell Gate. It was most likely the modern Astoria peninsula and Astoria Park coastal areas. Southward, surrounding Dutch Kills creek, "the crack military organizations encamped on the hills were the Fifty-fourth and Seventy-first Regiments of infantry."[178]

The Royal Artillery under Brigadier General Samuel Cleaveland was stationed near its battery north of Hallett's Cove, which bombarded the Americans in September 1776 and was manned and ready for the war's duration. Hessians were garrisoned at the strategic and heavily traveled Narrow Passage (along the road to Hell Gate, later Woodside Avenue). Other units encamped in the western Newtown area were the 17th Regiment of Light Dragoons and the Maryland Loyalists. These dragoons were the British horse-mounted force in Newtown from late August into September 1776.

Colonel Samuel Birch of the British 17th Light Dragoons was known to have scoured Newtown and the other Queens County towns, in search of fleeing Whig civilians and rebel soldiers. A contemporary 1776 map (page 172) shows, near the northwestern point of Long Island, at Berrien's Island, a "Birch P[oint]." This is a rarity, since this point is not a formidable navigation point as is Lawrence Point, just to the west. The 1776 Charles Blaskowitz map is the only map with a "Birch P[oint]." Curiously, this Blaskowitz map shows Lawrence Point as "Bowry P[oin]t." The painter Blaskowitz refused to give the rebel Lawrences their local place name.

United Empire Loyalists in the New York City and Long Island area, of course, swore allegiance to the king, and were treated well enough to survive the war and occupation. Local Loyalist militias were forcibly recruited by British authorities after the conquest. Newly organized Queens Loyalist companies and battalions served the British army after this mandatory conscription in September 1776. These men would serve and fight for the British armed forces throughout the war. Some Loyalist refugees were given possession of the houses of escaped or captured rebels. Local Loyalist militias and army units, such as (Oliver) DeLancey's Brigade and the Queen's Rangers drew troops from and encamped units throughout Newtown. These units served on Long Island and elsewhere in various capacities.

The roads and hills and marshlands of neighboring Woodside had numerous British and Hessian troop encampment sites and homes that billeted the officers. This author has borrowed from Woodside's own rich history to help to tell the story of greater Long Island City. British general William Howe rode to Hell Gate with his officers to survey the newly conquered Newtown. General Howe was the highest-ranking soldier on both sides in Long Island City during the Revolutionary War. It is a known fact that the following British officers and their troops set foot and encamped in western Newtown, the future Long Island City, all of whom are mentioned in these pages.

All the highest-ranking British officers were in western Queens County in September 1776. General William Howe, Lieutenant General Henry Clinton, Lieutenant General Charles Cornwallis and Lieutenant Colonel Samuel Birch were there. British Royal Navy admiral Richard Howe later navigated the tides that brought some of his warships through Hell Gate. Major General James Robertson led part of the British army from Bedford in Kings County northward, to Newtown, to cover all western Queens. General Robertson was a major British political and military leader, later appointed provincial governor of New York. He stayed at the William Lawrence house, at Newtown Road and the future Grand Avenue (30th Avenue) and Steinway Street. Francis Lord Rawdon was a highly decorated and trusted British officer during the Revolutionary War. In 1776, Lieutenant Rawdon was appointed aide-de-camp to Lieutenant General Henry Clinton. After a major naval defeat at Charleston, South Carolina, in June 1776, Lord Rawdon sailed with Lieutenant General Clinton and the fleet to New York to regroup and to undertake major operations against the American rebels. Lord Rawdon later billeted, for a time, at the Jacob Blackwell house along the East River in western Newtown, an area later named Ravenswood, in Long Island City.

During the military campaigning season, a British officer or soldier would bring the fight to the enemy wherever they were ordered to go. Each division, brigade, regiment/battalion and company had its bivouac site assignment each winter, whether near or within a secure region or back at the Britishers' New York City home base.

The Hessians were German auxiliaries, hirelings or mercenaries, hired out by their princes to the British king for service in North America. They were considered foreign invaders, rented soldiers, a readily available reserve army—at a cost—for the great powers of Europe. The term "Hessians" was an American synecdoche (a term for when a part is made to represent the whole) for all German soldiers deployed by the British during the Revolutionary War. The Hessians were from the German state of Hessen, which sent the majority of troops to America. The first soldiers to arrive in America were from Hessen-Cassel, as true Hessians served here in New York in August–September 1776.

The Waldeckers, Brunswickers and others were not at the Battle of Long Island, as they and other Germans arrived later in 1776, where they bivouacked and fought elsewhere.

The Hessian commander at the Battle of Long Island was Lieutenant General Leopold Philip de Heister (1716–November 19, 1777), from Hesse-Cassel. Varied texts have spelled the name De Heister, de Heister, Heister and von Heister. "Von Heister" is the German name. The nobiliary particle in France, and in early Great Britain, was "de," a result of the Norman conquest of England in AD 1066. The German "von" is evidenced by Carl von Donop and Baron von Steuben. On August 27, de Heister led his Hessians in a frontal attack on the entrenched American positions on the Brooklyn high ground, acting as a diversion to the main flanking assault. The American brigadier general William Alexander, Lord Stirling, after heroically enabling the escape of hundreds of defeated Continental soldiers, surrendered to de Heister rather than to the British. The American Revolution historian Barnet Schecter, on a trolley tour of the Green-Wood Cemetery, related how the British officers held the Hessians in low esteem. They seldom recognized their titles of nobility, such as "von" or "de," before their German surnames.

de Heister's Hessian troops replaced the British troops that moved out to invade New York. Both he and General Clark stayed for three weeks at the William Lawrence house after Robertson's troops shipped and marched out. There were ten thousand British troops encamped in the Long Island City and Woodside areas, most of whom marched into and saturated the countryside.

In September–October 1776, Grenadier Regiment von Rall bivouacked in western Newtown and included the following units: First Battalion Grenadiers von Linsing, Second Battalion Grenadiers von Bloch and Third Battalion Grenadiers von Minnigerode, all of which were encamped in the future Astoria. It is interesting to speculate on the proximity of Colonel von Rall's grenadier battalion or, perhaps, the colonel himself to the homes and properties of Dr. John Berrien Riker and other Riker family members. Three Hessian battalions are shown on the 1776 French maps on pages 136 and 138; those of Colonel von Rall set foot on this Astoria ground. The Hessians commanded the high ground in northwestern Queens County around the site of the current St. John's Preparatory High School in Astoria.

An ancillary connection to the Revolution and to the future Long Island City was the grounds of the old Wolcott Mansion. The Hessians trod heavily on these local hills and the site of the Wolcott house, extant in 1776. The grandson of a Declaration of Independence signer from Connecticut, Oliver Wolcott, Frederick H. Wolcott lived at the house circa 1850 to 1883. 21st Avenue was formerly named Wolcott Avenue, running north of Ditmars Boulevard and south of parts of Old Bowery Road, now 20th Road.

There was major British naval activity in the East River at Hell Gate on September 8, 1776. The Horn's Hook name, variously spelled, was derived from the Dutch *hoek*, meaning a corner or point of land. Horn's Hook on the upper east side of Manhattan Island overlooked Hell Gate, the treacherous pinch-point of the East River between Long, New York and Buchanan's (now Ward's) Islands. The navigating ship captains had to pay the utmost attention to the variables that created the volatility. Ocean tide and ancient rock made Hell Gate so hellish. The Horn's Hook bluff was only thirty to forty feet above sea level, not exactly a commanding height or dominating fort, which made it very vulnerable to direct, close-range, British ship-borne cannon fire. Though quite vulnerable to land-based cannon fire, maneuverable medium-sized warships could pulverize the stone, wood and earthen forts of the Revolutionary era. The American fort at Horn's Hook was both strategically and precariously situated.

Colonel William Thompson, commander of Thompson's Pennsylvania Regiment, helped fortify Horn's Hook. Thompson's Battery there was a nine-gun cannon battery planned in February 1776 for the defense of Manhattan Island.

The 14.9-acre Carl Schurz Park

> overlooks the turbulent waters of Hell Gate....Jacob Walton built the first house on the site in 1770. During the Revolutionary War, the Continental Army built a fort surrounding the Walton residence to guard the strategic shipping passage of Hell Gate. After a British attack on September 8, 1776, the house was destroyed and the Americans were forced to retreat from the fort, which the British retained until the end of the war in 1783.[179]

American artillery at Horn's Hook was of the highest strategic importance in this section of the East River. "A battery was put here by Washington in the Revolutionary War, but it failed to discourage the British navy from sailing up the East River in 1776 and destroying all the buildings on the bank."[180]

Unlike in Charleston Harbor seventy days earlier, here, the British Royal Navy was stronger than the small American fort. The Americans at this Horn's Hook artillery battery and the East River shores of western Queens County were forever linked by cannon fire. Some cannonballs are forever in the Long Island City ground, the ancient dirt now deep under the modern age of concrete.

The British army was pushing closer to New York Island by trying to send some troops from western Long Island to Blackwell's (Roosevelt) Island, across the East Channel of the East River. American cannon fire from the Manhattan side of the West Channel of the East River fired at the advancing redcoats. "This cannonading continued for several days by which the enemy was so emboldened that on Tuesday they crossed in considerable numbers to Blackwell's Island, but the shot from our Batteries proving too warm for them they soon recrossed the river."[181] Due to the "warm" cannon fire from the Americans, the British were satisfied to remain on Long Island. They would be there, in relative safety, for only a short time. The British and Hessians were not on Long Island to remain safe. They were there to be in harm's way very soon, as would be the Americans on Manhattan Island.

From Hallett's Point, British cannon had a maximum range of approximately two thousand yards, so, at these meager distances, the wrecking of one's fort or redoubt was a very real possibility. Bombardments commencing on September 1, 1776, would surely test the accuracy and mettle of artillerists from both camps.

> *The English commander considered it desirable to destroy a very strong redoubt, at a place called Hell Gate....Four batteries were accordingly erected by the Royal Artillery on the opposite shore, mounting three 24-pounders, three heavy and three medium 12-pounders, and ten small mortars.* [On the British entering the battery in the days afterwards, they found] *the enemy's guns dismounted, and the works so shattered, that the troops might have marched in with little or no impediment. In the Brigadier's report, he said, "The distance was near 700 yards, and though the enemy threw a number of shells from six mortars, we had only on this occasion two men killed, and one lost an arm."*[182]

These two British artillerists were combat deaths on Hallett's Point, the future Astoria peninsula. War had found its way to our good Long Island City shores.

The entire name of the image on the following page is *View of the opening of our Batterys at Hell Gate upon the Rebel Works at Walton's house on the island of N. York 8 Sept.r 1776*. Careful scrutiny of this important historic sketch has revealed that the view is from Hallett's Cove facing northwest. The British cannon and mortar batteries at Hallett's Point on Long Island are on the right. The battery was just north of its namesake and well-known cove.

View of the opening of our Batteries at Hell Gate…8 Sept. 1776, by Archibald Robertson, a famous British landscape painter and portraitist. *Public domain. Spencer Collection, New York Public Library.*

The built-up American fort, with nine guns, is to the distant center left on Manhattan Island at Horn's Hook. The American fort at Horn's Hook was an important strategic point protecting the "back door" to New York Harbor and New York City. Beyond the fort is the Walderon/Walton house at the approximate site of the 1799 Gracie Mansion at the modern Gracie Point.

The Dutch colonial name of Horns Hook has fallen into disuse, yet the modern NOAA navigation chart no. 12339 still defines the three major land points surrounding the Hell Gate as Horns Hook (on Manhattan), Hallets Point (in Queens County, on Long Island) and Negro Point (on Ward's Island). The origin of the name Negro Point is a historical nod to the knowledgeable and skilled "Negro" (Black men of African descent) river pilots. The term here, should anyone protest or cause a fuss about a word, is not used as a derogatory. The name is a salute to the sturdy and experienced African slaves or free Black men, "Black Jacks," who safely piloted ships through this rough tidal strait called Hell Gate, and other areas of navigational difficulty. It was not uncommon during the colonial period to find Black men in the seafaring services as sailors and stevedores.

This Hell Gate cannon engagement occurred on September 8, 1776. Buchanan's (now Ward's) and Montresor's (Randall's) Islands, just north, were on the verge of capture. Harm from American artillery directed at

156

the British on the local Queens County shores was nearly neutralized. Western Newtown was conquered. Next in the British war plan was to invade New York Island.

Whereas accuracy may suffer over longer distances, a concerted effort by multiple guns firing a bracketing fire will hit you or your breastwork, redoubt or fort. There was seldom adequate cover from a freshly fired iron cannonball. If a man was where the cannonball was going, he would either die or be severely injured. He would be rendered useless to the battle. There are recorded incidents where two and three men were killed by a single cannonball. The fascinating 1776 Charles Blaskowitz map in this book (page 126) corroborates the exact locations of the British Hallett's Point batteries. By September 9, 1776, the British were in full control of western Queens County, to include all the future Long Island City. A Founders Online footnote to a letter by Major General William Heath at Kingsbridge to General Washington reads, "At flood tide on the night of this date, the British brought these transports undetected through Hell Gate, and at daybreak on 10 Sept. two battalions of light infantry were ferried to Montresor's and Buchanan's islands, nearly opposite Harlem, where the British encountered virtually no Continental resistance."[183] The two strategic islands north of the Hell Gate, Buchanan's and Montresor's, were now in British hands.

Directly across the narrowest part of the East River, a mere three hundred yards wide at this point, the Queens shoreline north of Pot Cove was secured to beyond Lawrence Point.

Captain John Montresor was a British officer and cartographer who surveyed and drew numerous informative maps of New York for the British government. His maps were created prior to and during the Revolutionary War. Captain Montresor is most noted for being the British engineer who built Fort George in southernmost Manhattan in 1765. While it was under American control, Continental and militia troops with smallpox were sent to Montresor's Island, which was designated a quarantine area. On September 10, 1776, the British landed on Montresor's

Captain John Montresor, a British engineer and cartographer, purchased his island north of Hell Gate in 1772. His great maps can be seen and studied today. *Public domain. Painting by John Singleton Copley, circa 1771.*

Island and captured it, inching ever closer to their prize, New York. "British forces occupied and fortified it September 1776 and used it as a base for operations against northern Manhattan. Attacked once by Americans, British held it until the evacuation in 1782."[184] The author notes that the British evacuation of New York occurred in 1783.

The total capitulation of western Queens County, by land and by sea, had been exacted. Preparations by the British were taking place primarily in Newtown, where the British forces were planning their next move to unseat the Americans from New York Island. The future Long Island City was now fully occupied by angry and highly motivated British and Hessian troops.

Montresor's Island, freshly conquered by the British, was less than two hundred yards across the Bronx Kill waterway from the mainland Westchester County and less than four hundred yards from Lawrence Point in Queens County. The British landing on both Montresor's and Buchanan's Islands would facilitate an assault on New York Island. The troops would protect warships and support vessels passing through the Hell Gate from points east. Let the author provide a reminder that in the modern city of New York, four of the five boroughs, except for the Bronx, are on islands: Staten, Manhattan and Long.

Of importance to Newtown, Queens, is that Montresor's Island is directly across the East River from Lawrence Point and the northern entrance to Hell Gate. The Continental artillery, a novice force compared to the seasoned and better-trained British artillerists, inflicted some damage, for sure, yet not enough to dislodge the sturdy British batteries. One British soldier, napping in the grass on Montresor's (Randall's) Island, was struck and killed by an American cannonball, fired from New York Island, across the narrow southern entrance to the Harlem River. Catching some permanent shut-eye, the soldier never saw it coming. Inglorious, indeed.

On Staten Island, a "Peace Conference" between the British admiral Richard Howe and three American emissaries from the Continental Congress took place on September 11, 1776. The Americans were Benjamin Franklin, John Adams and Edward Rutledge, sent to speak with the British delegation. The British attempt to broker a hard peace was unsuccessful, the delegates retired and war operations resumed. The Revolutionaries were true to their cause. From Long Island, the British were about to bring their hard truth to New York City.

An indirect Long Island City link to Benjamin Franklin was that in June 1776, Colonel Heard of the New Jersey militia captured Benjamin's illegitimate and estranged son, William Franklin, the royal governor of New

Lieutenant General Charles Cornwallis, perhaps the most effective British army general, helped defeat the Americans at Long Island in 1776. He would ably serve the cause of Empire. *Public domain. Painting by Daniel Gardner.*

Jersey. Colonel Heard and his New Jersey militia were in Hallett's Cove and Newtown in January 1776.

The name of Cornwallis is perhaps the most recognizable of all the British officers during the American War of Independence. More so than those of Howe, Clinton, Burgoyne or Tarleton. Lieutenant General

Charles Earl Cornwallis (1738–1805), in the late summer of 1776, trod heavily on western Queens County. Cornwallis's troops, his Thirty-Third Regiment of Foot, were encamped along Dutch Kills Road, now 39th Avenue in Sunnyside and Woodside. Maps from 1776 have shown the precise locations of his unit. Generals Cornwallis, Vaughan and Leslie and Hessian colonel Donop stayed at the old Alsop mansion, a short horse ride from this troop encampment and cantonment. The British army and its Hessian auxiliaries were spread neatly across all of western Queens, from Hunter's Point to Bowery Bay.

The HMS *Rose* sailed north up the East River on September 12. Jacob Polhemus, a Kings County Loyalist and a relative of Patriot major John Polhemus, was suppling the HMS *Rose* off Bushwick Creek, just south of Hunter's Point. Here Jacob's cow was killed by strong American cannon fire from New York Island hitting the HMS *Rose*. "The frigate returned the fire, but her shot fell short….Night coming on, the firing ceased on both sides; and under cover of darkness, the frigate changed her position, and anchored between Blackwell's and Long Island, under protection of an intervening point of land."[185] The HMS *Rose*, under fire from American batteries, was aided by nightfall, which cannot stop cannon fire. It sought the incomplete cover of Blackwell's Island (now Roosevelt Island) by anchoring in the East Channel of the East River. The island provided some concealment, yet the ship's highest masts could be spied by the Americans at daybreak.

A September 13, 1776 letter from General Washington to Major General William Heath revealed, "Dr Sir, Let there be the most vigilant lookout kept. you know I suppose that four More Ships two of the(m) 40 odd Guns are gone up the East River. I am Yr Most Obedt Servt, Go: Washington." A footnote from the Heath Papers stated, "On the afternoon of this date, the British warships *Phoenix* and *Roebuck*, accompanied by the frigates *Orpheus* and *Carysfort*, sailed about three miles up the East River to the mouth of Bushwick Creek on the Long Island side of the river. The *Phoenix* lost one man to the fire of American batteries on Manhattan Island."[186] The British Royal Navy was within sight of Queens County, and five warships were coming closer.

In researching this vastly important topic of long-ago events, there are numerous errors and contradictions extracted from period and later sources. Texts, documents, maps and individual memoirs reveal much truth, most of it irrefutable. As a twenty-first-century historian, it is easy, 247 years after 1776, to point out errors made in the historical record. We are, as we always are, hostage to the written record and the research that subsequent historians have gathered and interpreted. Not all written history is fact. The job of the modern historian is to gather all information available and interpret and try to separate provable fact from fiction. Sometimes this cannot be done. There lies the beauty of historical inquiry.

George Washington's headquarters on the night of September 13–14, 1776, was at the Robert Murray house on the Heights of Inclenberg, near the current 36th Street and Park Avenue. Robert and Mary Murray were wealthy residents of New York, and their hospitality would soon be legendary.

In an incident of great importance to the cause of liberty, the following occurred down the East River.

> In the middle of the Aug–Sep 1776 battles for New York is an event of great interest to the United States. On September 14th, "Just after dinner 3 Frigates and a 40 Gun Ship (as if they meant to attack the city) sailed up the East River under a gentle Breeze toward Hell-Gate and kept up an incessant Fire assisted with the Cannon at Governor's Island; The Batteries from the City return'd the Ships the like Salutation; 3 Men agape, idle Spectators, had the misfortune of being killed by one Cannon-ball, the other mischief suffered on our side was inconsiderable Saving the making a few Holes in some of the Buildings; one shot struck within 6 Foot of Gen. Washington as he was on Horseback riding into the Fort."[187]

The British warships, sailing upriver with the flood tide, challenged the American cannon batteries on York Island. In lower Manhattan, it seemed that the entire flame of Revolution being carried by General George Washington was one cannonball from being extinguished.

At the Alsop mansion on September 14, 1776, the final stages of the massive troop marshaling operation in western Queens were taking place. A large maneuver and attack were imminent. The Continentals knew not where this attack would come from. The British army knew exactly how and where and when.

> In 1776, the Alsop house was the abode of Lord Cornwallis, Colonel Meadows, Sir Henry Clinton and a retinue of military men of less repute. They slept there the night before the day of the capture of New York, and there is in the vicinity a great stone on which Cornwallis and Meadows stood on the eve of battle, exchanging ideas.[188]

The major assault of New York Island was being planned by the British generals, while they dined and lived finely in the confiscated homes of western Queens. The houses of Richard Alsop, Jacob Blackwell, Nathaniel Moore, Walter Franklin and other prominent Newtown residents were commandeered for lodging and for the brainstorming of the master plan to take New York Island.

At the Richard Alsop house was Brigadier General Leslie, and on the surrounding property was his light infantry, as well as the British reserve under Lieutenant General Cornwallis and Major General Vaughan. There and at locations northward was Colonel Donop with his Hessian grenadiers and chasseurs. The nearby Franklin-Sackett (later DeWitt Clinton) house was temporary home to a General Warren. The British army was here, in western Newtown, to include the modern Elmhurst, Maspeth, Woodside, Jackson Heights and Long Island City. The British were rearming, massing and planning. Americans beware.

British Naval Operations in Long Island City Waters, 1776

As early as September 3, 1776, the HMS *Rose* sailed into and up the East River. It had a complement of 160 men, commanded by Captain Wallace.[189] The larger British vessels, those over 44 guns, could not, without a great measure of risk and difficulty, sail up the East River. Attempts to traverse the narrow, treacherous and, at certain sections, shallow Hell Gate must ensue. The HMS *Eagle* was the 64-gun flagship of Admiral Lord Richard Howe. The American *Turtle*, an early submarine, attempted unsuccessfully to attach a bomb to the HMS *Eagle* on September 6–7, 1776. On September 13, 1776, the HMS *Phoenix* (44 guns), HMS *Roebuck* (44), HMS *Orpheus* (32) and HMS *Carysfort* (28), joined the HMS *Rose* (20) in East River battle operations.

In the Long Island Sound and in the upper East River as far as the northern edge of Hell Gate was the HMS *Brune* (32), a ship captured from the French years earlier. The HMS *Niger* (32), commanded by Captain George Talbot, most likely fired its cannons at the Francis Lewis house in Whitestone, Queens. It patrolled various northern East River coasts, from Whitestone to Stony Point, north of Montresor's Island, across from Lawrence Point. Later in the war, the HMS *Niger* would attempt a run through Hell Gate. A third yet smaller vessel in this fleet was the HM

Brigantine *Halifax,* a schooner.[190] From 1776 to at least 1781, the coastal guard on land and corvettes and guardships patrolled the waters around Riker's Island, at Bowery Bay and along the Astoria shoreline. A corvette is a small, maneuverable sailing vessel used in shallower waters. Corvettes were used for coastal patrols, for engaging enemy forces in minor operations, for fleet support and for showing the flag. All the British vessels sought to intercept whaleboats from Connecticut and southwestern Westchester County conveying Patriots preying on the north shore of Long Island. Bowery Bay at the Lent-Riker-Smith house was a very busy supply point during the war.

NEWTOWN CREEK DURING THE AMERICAN REVOLUTIONARY WAR

After the disastrous Battle of Long Island on August 27, 1776, the victorious British and Hessian troops swept into Queens County. Invading troops approached by land south and east, and some crossed Newtown Creek to get to western Queens. Newtown Creek is a tidal creek and a tributary of the East River, running three and a half miles inland and separating Kings and Queens Counties for most of its length. Its mouth is at the East River. Dutch Kills creek was a tributary of Newtown Creek and supplied water to the Ryerson Mill. The western Queens County towns that border along the creek are the modern Hunters Point and Blissville, both part of Long Island City, and Laurel Hill and Maspeth. A major British army and naval depot existed at Maspeth at the head of the creek, protecting and supplying the massive encampments in the area. The shorelines had small docks in which to conduct trade and to supply the hordes of occupying British and Hessian troops. The smaller warships and sloops were sent to these calmer waters but could not easily hide near the mouth of the creek. When the tide is contrary to your desired direction of travel, only strongly rowed boats or favorably wind-aided boats can cross the full tide.

The strategic Alsop house had Royal Navy guard boats, both rowed and sailed, to protect the various landings along the creek. "Newtown Creek, during most of the great conflict, was a secure retreat for all sorts of British vessels. Naval Boats were always nigh at hand on patrol Duty doubling their security."[191]

September 15, 1776

The painting below, *The British Landing at Kip's Bay, New York Island, September 15, 1776*, depicts the massive amphibious assault of New York Island on September 15, 1776.[192] Artillery positions, engineered earthworks and redoubts lined the eastern Manhattan shore from the Battery and Wall Street up to the Stuyvesant farm and more sparsely from Kip's Bay, Turtle Bay, up to the battery at Horn's Hook at the present Gracie Point. Although some of the American cannons and ordnance were subpar compared to British guns, the fear of the American cannonball did exist. British and Hessians on Long Island had to move troops, equipment and cannon from western Queens County to Newtown Creek for the invasion.

On the morning of September 15, 1776, "the troops encamped on the Brinckerhoff, Morrell, Bragaw and Moore farms, broke camp and joined their comrades in the camp at Laurel Hill, and the cedar lots on the DeBevoise farm. Cornwallis gave a grand breakfast to his aides de camp, cooked on the great hearth in the Alsop mansion."[193]

"Newtown Creek, on the fifteenth day of September, 1776, encouraged a plot against the city on the yonder side of the river."[194] The ships bombarding

The British Landing at Kip's Bay, New York Island, September 15, 1776, by Robert Cleveley. Five British warships fire cannon broadsides at meager American defenses. *Public domain. National Maritime Museum, Greenwich, London.*

rebel positions from one hundred yards offshore launched superior naval firepower to "prep" the American defenses.

Off the eastern Manhattan coast at Kip's Bay, five British warships, the HMS *Phoenix, Roebuck, Orpheus, Carysfort* and *Rose,* "formed an end to end cordon with a combined broadside of more than 80 cannon to cover the landing of 4,000 troops."[195]

> *The ships opened up with a horrendous explosion. With springs on anchor cables to maintain broadside positions, they continued to pour a tremendous bombardment over the town, woods and entrenchments using solid shot, mortar, fire bombs and swivels loaded with grape shot. So fierce was the torrent that many soldiers reported later that they thought the sound alone was enough to cause their death.*[196]

As the mighty British warships were laying down covering fire, pulverizing or "prepping" the American coastal defenses, the First Division of the British army was en route from Queens, via the East River. It was commanded by Lieutenant General Henry Clinton. In his command were Generals Cornwallis, Leslie and Vaughan and Colonel Donop. His forces "lay in boats a sufficient distance up the [Newtown] creek to be concealed from the view of the Continental Army."[197]

This great flotilla of four thousand men, on eighty-four flatboats and bateaux, consisting of the light infantry, British reserve, Hessian grenadiers and chasseurs, "embarked at the head of Newtown creek, and landed at noon at Kip's Bay, under the fire of the British ships."[198] "Crammed on board were the 42nd Infantry (the famed Black Watch), the 33rd Regiment, 2nd, 3rd, & 4th Brigade of Guards (from Bedford), a Brigade of Hessians from General De Heister's Corps, additional British Light Infantry and Grenadiers from Hell's Gate, Hessian Grenadiers and Jaegers also from Hell's Gate."[199] The Hessian positions at Hell Gate are seen in the 1776 French maps on pages 136 and 138. British lieutenant Rawdon and Hessian colonel von Donop were just two of the famous invaders who encamped in Long Island City to be rowed out of Newtown Creek to assault New York. The earlier quotes have excellent corroborative Astoria-area troop locations for the Hessians north and east of the Hell Gate. The Hessians had a camp of grenadiers on the hills east of Hell Gate and pickets and chasseurs, in smaller numbers, that had lain closer to the East River.

The Invasion of New York

The first wave of British and Hessian troops landed mostly, if not entirely, unopposed. The green, inexperienced and overwhelmed Connecticut militia had to flee their inadequate defensive redoubts and breastworks. The retreating Americans could not load and fire their muskets while running away. Some Americans had only long wooden pikes as weapons. The superiority of force and numbers made flight the more prudent choice. Running for their lives, the horrified troops knew full well that this battle on this day, at Kip's Bay, as they were, could not be won. In a panic only a retreating soldier can know, the main goal was to save their own lives.

General George Washington, on September 15, 1776, having ridden south from his Harlem headquarters, tried to rally his frantically fleeing militia. Pursuing enemy troops were too close for them to mount an effective counterattack. As his troops continued their mad flight, Washington reportedly said, in absolute exasperation, "Are these the men with which I am to defend America?"[200]

After the first wave of four thousand troops out of Newtown Creek, another nine thousand had landed on Manhattan Island by the end of September 15. The Continental army was in quick-march mode, moving north to the fortifications at Harlem, well north of the present 110th Street. "Additional launches included light artillery, mantelets (wooden structures used in building the inner side of batteries and redoubts), entrenching tools, ammunition, and supplies."[201] The massive amounts of wood to build new and reinforce existing fortifications were from the ancient forests of Queens and Kings Counties.

Commanding many troops in western Queens, General Robertson sent a detachment of troops over to Manhattan for the Kip's Bay landings. He marched his main force along the Old Bowery Road (now 20th Road), past the old Captain Samuel Moore and Jacobus Lent houses, to the shoreline and on to Flushing and Whitestone. These troops eventually crossed the eastern portion of the East River to Westchester County.

Until the conquest of Kip's Bay and the rebuilding and manning of the fort at Horn's Hook, the lower East River was not completely under British control. On Long Island, only now could the waterfront and shoreline of western Newtown be fully occupied and utilized. Hallett's Cove, Bowery Bay, Dutch Kills, Middletown, Dominie's Hook: all the future Long Island City was now safely in British hands. The occupation has begun.

Most 1776 maps omit entirely the British and Hessian troop movements and encampments in Queens County in August–October 1776. Maps show British troop maneuvers from Brooklyn (Kings County) to crossing the East River directly to Manhattan (York Island, New York County). Activities in Queens County are largely forgotten or omitted as not essential to the entire scheme of movement, battle and pursuit. In terms of the most important events of the Revolutionary War, the activities in Queens County were massive troop movements, bivouac, master planning, a significant cross-river cannonade, the base camp for a major invasion and a long-term military occupation.

The town was rapidly subdued by the British. What little opposition remained had either escaped to the mainland or was captured. Many Whig and Patriot men fled, leaving their wives, families, farms and possessions behind.

The following four maps show great coastal detail. Since New York Island (Manhattan) was the site of the invasion of New York, this landing at Kip's Bay was given detailed scrutiny. Long Island, specifically western Queens and Kings Counties, had been the base of the great British military operations for the past three weeks, August 29 to September 15, 1776. Ten thousand British and Hessian soldiers in western Queens County encamped, drilled, rearmed and prepared for maneuver and battle. They were joined by other forces from neighboring areas. The king's troops were on the land and waterways that became Long Island City. These western Queens lands are given scant detail in the four maps.

The king's forces, fresh off their nearly complete battlefield victory, were trying again to catch up with the Americans, those "Damned Rebels." The attempts, still unsuccessful, to capture General Washington on Long Island had shifted to a new island.

British grand strategy focused on New York City. It was British thinking that control of the continent lay in control of New York. New York, subdued, could be a massive base for British naval and army operations.

Most of the highest-ranking British and Hessian officers—Clinton, Cornwallis, Percy, Leslie, Vaughan and von Donop—slept in western Queens County the night before the invasion.

To the Loyalists on Manhattan Island, this was liberation by the king's forces. To the Patriots, it was fight overwhelming force and die, or retreat. On the map on the following page, notice the Murray farmhouse on the high hill, colonial roads and the modern road grid to clarify terrain and places. The Beekman house, General Howe's next headquarters, is north of Turtle Bay. The Heights of Inclenberg became Murray Hill, and the old and important Post Road was demapped and built on, parts of it under repaved city avenues.

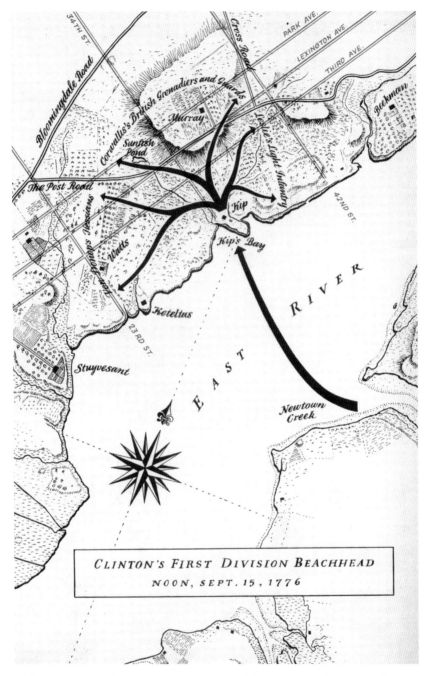

"Clinton's First Division Beachhead Noon, Sept. 15, 1776." Out of Newtown Creek poured the first four thousand British and Hessian troops to invade New York. *Bruce Bliven Jr.,* Battle for Manhattan, *1956.*

At Hell Gate on September 15, 1776, two miles farther north up the East River, the treacherous waterway was confirmed to be of major tactical value to both the British and any enemy. Hell Gate was important as a second water entrance to the city and harbor. The Horn's Hook fort had been destroyed by British cannon on September 8; the Americans could not have returned and tried to rebuild the fort. On September 15, the British bombarded the fort once more to ensure its evacuation. The British were on their way. By land from Kip's Bay, the British took the position by day's end and rebuilt, improved and occupied the site for the duration of the war. George Washington's army was in retreat and soured by this awful day.

Back in Newtown, "Richard Alsop kept strict account of his losses by the lusts and recklessness of the British, and it is safe to assume that he was profitably reimbursed. A page of his account books for twenty-four days in September 1776 is preserved, and it is a document of interest. It totals 320 pounds, 15 shillings."[202]

After British general Robertson left western Queens on September 15, Generals Clark and de Heister occupied the William Lawrence house. They would occupy the house for three weeks, with hundreds of British and Hessian troops encamped nearby. Good news was to be found when Continental major general Nathanael Greene, who had reconnoitered Hell Gate and western Newtown by horseback one month earlier, rendezvoused with his troops by September 15, 1776. Having recovered from near deadly fever, General Greene would soon lead American troops into battle.

A Manhattan-centric book and map reveal zero features of Queens County, including a nondescript shoreline and an undetailed land mass. This is part of

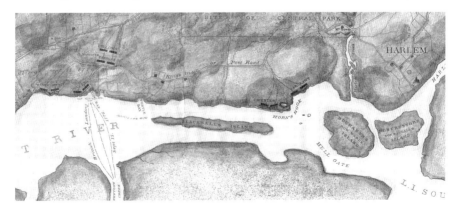

This 1878 map by Henry Johnston was based on earlier Revolutionary-period maps and documents. The details of Kip's Bay and Horn's Hook are exceptional. *Public domain. Henry Phelps Johnston*, The Campaign of 1776 around New York and Brooklyn.

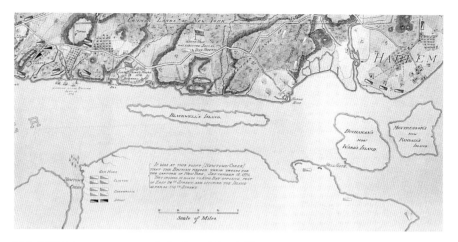

This 1895 Johnston map reveals the Long Island City coastline at Newtown Creek, the massing troops and the detailed invasion operations across the East River. *Courtesy Fraunces Tavern Museum.*

a much larger map; the focus here is on American defensive positions on New York Island, the officers who commanded them and their routes of egress. Note the "Kings Bridge or Post Road" running north up Manhattan and the locations of Kip's and Turtle Bays and Horn's Hook and Hell Gate in relation to Queens County. Of the greatest importance are the five British warships at Kip's Bay, which bombarded American positions. Other sources have lined up five ships in a row, with a broadsides of eighty guns facing the American defenses. On the East River is drawn the route the British and Hessian invaders took as they exited positions along Newtown Creek in Queens to assault New York. It was twelve noon. Here, again, the British were bringing the full force of their war machine to General Washington and his army. The East River would no longer separate the two armies.

This map displays magnificent detail showing who was where along the East River on September 15, 1776. To the east, on the map bottom, the explanation reads, "It was at this point [Newtown Creek] that the British massed their troops for the capture of New York, September 15, 1776. They crossed in boats to Kip's Bay opposite, foot of East 34th Street and occupied the island as far as 110th Street."[203] The massed British and Hessians are shown leaving the mouth of Newtown Creek, four thousand strong, in the first wave invading New York, still in the nervous hands of the awaiting Americans.

British positions to the right, on the Astoria (Hallett's Point) peninsula, had a formidable artillery battery, and there were three coastal troop positions to the northwest corner of Queens, Lawrence Point. Across the East River, to

This Charles Blaskowitz map of 1776 is an excellent source that must be described in greater detail. Scores of troop flatboats exit Newtown Creek as the British invade New York. *Public domain. Charles Blaskowitz map, 1776.*

the west of (above) Blackwell's Island, is a very meticulous rendering of the eastern Manhattan shore. Shown are both the fleeing Americans and the invading British and Hessians. Four British warships assist the "Landing of the British, Sepr. 15, 1776." (It should be five ships.) At Turtle Bay, on the conquest of New York, was "Sir Wm. Howe's Hdqrs 1776" at the Beekman house. Interestingly, just up the road, to the north (right), was the Dove Tavern near where British troops later garrisoned and where American spy Nathan Hale's fate would be sealed.

> *Embarkation of the British Troops at the Head of New Town Inlet, and their Landing in two diferent [sic] embarkations-upon New York Island. Commanded by Lieutenant General Clinton & Lieutenant General Earl Percy at Kipp's Bay, under the Fire of two forty Gun ships and Three Frigates Septembr 15th.[204]*

At "Newtown Inlet," on Long Island, separating Kings and Queens Counties, scores of British flatboats and other rowed vessels poured out of

Newtown Creek to invade New York. Across the East River, at Kip's Bay, five "ships of war" were strategically situated, bombarding the weak American defenses at that point of Manhattan, north of the city. It started as the five warships fired broadsides from their eighty-plus guns, a mighty force of arms from only part of a grand British naval fleet. It was a very successful bombardment as it scattered the Americans. The map on the previous page is only a part of the massive 1776 Charles Blaskowitz map.

Part of the 1776 Blaskowitz map is a close-up of the ancient, colonial northwestern Newtown, now Astoria. Covered is the Queens County shoreline from Ravenswood in Long Island City to the former point now under LaGuardia Airport. The 1753 Jacob Blackwell/Joseph Hallett mill was later Suydam's mill on Sunswick Creek at Hallett's Cove. The word "Mill" is written in the unnamed Hallett's Cove in the bottom left, under the letter *G*. On land, note the letter *G* at Hallett's Cove, reporting the British artillery battery, and the letter *F* depicting the British line of defense to secure northwestern Queens County. Here is western Newtown, Hell Gate Neck and all the future Astoria. The British warship "*LeBrun*" is anchored at the northern end of the treacherous Hell Gate. This warship did not negotiate

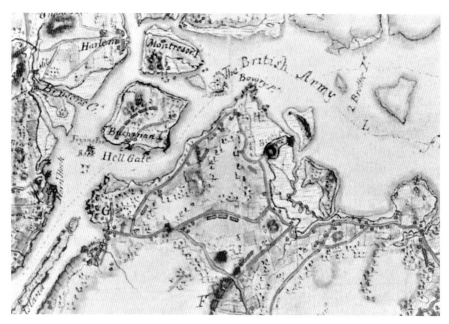

The "*LeBrun*," officially the HMS *Brune*, patrols the upper East River off northwestern Newtown, Queens. Troop positions are drawn on this finely detailed Revolutionary War map. *Public domain. Charles Blaskowitz map, 1776.*

Hell Gate from south to north. The HMS *LeBrun* was, as of late August 1776, patrolling the western end of the Long Island Sound and the eastern East River. In this close-up of the map, the viewer is able to see upper Hell Gate and "Bowery Point"; this is perhaps the only map naming this area as Bowery Point. It was referred to—and is today on NOAA navigation charts—as "Lawrence Point." British cartographers were loath to use the place names of rebels.

After the twelve o'clock landing at Kip's Bay on September 15, 1776, by late afternoon, it is rumored that Mary Lindley Murray, wife of Robert Murray, delayed the British general Howe and his conquering officers with hospitality. Delayed also were the conquering troops from chasing down half of the rebel enemy, five thousand strong, nearly trapped in lower Manhattan. That historical tale is in question and debatable, the delaying aspect being suspect yet written about as truth. One of General Howe's headquarters on New York Island was to be the Murray house. General Washington had been there only a day earlier.

The nature of writing history inherently lacks perfection due to some historical facts being in dispute or subject to disparate or new interpretations. History walks wearily under the weight of revision and new scholarship. An author may simply write about an area that they have never been to, but while the scholarship may be bountifully available and present, to walk and feel and view the terrain of a place is key to a better overall understanding of a site. Some modern maps present excellent graphics yet are greatly diminished by blatant factual and spelling errors.

Around 34th Street, between First and Second Avenues, is the former site of the filled-in and long-gone Kip's Bay. There was no ferry point here in 1776. Note the *Donna M.* dock barge that allows commuters and sightseers to board ferryboats to Long Island City, Roosevelt Island, Astoria, East 90th Street in Manhattan, and through Hell Gate to the Bronx. Besides kayaking, the local ferries are the best way to envision ships on the East River in 1776.

The historical signage reads, in parts important to Long Island City:

> *Using 75 flatboats, and other small craft, which had been hidden at the mouth of Newton Creek (Queens), and under the furious, if ineffective, bombardment from the guns of four warships, the Americans abandoned their position. Washington's army withdrew in disorder but was saved from destruction by a rear guard of the Continental Army's Maryland Regiments. The invaders seized Inclenberg, home of Robert Murray (about*

The modern East 34th Street East River ferry docks, at Kip's Bay, are a hub for numerous commuter and tourist ferries. The informational signage misinforms with errors. *R. Melnick photo.*

37th Street and Park Avenue), giving rise to the apocryphal tale of Colonial sympathizers entertaining English Generals to delay the British while the American army escaped.[205]

As a local historian thoroughly immersed in this and other 1776 events, the author wishes to point out some errors that, on this sign, misinform the reader. One glaring error is the misspelling of "Newtown Creek" as "Newton." That is bad. It has always been, since the English period, Newtown Creek. The flatboats were towed up the East River by the warships and sent down creek to the creek headwaters, where the boats were hidden. Also, there were five British warships firing broadsides at Kip's Bay, not four. The fire was not ineffective. They may have overdone the volume of fire, but it was not ineffective. The bombardment did its job precisely, pulverizing the meager coastal defenses, causing the Americans to flee and allowing for an uncontested British landing, resulting in zero casualties. Plus, the bombardment of Kip's Bay sent a severe message: The king's army is coming to your island. Now!

A final necessary criticism: Washington's army withdrew in disorder, but it was not here where he was saved from destruction by a Maryland regiment. The famous rearguard action by the Marylanders that saved Washington's army took place on Long Island on August 27, 1776, not at Kip's Bay on September 15. These things will not burden the commuter and tourist, but they sorely vex the historian. New York, we can do better.

SEPTEMBER 16, 1776

John Alsop (1724–1794), a New York delegate to the Continental Congress since 1774, elected not to approve the Declaration of Independence and resigned his seat in mid-July 1776. His reasons were that he had wished for a peaceful reconciliation with the colonies' parent country, Great Britain. The British army was in the midst of conquering New York City at the southern portion of New York Island; the Congress in Philadelphia was not yet aware of these military actions to the north. Alsop, still a Whig and a Patriot, with a great mercantile business in New York and family in western Queens County, was still a wanted man. He requested from Congress a letter allowing him passage in and out of American defensive lines. John Hancock, president of the Continental Congress and first signer of the Declaration of Independence, signed this letter in Philadelphia on September 16, 1776, the day after the September 15 British and Hessian landing at Kip's Bay. This document makes September 16 a remarkable day for western Newtown. The Alsops lived here. At great peril to his person, John Alsop had a great chance to make his name famous by signing the Declaration.

In summary, the letter instructs all Continental officers and guards along the defensible American lines to allow John Alsop passage through their lines. "To all Continental Officers Guards & others whom it may concern, Permitt the Honrble John Alsop Esqr. to Pass and Repass without hindrance or interruption. Given under my Hand at Philadelphia this Sixteenth Day of September 1776. John Hancock Presidt."[206]

John Hancock's signing of this letter for John Alsop did not reflect the harsh reality in New York City. This was a very interesting and tenuous situation for John Alsop. The document's historical background states:

Ironically, Hancock wrote this pass for a man who had resigned from Congress to protest the Declaration of Independence. John Alsop…had been an ardent supporter of the Revolutionary cause. He represented New York in both the First and Second Continental Congress, but still hoped for fair and honorable terms from England, and considered the Declaration of Independence to be too radical a step.[207]

Concluding the John-Alsop-as-Revolutionary file is that by September 16, 1776, John Alsop's house and property in New York City and his home in western Newtown had been confiscated and occupied by the British. If Alsop had wanted to go back to New York, his attempt would have been wrought with difficulty and peril. He was, up until July 16, 1776, a Patriot, a rebel congressman debating sedition and conducting treasonous business against the king. "It is unlikely that Alsop ever reached his New York City destination."[208]

September 1776 saw many Whigs retreat, relocate and regroup. John Alsop's capture by the British might have meant an inglorious traitor's death by hanging. To retreat to fight another day was a noble endeavor nonetheless. Dead soldiers, while often celebrated, do not get to continue the fight. By September 1776, the British had occupied New York City, ending the exiled John Alsop's effective contributions to the Revolution. Former Continental congressman John Alsop, a diffused Patriot and still a traitor to the British Crown, was forced to relocate to the home of his brother, in Middletown, Connecticut, where he sat out the war in retirement.

Upon the British invasion, the rattled yet determined Americans fled lower New York City to Harlem, where they would fight another day. The next day, on September 16, 1776, the battle on and around the Harlem Heights produced for the Americans an inconclusive stalemate yet a morale-building "victory" for the Continentals. The Americans, routed on August 27 and on the previous day, September 15, fought well enough for the British to realize that the rebellion would not go down easily. Some of the cowards of the previous day got tough fast and stood their ground.

The western two-thirds of Queens County on Long Island was now entirely British. Their Royal Army and Navy were in command and in control. Long Island was occupied from New York Harbor and the East River to Hell Gate. North of Hell Gate was a small fleet of British ships. Any point on York Island south of Harlem was now British occupied. New York City was theirs. To take full control of New York Island was being planned. The former Sargent's Battery on Horn's Hook overlooking Hell Gate was now British. British guns would now command the strategic Hell Gate, and the fort would be garrisoned by the Hessians for the foreseeable future.

The active war had left Queens County via western Newtown, the future Long Island City, on September 15, 1776, and crossed the East River. The remaining troops dug in as the British occupation began. The war for American independence took the fight to upper New York Island, Upstate New York, New Jersey, Pennsylvania and, after 1779, to Georgia, the Carolinas and Virginia. The Revolutionary War was in full swing. Life in western Queens County, western Newtown, was about to become extremely difficult, as the victorious British army and their Hessian allies would be here for an extended stay.

Major General Heath reported to General Washington that a British warship was off the coast of southern Westchester, near Lawrence Point in Queens. The 36 guns he speaks of are the HMS *Brune* of 32 guns. Its guns and those of other vessels would guard the northern entrance to the Hell Gate for the foreseeable future. The HMS *Brune* is called the "Le Brun" on the 1776 Blaskowitz map on page 172.

Noteworthy to Long Island's Revolutionary story is a death that occurred on September 20, 1776. General Nathaniel Woodhull, captured near Jamaica, Queens County, on August 28 and mortally wounded then, died in captivity at New Utrecht, Kings County. His important mission to clear western Kings and Queens Counties of cattle that would surely have helped feed the British went unfulfilled. Long Island's highest-ranking militia officer was dead. He left behind his wife, Ruth, who was the sister of William Floyd, a signer of the Declaration of Independence.

The "Great Fire of New York" burned about one-quarter of New York City on September 20–21, 1776. Between four hundred and one thousand structures were destroyed. The fire started at Whitehall Slip and devoured buildings west of Broadway to the Hudson River. Queens County residents saw the massive blaze from hilltops and shorelines.

General James Robertson, fresh from the short military occupation of western Queens County, was instrumental in containing and extinguishing the great fire. On September 15, General Robertson marched part of his army along 20th Road, then Old Bowery Road, to Bowery Bay Road and beyond to Flushing and Whitestone. A smaller portion of Robertson's troops followed the first wave of troops from Queens County to Kip's Bay, making the general's force available to fight the Great Fire of 1776.

Posing as a "Dutch schoolmaster," Captain Nathan Hale of the 19th Connecticut Regiment of the Continental army was captured as a spy on Long Island on September 21, 1776. The main events of Hale's mission occurred outside of western Queens, our area of focus. After his capture, Captain Hale was brought to British general William Howe's headquarters at the Beekman house. The Beekman homestead, on a modest shoreline elevation, stood near the modern East 51st Street near First Avenue and can be seen on four maps in this book. Hunter's Point residents could see the Beekman and Kip houses across Blackwell's Island and the East

River. Without a trial and sentenced to death by General William Howe, Continental army captain Nathan Hale was hanged as a spy on September 22, 1776. British captain John Montresor witnessed the hanging and spoke the details to posterity.

Tories vs. Whigs in Newtown

A very prominent family in Newtown was the Rapeljes. Primary and secondary source books and gravestones report four different spellings of the family name, which sometimes made following a character or family line difficult. George Rapelje was the epitome of the harsh Loyalist: harsh toward anyone who was formerly a Whig or, perhaps, secretly a Whig and avoiding being found out by the likes of Rapelje. "Distinctive among the cruelties of the Newtown Tories towards their neighbors was that of George Rapelje."[209]

Although he lived more than a mile outside of this book's Long Island City purview, this George Rapelje was notorious throughout all Newtown. His end was to remain in British favor while turning in anyone who spoke sedition or whispered rebellion. He was either respected for his zeal to assist the authority of the Crown or loathed by any former Whig now under British occupation.

> *This British sympathizer did all he could to persecute his American neighbors and to aid the British, so that he even became a paymaster to the English troops, and when assessments were laid upon the townspeople to provide food for the British soldiers, George Rapelje was appointed to collect these, and he did so with great pleasure, cheating many of his neighbors so greatly that he and his wife Polly had to flee Newtown after the War, and never returned here.*[210]

Chapter 8

Occupation Here, War There: Newtown Occupied, 1776–1783

The British army conquered western Queens County, the future eleven square miles of Long Island City, by early September 1776. All Patriots had better have fled, or the hangman's rope awaited traitors to the British Crown. What lay ahead for captured Patriots was an agonizingly slow demise in an inhumane sugar house or prison ship.

The British now commanded all of Newtown and the surrounding salt waters. It was martial law. Every house and homestead was soon to shelter British officers and some soldiers. Sign the oath of loyalty to King George III, or you are under arrest. You will decide now. Unfair treatment awaited the subjugated Whigs who signed oaths of loyalty, yet they were not in jail, and they were still alive. Total acquiescence was in order for the subjugated citizen to survive the war. "With silent eloquence all these olden manor houses tell of British pomp and Hessian vandalism, for not one was exempt from the events which marked the customs of warfare."[211]

Once the main British forces crossed the East River to pursue the retreating Americans, part of the British army and some Hessians were left behind in Queens County to occupy. The British were to establish long-term encampments, with troops ready to rotate to combat areas or protect the seat of British power in North America, New York City. In Dutch Kills, where the British chose to billet and encamp, the Brinckerhoff and Bragaw houses were in full use by their idle yet occupying troops. Houses sheltered officers, and ovens baked breads for the soldiery. The Long Island—now Brooklyn—Historical Society may still possess the windowpanes of local homes where British officers etched their names, perhaps eyeing a sort of morbid immortality—or, perhaps, as a reminder to the reader of past revolutionary times.

"The Hessians, with characteristic wantonness, celebrated the flight of William Payntar to Staten Island, by using his mahogany furniture for fuel, and orderly denuding the house of every article of value."[212] William Payntar was not in the main Payntar house in 1776; it was occupied by the Bragaws, who built it. Some families had more than one dwelling in a certain area.

All western Newtown houses were occupied. British and Hessian soldiers billeted in houses as they were available, in barns, in tent encampments or in a cantonment of constructed huts partially in the earth.

> *Persons whose homes were confiscated in this manner had by far the best of the bargain compared with their less fortunate neighbors upon whom may have been quartered as many as twenty British Regulars, to be fed and given the best fire in the house.*[213]

Confiscation of homes, farms, wagons, equipment, animals and food was always the rule in this harsh military occupation of western Queens County. Loyalist sons and young men were often forced into subscription or joined Loyalist companies to assist the ruling British military. In this martial law situation, British military control was the rule. They could, in a moment, decide your fate. Even the most giving and fawning Newtown Loyalist had to acquiesce to the British military officer corps. During martial law, every nonmilitary person and soldier alike was subject to the arbitrary rule of the ranking officer in command of that place. Some Loyalist residents of western Queens County were quite at ease serving their ruling British masters and abusively treating loyalty-oath-taking former Whigs and Patriots. The British officers billeted in the best houses, preferably with obsequious Loyalist hosts, and dismissed regard for the rightful owners' rights. The rights of the citizenry are not an issue to an occupying army. "Local residents had to house the soldiers and help feed them, and food prices for everyone soared. To many the soldiers seemed little better than robbers."[214]

A high level of revelry surrounded these officers' residences. Dinners and dances were often given. In some cases, in disregard for the homeowner, whether strongly Loyalist or subjugated Whig, the parlor was used as a stable for the British dragoons' horses. "Headquarters" was a term used liberally. Besides the actual General William Howe headquarters, each unit had a main command center. From company to regiment/battalion to brigade and to division, each commanding officer established his "headquarters" in a Newtown home.

During the seven-year occupation, both Tories and silent supporters of the revolution found these thirty-six thousand British troops as unruly as any large army without much fighting to do would be. The war was raging elsewhere in the colonies. Training and military discipline were not combat. With no enemy in sight, occupying troops were easily bored, as idle minds are the devil's workshop. It took this many troops, rotating in and out of combat or moving to other British occupied areas, to control New York City, the base of British military operations in North America. "The British troops had no respect for the homes of patriots, especially where the men were absent fighting against King George's redcoated soldiers."[215] The furniture and outbuildings of many Patriot homes were used as fuel by the British and Hessians alike. The term "vandalism" may be applied to these actions, yet from a British perspective, it was rebel property confiscation and reuse. Some reuse was, of course, the burning of the wood from deliberately broken furniture and dismantled structures for fuel.

Once the occupation was established, the British Royal Navy kept a corvette stationed at Riker's Island. These essential vessels operated in shallower, less navigable waterways, of which New York had many. The future Long Island City had numerous smaller waterways, such as Newtown Creek, Dutch Kills and the hardly navigable Sunswick and Luyster Creeks. On the nearby Bowery Bay coast, the Jacobus Lent house was a "quaint cottage [that] contained many curious relics and was the favorite stopping place of British dragoons seeking bread and whisky for themselves and watering their horses at the trough by the roadside."[216]

New York had a large standing British garrison, the bulk of which was in western Long Island. Southern New York Province was entirely British. Troops stayed here year-round. Some troops wintered here in western Newtown and waited for springtime to go to where their commanders were sent. They had to maintain a large force in case of attack on the city and to defend the region's supply routes and resources. Harsh treatment of Patriot families or their former homesteads ensued. "The Tory residents took advantage of this opportunity to show their dislike for all American patriots. The homes of the latter were raided and their occupants subjected to all manner of insult. Believing in the justness and ultimate success of their cause the patriots withstood it all and repaid evil with good."[217]

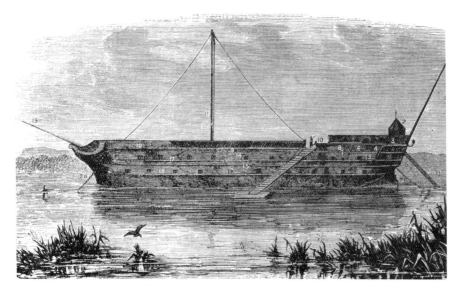

The notorious British prison ship *Jersey* anchored in Wallabout Bay, Kings County. Over eleven thousand Patriots died in these ships, more than in actual battle. *Public domain. The New York Public Library.*

The occupation army, camped in close proximity, was beset by debilitating sanitary and health issues. "In homes where the Hessians were quartered, their habits being unclean, a dreadful fever took root, which was to recur in the hot summer months for several years after the Revolution was over, killing many residents."[218]

Although well out of our Long Island City purview, the Wallabout Bay prison ships in Brooklyn are the subject of books and fully worth mentioning.[219] The *Jersey* was the most notorious of them all; some others were the *Scorpion*, *Stromboli*, *Hope* and *Hunter*. No longer sailing vessels with masts and sails, these ships were stripped of all functionality save for their ability to not sink at anchor as a floating prison hulk. Not a few soldiers in the Newtown North and South Beats and Queens County militias were captured at the Battle of Long Island. Most were thrown into these fetid floating prisons to die. Richard Bragaw, a local resident who lived along the old Dutch Kills Road, was captured near Jamaica, Queens County. Bragaw was seized along with General Nathaniel Woodhull on August 28, 1776, while conducting a major strategic cattle drive. General Woodhull was mortally wounded. Bragaw was thrown into the *Jersey*. Captain Richard Lawrence was "captured after the Battle of L.I., he was held prisoner in

The old Morrell House at Woodside Avenue and Middleburg Avenue, now 39th Avenue. Note the LIRR train and the Hell Gate Bridge in the distance (*right*). *QBPL*.

the sugar house in New York City."[220] Another local man, John Lawrence, was thrown into the *Jersey* in 1781.

The sturdy Morrell house, the expanse of property and the informative vistas must surely give way to the chickens in the foreground. In this excellent Eugene Armbruster photo above, to the right are a Long Island Rail Road train and the 1916 Hell Gate Bridge.

John Morrell the elder was born in 1703, built the house circa 1735 and built a forge here; he died in 1768. His only son, John, born in 1733, succeeded to his estate. His wife, Elizabeth (1737–1808), was from the prominent local Skillman family. The house was built on the south side of old Middleburg Avenue (39th Avenue) between 51st and 52nd Streets. The father and two sons were Patriots who had to flee their home and county after the Battle of Long Island, leaving behind Mrs. Morrell, her younger children and the farm.

The British army's advance guard of the light brigade and grenadiers were riding down the road from Newtown toward the Narrow Passage when they came on the Morrell house. These troops, fresh off their victory over the Americans at the Battle of Long Island, were seeking a large area to encamp and regroup for the next battle, date and place unknown. Mrs. Morrell, wife of John, was anxious for her Patriot husband and sons, who were at the recent battle and were involved in the defeat. Where were they? Were they still alive? Captured? Or had they safely fled? To a mother, the battle death of a husband or son is never glorious.

A group of British army soldiers "on the gallop emerged from Woodside at the turn below on the Astoria Road" (Woodside Avenue, a.k.a. the Road to Hallett's Cove) and dismounted their horses at the door of the Morrell house. Mother Morrell was politely greeted by a gentlemanly British officer. "I am Major March, in command of the Advance Guard, First Division under Lieutenant-General Sir Henry Clinton, who will soon be here with the main army: but first secure all your cattle and poultry, or I won't be responsible for them."[221]

Major Thomas March, of the Third Battalion of Grenadiers, then pointed to the nearby hills, where ten thousand men were soon to arrive and pitch their camps. Other units would march even farther west in the next few days and encamp. He then asked her to prepare a dinner for the officers soon to arrive, which he said he would pay for. This was still British troop maneuvering in search of the rebel enemy, not yet the army of occupation. Mrs. Morrell and her younger children, having been advised to do so, secured the livestock under lock and key and could only hope that the slightest protections offered by Major March would keep her farm from being rudely plundered.

Of strong importance to this narrative is the fact that Mrs. Morrell was understandably forthright with Major March. Francis Skillman reported, "John Morrell, with his two sons, John and Abraham, were absent with the patriots, being a very active family in the service of their country—a condition which Mrs. Morrell did not hesitate to confide to Major March. Nor was her confidence misplaced; his influence ever after protected the family against marauding Tories."[222] After Major March left to assign new positions, "the glancing bayonets of the main division" passed through the Morrell gate and along Dutch Kills Road to encamp. It was undoubtedly quite a scene, this grand military review before their very eyes.[223] The importance of Dutch Kills Road was immeasurable. It connected points in western Queens County from Ridge Road at Queens Plaza in the west and Woodside Avenue to the east. One hundred yards north was the "Narrow Passage" that led to the road fork heading north to Bowery Bay Road and north and west onto Newtown Road, also called the Road to Hallett's Cove.

John Morrell's farm was occupied by the British, as he was a soldier in Washington's army. Private Morrell served in 1776 in Captain Abraham Riker's company in the New York Line. He may have signed an oath of loyalty to the king and been allowed to return to his ancient home at a later date. On his return, an angry British officer hanged Morrell from a tree limb in his own orchard. Luckily for Morrell, a higher-ranking and sympathetic

British officer cut him down. A differing account reveals, "Among the numerous fruit trees there still remains the one from whose limb old Morrell was suspended by Hessian soldiers to extort from him the hiding place of the money."[224] Considerations of his rumored stash of gold also motivated Tory marauders and uncontrolled Hessians. Major March was off with the British troops fighting elsewhere. He could not protect the Morrells any longer. "On the farm of the Morrell Family is the well which supplied water to the Hessians in 1776 and the tree from which Morrell was suspended until he divulged the hiding place of his gold."[225]

The Morrell house had once lain just across the Long Island City line in Woodside. Some later maps show two different Morrell houses, one north and one south of Middleburg Avenue. The rough border between Sunnyside, a part of Long Island City, and Woodside is roughly 49th or 50th Street and part of the length of the old and mostly de-mapped Bowery Bay Road. Patriot John Morrell survived the upheaval and died at the age of eighty-two. "John Morrell...died quietly in 1816 and was interred in the little family cemetery in the center of the farm, a lonely and deserted spot today, in the midst of strangers who now own the soil, but the stranger may without trespass visit the grave of John Morrell, the active partisan of 1776."[226] Based on a 1903 Belcher-Hyde property map at GAHS, the approximate site of the Morrell family cemetery is discernable. According to the excellent photographer Eugene Armbruster, on whose photos is written vital information, the John Morrell house was destroyed by fire on November 6, 1925. A recent 2023 recon of the 52nd Street, Woodside, Morrell family burial ground site shows no remnant in the approximate vicinity or any commemorative signage. Here, the Patriot Morrell family and their revolutionary sacrifices are forgotten.

A major consideration for a practical and sanitary military encampment is a clean source of drinking water, like a freshwater brook or a water well. The Morrell property provided this highly sought-after commodity. Just south of the Narrow Passage was "the old farmhouse of the Morrell family, which, although much altered, is in a good state of preservation. The old well still gives as good water as when it supplied the Hessians of 1776, who were camped all over the farm."[227]

A permanent regular garrison of passing troops, the wounded and the severely impaired was established from the Morrell farm at Woodside Avenue to the Skillman lands westward. Nearby was the residence and water well of Abraham Skillman, born in 1704. Two of Abraham's daughters married local men: Hester wed William Payntar, and Elizabeth was betrothed to

John Morrell. During the Revolutionary War, Skillman's well was poisoned. "This was a great mystery. Of course no one done it."[228] The perpetrators were unknown; the unsavory and punishable deed was most likely the work of Patriots, but the blame "was laid to a negro."[229] A Hessian regiment encamped on the farm and was taken ill by the befouled water well. Years later, Francis Skillman wrote that "Skillman's silver was concealed among the stones at the bottom of the well while soldiers were there."[230]

On the 1903 Belcher-Hyde property map, a small graveyard west of Woodside Avenue/Hurl Gate Road shows the 1816 burial site of the patriot John Morrell. "Seven headstones of the rudest kind mark the graves of the departed members of the family and many old bullets and flints have been plowed up at various points."[231]

A 1903 map mislabels one road as being Woodside Avenue when it was not, causing confusion. The 1816 Morrell family burial ground lay west of 52nd Street, once Dickinson or Dickson Street and the furthest extension north of Celtic Avenue starting from near Newtown Creek. The road went to the point where it intersected with Dutch Kills Road and Woodside Avenue.

The Cornelius Rapelye house in 1776, later the Wyckoff house, was along the strategic Bowery Bay Road and stood east of the modern Hobart Street near 30th Avenue (formerly Grand Avenue). It was located near the north

The Rapelye house, here named after Wyckoff, was built prior to 1756, along the strategic Bowery Bay Road. Cornelius Rapelye owned the house in 1776. *GAHS collection.*

end of the Boulevard Gardens cooperative housing complex in Woodside. The house was east of Bowery Bay Road, facing south, with the porch facing east; this photo's view faces northwest. The road ran north to south to the west of the house. "Robberies were frequent, and Newtown became a prey to depredation, alarm and cruelty. The civil courts were suspended, and martial law prevailed through seven long years."[232]

Incidents of scavenging, marauding and plunder by the armed occupying British and Hessian troops were many. Every part of the future Long Island City was trod on heavily by these martial occupiers. Unlawful property incursions and material thefts often went unpunished by the British military authorities. Such nefarious martial rapaciousness would not be confined to 1776. The British were here to stay. Soldiers scavenging for food were rampant. It's been said that a chicken's cluck can be heard for miles by hungry men. The Cornelius Rapelye house on Bowery Bay Road had a life-and-death episode occur there further into the long occupation.

In its later years, the Rapelye house was renamed the Wyckoff house and, later, the David Purdy house. Some maps differ on the exact placement of the house. Perhaps controversially yet true to the correct study of history, leaving no omission, the photo caption reads, "Wyckoff House, Grand Ave & Nigger Lane, Astoria. (Built prior to 1756)." The information was written on the photo in white ink, as was the case with many photos of the time; it was more than likely written on the freshly developed photo. Notice two small children and one larger child sitting on the porch steps, accompanied by an adult servant or family member. A boy in a dark suit stands nearby. The ancient house was razed circa 1920, if not earlier.

A quarter mile to the south was the Nathaniel Moore house. "During the next seven years, while the British held New York and large numbers of English and Hessian troops were quartered at Newtown, Moore's house remained a gathering place for loyalists."[233]

The situating of in-ground hut structures is a cantonment, whereas a tent bivouac is an encampment, or camp.[234] There were cantonment huts behind (to the north) the colonial homes along the old Dutch Kills Road, now 39th Avenue and also along the future Skillman Avenue. There was high ground rising above the sea-level saltwater creeks, where the British could overlook the domains that they conquered and occupied. At their peak, thirty-six thousand soldiers of the British army camped along the heights of Woodside, the hills of Sunnyside and nearby lands providing dirt and stone hillsides to dig into. "They built huts, trenches, and earthworks on the Sackett, Morrell, Bragaw, and Cumberson farms."[235]

An excellent sketch of the Hessian and British-style huts built into the sturdy hills near Dutch Kills Road. Hut remnants survived until circa 1903. *Public domain.* Leslie's History of Greater New York, *Daniel Van Pelt, 1898.*

The encamped soldiers built entrenchments, latrines and earthen and wooden huts along the hills of Sunnyside and Woodside. "Until the massive regrading of the area for the Sunnyside Rail Yards in 1905, the foundations of these huts could still be seen."[236] From today's Woodside westward to Queens Plaza, a number of troops had huts dug into the hillsides, and tent encampments were erected as needed. Heavy demands were made on the occupied local households. Payments for farm produce and services for the Crown were infrequent and often withheld as punishment for infractions, sometimes for just having Whig leanings. Often, payment by the British to a subjugated Newtown resident did not exist. On this colonial road, the homes of Brinckerhoff, Bragaw and Morrell, Patriots all, were occupied by the British.

Some of these properties were within the borders of Sunnyside, part of Long Island City, and some in Woodside. Other nearby British camps were in Newtown Village (Elmhurst) and Jamaica, Queens County. The thatch- and sod-roofed wooden huts were built into the ground, with wood beams and stacked stones as supports. A small fireplace in the huts was the only warmth for the troops during the harsh winter months. A sturdy roof was necessary, yet not always guaranteed, to ward against hard New York rains, winds, snows and deep freezes.

The Alsops were a very prominent Newtown family. One Richard lived in the house just north of Newtown Creek, at the southern terminus of Bowery Bay Road. The Alsop family cemetery lay northwest of the house. Another Richard, John's brother, lived in Connecticut and died there in 1776. John Alsop, a stronger Patriot than Richard, lived elsewhere in western Newtown; his exact home location in 1776 is hard to verify. There was a John Alsop house east of Lawrence Point along the Old Bowery Road; its construction date is unclear, yet photos of the house exist at the Queens Borough Public Library.

The Richard Alsop home was a perfect case of a house divided. Their politics willfully far apart and beds forced close together, their home was occupied. The grand home saw the Alsop family as both willful allies and forced allies of the Crown. There would be no dissent here. Mrs. Abigail Alsop was a fervent and intense Tory, and her husband, Richard, was obsequiously a former Whig. Mrs. Alsop's service to the British occupiers was exemplary, as the "generals and colonels paid her marks of great distinctions."[237] Richard's Tory wife held sway over the household, and "trusting in the control his wife had over him, they probably regarded him as harmless. He never again did ought to give offense."[238]

Friends of Richard Alsop were notable local men. Key players in the Whig politics of Newtown were Robert Blackwell, Jonathan Lawrence, Samuel Moore, Jeromus Remsen, Samuel Riker, Samuel Morrell and others from eastern and southern parts of Newtown, "all of whom, with [Richard] Alsop, signed the document sent out by the Committee of Correspondence in 1774."[239] Heavy suspicion fell on Richard Alsop based on the colleagues mentioned earlier and his own actions. "Richard Alsop was a patriot and made himself very conspicuous at the commencement of hostilities, but the occupation of his grounds by Colonel Ruggles and his little regiment for eight years, kept his spirit in complete subjection."[240] The Alsop house was strategically and conveniently placed. It served as a vital military post between Newtown and New York. Travelers and military used it as an inn or a stop along the way, a last rest stop on the continuing journey. This house was well protected. "Beside affording his house protection against the raids of the foraging hordes, Alsop realized great sums of money from the British exchequer."[241]

The hardships suffered by local farmers were many. The only profit to be made was by the British overseers, not the subjugated farmers. The majority portions of their hay, straw, rye, corn, oats, provisions and animals were gathered for the use of the army, each and every year. Payments to the farmers were disbursed according to the whims of the king's commissioners and their price fixing, based on the weight or size of the product or produce. "If the seller demanded more it was at the risk of losing the whole, at best, at worst, crop confiscation or personal imprisonment."[242] Loyal Tory farmers and landowners had to adhere to the rules of the military occupation. British lieutenant general Charles Cornwallis billeted at the former Whig Richard Alsop's house. Maps and sketches show that the Alsop house was not within the grounds of the later Calvary Cemetery, as is the Alsop Cemetery. The house was east across the road that became Laurel Hill Boulevard, then the southernmost part of the road from the future Penny Bridge, then a ferry point, north to Bowery Bay.

The highest-ranking and successful British officers and a handful of American officers passed through the future Long Island City. They were here, on missions, fleeing, capturing, encamping. The British army marched through this town. War passed through this town. Pieces of war and colonial life lie forever buried under the modern Long Island City.

Chapter 9

OCTOBER–DECEMBER 1776

OCTOBER 1776

In past teachings of America's struggle to bring itself into existence, the views of and arguments for the British colonial powers were given less space in the textbooks. These views, then prominent in the monarchies of Europe, were considered old hat and draconian by the forward-thinking Americans, who had new and better ideas on governance. The majority of Queens County residents wanted to remain within the British realm. "It is not often taught in our schools that so many of the early Americans were appalled at the idea of Independence from their mother country, England. After all, they were, firstly, Englishmen."[243] History reports back to us that the American republican experiment, though flawed, was worth the rebellion that made it so.

In September and October 1776, the HMS *Brune* (32 guns) patrolled to the north of the Hell Gate, off Montresor's Island to the eastern end of the East River. The two frigates HMS *Niger* and HMS *Brune* had sufficient armaments to project British might, where necessary, up to a half-mile inland and along the coastlines. The HMS *Brune* patrolled and fired on American guns on the continent, lower Westchester County, across the river from Lawrence Point in Queens County.

The HMS *Roebuck* (44 guns) and HMS *Phoenix* (44), pictured on the following page, with three other ships, did navigate and help to conquer the lower East River from September 13–15, 1776.[244] Shown is a famous

Above: British Royal Navy warships sailed up the Hudson River on October 9, 1776. The HMS *Phoenix* and HMS *Roebuck* fired their guns from the East River near Queens one month earlier. *Public domain. Painting by Thomas Mitchell.*

Left: Admiral Richard Howe, Fourth Viscount Howe (1726–1799). Richard Howe was the older brother of the British commander-in-chief, General William Howe. They brought war to America. *Public domain.*

painting depicting a British Royal Navy action on the Hudson River on October 9, 1776. This event did not occur in local Long Island City waters. It is absolutely necessary to provide this fact. New York's great bay and rivers projected British sea power. This provided His Majesty's army with greater maneuverability and the means to land a large force nearly anywhere in New York's saltwater realm. Here are the HMS *Tartar*, HMS *Roebuck* and HMS *Phoenix*, plus support tenders and boats alongside and aft, testing the American guns at Fort Washington and Fort Lee.

The vibrant and battle-hardened admiral of the British Royal Navy fleet in North America commanded all New York City waters after November 1776. This 1790s painting does not do justice to the forty-year-old (in 1776), Admiral Richard Howe. His naval ships and force logistics facilitated major amphibious landings at Gravesend Bay, Kip's Bay, Pelham Bay and Fort Lee, and the ships fired their guns from the Hudson and East Rivers. Admiral Howe's navy faced limited naval opposition around New York until a French squadron arrived in 1778 to harass and battle the British and to draw their ships elsewhere.

ON OCTOBER 12, 1776, in a feat that was considered reckless, Admiral Richard Howe sailed part of his fleet through the turbulent and treacherous Hell Gate. The naval maneuver was a major "feat of navigation and seamanship through Hell Gate, only one boat was lost."[245] The East River's Hell Gate proved to be a major obstacle to British Royal Navy operations and mercantile shipping during the Revolutionary War. However, wartime will make attempting certain difficult feats worth the risk. Admiral Howe sailed on warships in the East River, off the Long Island City and Hell Gate coastlines and in Newtown Creek. His flagship, the mighty 64-gun HMS *Eagle*, dared not venture into the East River.

From right after the September 15 invasion of New York to October 12, 1776, British general Clark and Hessian lieutenant general De Heister billeted at the William Lawrence house that General Robertson had vacated. "The Hessians remained 3 weeks and then left to join in the movement against New York," on October 12, 1776.[246] "Heister had his Hessians with him, and embarked, October 12, for Frog's Point, by way of Hell-Gate, with flat-bottomed boats and other craft."[247] The Hessians left this western Queens area on flatboats from Polhemus dock north of Hell Gate, two hundred yards north of Astoria Park, west of Shore Boulevard. The Polhemuses had numerous properties and houses in this area deep into the nineteenth century; remnants of their wooden dock may still be visible.

Part of the fleet that navigated the Hell Gate was the 28-gun HMS *Carysfort*, which sailed through with other warships, transports and flatboats to move the British army to Westchester County. The HMS *Carysfort* was one of the five British warships that bombarded Kip's Bay on September 15, 1776, prior to the invasion of New York. The *Carysfort* negotiated the Hell Gate en route to covering the British landing at Throgs Neck on October 12, 1776, confirmed by the larger 1776 Blaskowitz map. In coordination with the great nautical maneuver through Hell Gate on October 12, some British and Hessian units marched east from the Hell Gate along Old Bowery Road (now 20th Road) and around Bowery Bay to Flushing and Whitestone. They were soon to embark to Westchester County to pursue the Americans.

The combat operations in Newtown and Queens County, as of October 12, 1776, were finished.

Combat troops seeking battle with the Continental army were gone. The maneuvers to war moved to the North American continent. Queens County and western Newtown were now facing the onset of years of military occupation. The conquering British army and their Hessian allies were here to stay.

By October 12 through to October 18, the full sixteen-mile length of the East River was now secured and occupied by the British Royal Navy. The next battles of the war would take place in Westchester County, New York.

Previously, British forces captured and occupied Staten Island, western Long Island, lower New York Island and the small but well-situated East River islands. Island hopping was the British strategy until continental terra firma was gained and secured. The British frigate HMS *Niger* was located in the upper East River just off Hunt's Point (now in the Bronx). The HMS *Brune*, HMS *Senegal* and HMS *Halifax* were nearby. Their cannons could easily hit the local homes along Old Bowery Road. The *Niger* was helping protect the northern end of Hell Gate, which was the northern "back door" to New York Harbor. The eastern edge was Lawrence Point in northwest Queens County.

> *Before the late war, a top-sail vessel was seldom ever known to pass through Hell-Gates; but since the commencement of it, fleets of transports with frigates for their convoy, have frequently ventured and accomplished it; the Niger, indeed, a very fine frigate of thirty-two guns, generally struck in some hidden rock, every time she attempted this passage.*[248]

The above passage occurred later in the war but proves the treacherous nature of the aptly named Hell Gate.

A "petition by Queens County Freeholders to the British authorities" was offered so that "Queens County might be restored to Royal favor."[249] The petition was signed by the inhabitants of Queens County on October 21, 1776. If a Whig sympathizer did not escape from all of Newtown, he would have only one option: to acquiesce and sign the oath of loyalty to the British Crown. He or she would still be treated harshly and unfairly by the Tory co-inhabitants, they knowing full well of the Whig's leanings. The Tories and Loyalists now had the upper hand. Survival was the goal. Stating your allegiance to the cause of America was now silenced, if you wanted to "live" under British martial law and occupation.

Henry Onderdonk Jr. lists 1,293 Queens residents who signed the October 21 petition. Their last names echo those of the Patriots from Newtown who fought or fled for their lives and honor: Morrell, Hallett, Lawrence, Fish, Suydam, Remsen, Rapalje, Ricker, Berrien, Luyster, Polhemus, Brinckerhoff, Bennett, Titus, Alburtus, Moore, Debevois, Duryee, Ditmars, Ryerson, Sackett, Bragaw, Welling, Way, Alsop and Penfold. This list is long, yet it reflects and represents the family names of the subjugated citizens of Queens County, whether overtly Tory or silently Whig. Many of these names reoccur in the annals of the history of Newtown via future leaders of the area or in many now-defunct street names.

The Hessians, who so rudely encamped in western Newtown, on the hills of northern Astoria and above the ancient Shore Road, saw plenty of military action in the months following their October 12 departure from Queens. The British and Hessians brought battle to the Continentals on October 28, 1776, at White Plains in Westchester County. Lieutenant General De Heister, Colonel Donop, Colonel Johann Rall and Lieutenant Colonels Block, Minnegerode and Linsingen, all once in western Queens County, were now on the march in New York, most never to return to Queens County.

From October 1776 going forward, there was a British naval fleet in New York Harbor. Nearly all areas of the five future boroughs of the city of New York were under British control. It was a conquering fleet from August to October 1776, afterward an occupying naval fleet. Ships would rotate in and out of combat zones and defense zones. All the mighty British naval ships that saw action on the East River in September–October 1776 would serve the Crown in distant North American waters. Some East River vessels did not make it to the end of the war. On local land, Americans were nowhere to be found, and the British moved about as they wished in Kings and Queens Counties. Britannia reigned throughout all the old town of Newtown and the future Long Island City. The British occupation was total. Your will was theirs.

NOVEMBER 16, 1776

The capture and surrender of Fort Washington, also referred to as Mount Washington, on upper New York Island was a decisive British victory. The Battle of Fort Washington was a disaster for the Continental army, as 59 were killed, 96 wounded and 2,838 taken captive and 34 cannons were surrendered.

Colonel Rall's Hessians, who encamped near Hell Gate two months prior, fought at and took part in the capture of Fort Washington. General George Washington's Continental army, now short three thousand soldiers, was entirely out of New York City—off New York Island, to be certain. Many prisoners were sent to the sugar house jails on New York Island and the Wallabout Bay prison ships on the East River to die.

In the months through the end of November 1776, the status of General Washington's surviving army was, at the time, not easily discernable. Every soldier's mettle was being tested. Some men were eager to desert the nearly defeated cause, longing for home, longing for their wives, while others were being rewarded for their valor and commitment. On November 21, 1776, the Continental "Congress commissioned [Nicholas] Fish a major in the 2nd New York Regiment of the Continental Army."[250]

The New York Loyalist Petition of November 28, 1776, commonly known as the "Loyalist Declaration of Dependence," was presented to the royal authorities in New York.[251] All Loyalists in lower New York Province had wished to be held in the favor of the Crown. Queens County Loyalists eagerly signed.

The thirteen-mile-long New York, now Manhattan Island, was completely conquered. The battle operations had freed themselves from the confines of New York islands. Staten, Long, Governor's, Blackwell's, Buchanan's, Montresor's and Riker's, and now New York Island, all witnessed troop maneuvers, subjugation and occupation. The war, with its two armies, was now in New Jersey, on the North American continental mainland. The British army would continue the pursuit. The Continental army still existed.

DECEMBER 1776

Lieutenant Robert Troup (1756–1832), captured at the Jamaica Pass early on August 27, 1776, prior to the Battle of Long Island, was confined to the British prison ship *Jersey*. He was part of a prisoner exchange in December 1776 and rejoined American forces to fight another day. Troup was great friends, King's College classmates and a New York militiaman with Nicholas Fish and Alexander Hamilton. The three would continue to ably serve the Patriot cause.

In early December 1776, the HMS *Niger* and its small fleet continued their patrols and dominance of the eastern end of, or upper, East River. They allowed supply vessels and warships from the Long Island Sound to the Hell Gate and, for some ships, passage downriver to New York City.

A British Royal Navy fleet under the command of Lieutenant General Henry Clinton took Newport, Rhode Island, on December 8, 1776. General Clinton had been at the Nathaniel Moore house from September 4 until very early on September 15, 1776. He led the vanguard of troops at the landing at Kip's Bay, the Invasion of New York.

Noteworthy citizens who were fortunate enough to escape the British army were now displaced from their ancestral homes and made refugees elsewhere. In their flight, these refugees could no longer avoid the mighty British Royal Navy, which, by November 16, commanded New York Harbor, the lower Hudson River and the full length of the sixteen-mile East River. Local Long Island City–area Patriots had their homes and farms confiscated and some family members arrested; their affairs were in disarray. Their families were scattered into uncertainty to places that they didn't know. The war was now in charge. Although they remained uncaptured and unwavering in their service, how might they still help the cause that left them refugees? "December 12, 1776, we find Col. Blackwell and Major Jona. Lawrence, members from Queens county, offering their attendance in the [New York State] Convention, if desired, although the county is in possession of the enemy."[252] The New York Provincial Congress convened, no longer in New York City but in counties north of New York City. The fine Newtown officers offered their services in the New York Congress yet were far from homes that they could not return to.

The good colonel who visited Hallett's Cove and Newtown, Queens, in January 1776, Colonel Nathaniel Heard, suffered property and pecuniary losses while serving away from his New Jersey home. The British exacted revenge on Colonel Heard. "When the British arrived in Woodbridge, in December, 1776, they confiscated his property and burned his home and out buildings."[253]

Lieutenant General Charles Lee, George Washington's second-in-command, may have actually set foot in Queens County around February 1776. Washington had dispatched him to New York and Long Island to begin to construct defensive positions in and around New York City. His reconnaissance may have taken him as far north as Hell Gate and northwestern Queens. On December 13, 1776, while Lieutenant General Lee was away from his troops, the British Light Dragoons captured him in Basking Ridge, New Jersey. This abruptly changed the dynamic of the war and of the American army. History has revealed that the capture of General

The *American* CRISIS.

NUMBER I.

By the Author of COMMON SENSE.

THESE are the times that try men's fouls: The
summer foldier and the funfhine patriot will, in this
crifis, fhrink from the fervice of his country; but
he that ftands it NOW, deferves the love and thanks of man
and woman. Tyranny, like hell, is not eafily conquered;
yet we have this confolation with us, that the harder the
conflict, the more glorious the triumph. What we obtain
too cheap, we efteem too lightly:—Tis dearnefs only
that gives every thing its value. Heaven knows how to fet
a proper price upon its goods; and it would be ftrange, indeed, if fo celeftial an article as FREEDOM fhould not be
highly rated. Britain, with an army to enforce her tyranny,
has declared, that fhe has a right (*not only to* TAX, but) "to
"BIND *us in* ALL CASES WHATSOEVER," and if being
bound in that manner is not flavery, then is there not fuch a
thing as flavery upon earth. Even the expreffion is impious,
for fo unlimited a power can belong only to GOD.

WHETHER the Independence of the Continent was declared too foon, or delayed too long, I will not now enter
into as an argument; my own fimple opinion is, that had
it been eight months earlier, it would have been much better. We did not make a proper ufe of laft winter, neither
could we, while we were in a dependent ftate. However,
the fault, if it were one, was all our own; we have none
to blame but ourfelves*. But no great deal is loft yet; all
that Howe has been doing for this month paft is rather a
ravage than a conqueft, which the fpirit of the Jerfies a year
ago would have quickly repulfed, and which time and a
little refolution will foon recover.

I have as little fuperftition in me as any man living, but
my.

* "The prefent winter" (meaning the laft)," is worth an
" age if rightly employed, but if loft, or neglected, the whole
" Continent will partake of the evil; and there in no punifh-
" ment that man does not deferve, be he who, or what, or
" where he will, that may be the means of facrificing a feafon
" fo precious and ufeful." COMMON SENSE.

On December 19, 1776, *The American Crisis*, by the author of *Common Sense*, is published. "THESE are the times that try men's souls…" Thomas Paine's stirring essays promoted independence. *Public domain.*

Charles Lee allowed General George Washington to lead his American army with diminished criticism and reduced the ever-present air of subterfuge against his leadership.

Thomas Paine published *The American Crisis* in the *Pennsylvania Journal*. *The Crisis* was a pamphlet series written to inspire Patriots to continue the cause. This gave soldiers and military leaders proper reason to continue the fight, although things at that moment looked bleak. These great works were said to have recharged the revolutionary spirit. "*These* are the times that try men's souls. The summer soldier and the sunshine patriot will, in this crisis, shrink from the service of his country; but he that stands it now, deserves the love and thanks of man and woman. Tyranny, like hell, is not easily conquered."[254]

General George Washington had this read to all his troops prior to the clandestine maneuvers against the Hessians at Trenton. By mid-December 1776, when the British and Hessian forces were sent into winter quarters, Colonel von Rall had been given command of the garrison at Trenton. Colonel von Rall and his Hessian grenadiers and jaegers had been in Hallett's Cove and in northwestern Queens from September to October 12, 1776. Though out of our western Queens County purview, the importance of the crossing of the Delaware River in late December is to be stressed.

This historic and meaningful event of December 25–26, 1776, was immortalized on a large canvas in 1851 by Emanuel Leutze (1816–1868). Of the many characters portrayed, both General Nathanael Greene and Lieutenant James Monroe had links to western Newtown, and they are depicted in the painting. This was a last gasp for the 1776 Continental army. The military assault was hindered by harsh weather conditions and extremely difficult logistics. Precise and stealthy operation by various soldiers, all Americans, all freezing their butts off, had a common goal on that frigid December night. This was the penultimate wartime "it's now or never."

The surrender of the Hessians to George Washington at Trenton, New Jersey, on December 26, 1776. Here, exiled Newtown resident Dr. John Berrien Riker saves a wounded Lieutenant James Monroe. *Public domain. Painting by John Trumbull, 1828.*

Important to the narrative is that the Third Virginians' Captain William Washington and Lieutenant James Monroe and their company formed the vanguard, an advance party that first crossed the Delaware River. They crossed at dusk on Christmas night, December 25, 1776. The Virginians were to secure strategic points and crossroads around Trenton, readying for the arrival of the Continentals.

General George Washington and most of his 2,400-man Continental army crossed the Delaware River on December 25–26, 1776. In what would be a historic and heroic crossing of the Delaware, morning light would bring about the Battle of Trenton. The painting shows Virginian lieutenant James Monroe and Dr. John Berrien Riker, from Newtown, Queens County, New York. This monumental victory of the Americans over the Hessians at Trenton lives in the historical annals as one of the greatest military operations ever conducted. "The Hessians lost 22 killed and 948 taken prisoner. Approximately 500 men escaped from the city and were used to form a combined battalion of foot."[255]

The impact of this battle is not so much in the capture of 948 enemy combatants—and their weapons, equipment and blankets—but in the lifting of American morale in those times which tried men's souls. These were not

"Sunshine Patriots." Major John Polhemus, a relative of the Hallett's Cove–area Polhemus family, who marched through in January 1776 with Colonel Heard's New Jersey troops, took part in the Battle of Trenton. Regarding Lieutenant Monroe: "As the attack ensued and the scattered Hessians formed to return musket and artillery fire, the Third Virginians rushed the enemy artillery. Captain Washington was felled, having been hit in both hands. Command of the company devolved on his young lieutenant, eighteen year old James Monroe, future president of the United States."[256]

A battlefield death makes an instant hero, if your comrades live to tell about it. Let the scrutiny of his decisions be for a later time. It is always tougher to live on, to drive forward, to never give up as long as you can walk and carry a musket, dig a redoubt, load a cannon or lead a bayonet charge. To die on the battlefield is to leave these earthly burdens to the living, your comrades in arms, they themselves trying not to die but to fight well and live free.

Late on Christmas night, December 25, 1776, Lieutenant Monroe and the Third Virginians began their fateful mission, to defeat the Hessians.

Monroe noted that the night was "tempestuous," and that snow was falling. While manning their post, the detachment was accosted by a local resident who thought the Continentals were British troops. Describing the incident many years later at a White House dinner during his presidency, Monroe recalled that the man, whose name was John Riker, was "determined in his manner and very profane." "Upon learning that the soldiers were Americans, he brought food from his house and said to Monroe, 'I know something is to be done, and I am going with you. I am a doctor, and I may help some poor fellow.' Dr. Riker proved remarkably prescient."[257]

As the Continentals got closer to Trenton, James Monroe's autobiography reveals heroic actions by the Virginians. They attacked Hessian pickets and rushed artillery and musket fire. Two Hessian cannons were attacked and captured in the fight, Captain Washington was wounded and Lieutenant Monroe was now in charge, on the fly, in a fluid battle situation. Get tough and push forward or die trying. Lieutenant Monroe, in charge of the corps for only minutes, "was shot down by a musket ball which passed through his breast and shoulder. He was also carried from the field."[258]

Lieutenant Monroe was brought to the same room as his wounded commander, Captain Washington, and had his severed artery clamped. His wound was dressed by the army's surgeon general, assisted by Dr. John

The touch-and-go moments of battlefield triage, 1776 style. Dr. John Berrien Riker is forever painted here, saving the life of the future fifth U.S. president. *Public domain. Painting by John Trumbull, 1828.*

Berrien Riker. Riker had been exiled to New Jersey after the Battle of Long Island in August 1776. "Riker's prediction of helping 'some poor fellow' came true as he repaired a damaged artery in Monroe's shoulder. What neither man realized at the time was that the intrepid physician had saved the life of a future president."[259] On his death in 1794, he was buried at the Riker Cemetery behind the Lent-Riker-Smith house, extant in East Elmhurst, Queens, where he rests to this day.

George Washington and his mobile army again, on December 30, 1776, crossed from Pennsylvania to New Jersey. They were to bring fresh battle to the British, this time on January 3, 1777, at Princeton, New Jersey.

THE YEAR 1776 WAS a very hard one for the revolutionary colonists, yet it ended in a battle victory. Would 1777 provide victory for the Continentals fighting for liberty or for the British fighting to preserve empire? Numerous British regiments stayed on Long Island at the times of year when a military campaign was out of the question, often December to April/May. The very secure wintering of troops occurred in the occupied towns across the East River from New York Island. In 1776, prominent local families in exile, such as Lawrence, Riker, Blackwell, Fish, Morell and others, continued the fight for independence. They would fight in major battles in New Jersey, Pennsylvania, Rhode Island, Upstate New York, on the Atlantic Ocean's high seas, in the Carolinas and in Virginia.

Newtown, Queens, was occupied territory. The hugely historic year of 1776 had ended. The Americans were fresh off a victory, taking one thousand Hessians out of the battle equation.

The year 1776 was a very tough one for all inhabitants. The Patriots had fled to fight another day. The Tories embraced the king's conquering army and did all they could to perpetuate the British Empire and its way of life. The British now occupied the lands of western Newtown, Queens County, the future Long Island City.

How the American War of Independence played out in Long Island City will be discussed in detail by this author in a second book to follow. The Revolutionary years of 1777 to 1783, the post–American Revolution period, findings and scholarship from 1776 to present and what can be found in the modern-day Long Island City will be greatly expanded on.

The year 1776 was not the end of this struggle for American independence from the British. Those seeking to live free would have to soldier on.

NOTES

Acknowledgements

1. The Who, "Slip Kid."

Chapter 1

2. Actual plaque on the Lent-Riker-Smith house, placed by the New York Community Trust, 1960.
3. *John Batchelor Show*, book review and discussion.
4. Dayton, "Popular Patriotic Songs."

Chapter 2

5. *Extracts from the Records of Newtown* (hereafter *Records of Newtown*), 86.
6. Onderdonk, *Revolutionary Incidents of Queens County*, 18–19.
7. Munsell, *History of Queens County, New York*, 336.
8. Ibid.
9. Onderdonk, *Revolutionary Incidents of Queens County*, 20.
10. Ibid., 43.
11. Hallett, *Hallett Family History*, 65.
12. Ibid., 66.

13. Fraunces Tavern Museum, placard.
14. Flag History, "Grand Union Flag."
15. Lewis, "Francis, Lord Rawdon—Colonel."
16. *Records of Newtown*, 88.
17. Ibid. Editor's note: American Revolution Scrapbook (GAHS), circa 1884.
18. Mystic Stamp Company, info sheet.
19. Historical Shop, Nicholas Fish information sheet, 1.
20. Onderdonk, *Revolutionary Incidents of Queens County*, 34.
21. Tiedemann, "Revolution Foiled," 417.
22. Cookinham, interview.
23. Ibid.
24. Adams, letter to Niles.
25. "By the King," Encyclopedia Virginia.
26. Onderdonk, *Revolutionary Incidents of Queens County*, 44.
27. Ibid.
28. Ibid.

Chapter 3

29. Woodbridge Township Historic Preservation Commission, informational signage.
30. Guerra, *NYCLPC Landmark Designation Report*.
31. Byers, *Small Town*, 6.
32. Onderdonk, *Revolutionary Incidents of Queens County*, 47.
33. Ibid., 45.
34. Ibid., 45.
35. Ibid., 47–48.
36. Stringfellow, "John Polhemus."
37. Onderdonk, *Revolutionary Incidents of Queens County*, 52.
38. Ibid., 52–53.
39. New York (Colony), *Committee-Chamber, New-York*.
40. Wikipedia, "John Alsop."
41. Peale, *George Washington*.
42. Onderdonk, *Revolutionary Incidents of Queens County*, 56.
43. Held, "Brooklyn Campaign."
44. Onderdonk, *Queens County in Olden Times*, 62.
45. Onderdonk, *Revolutionary Incidents of Queens County*, 62.

46. Greater Astoria Historical Society, *Long Island City Then & Now*, 68.
47. Wikipedia, "John Alsop."
48. National Archives, "Lee Resolution."
49. Ibid.
50. Washington, letter to Greene.
51. Greater Astoria Historical Society, December 10, 1774 document.

Chapter 4

52. Declaration of Independence, July 4, 1776.
53. *Newsday*, "July 2, 2018."
54. Heinl, *Military and Naval Quotations*.
55. The Green-Wood Cemetery, plaque.
56. Harvard University, "Unsullied by Falsehood."
57. Onderdonk, *Revolutionary Incidents of Queens County*, 76.
58. Ibid.
59. Munsell, *History of Queens County*, 337.
60. Ibid.
61. Onderdonk, *Revolutionary Incidents of Queens County*, 76.
62. "Unsullied by Falsehood."
63. Sethkaller.net, "1776 Safe Passage."
64. Ibid.
65. Ibid.
66. Onderdonk, *Revolutionary Incidents of Queens County*, 80.
67. Ibid., 81.
68. History.com Editors, "Sargent and Hutchinson Arrive."
69. Ibid.
70. Johnston, *Campaign of 1776*, 89.

Chapter 5

71. "Unsullied by Falsehood."
72. Ibid.
73. Onderdonk, *Revolutionary Incidents of Queens County*, 84.
74. McCullough, *1776*, 155.
75. PBS, *Liberty!*.
76. AmericanRevolution.org, "Hessians."

77. Onderdonk, *Revolutionary Incidents of Queens County*, 86.
78. Ibid., 89.
79. Lennon and McCartney, "Lucy in the Sky with Diamonds."
80. NOAA, Chart #12339.
81. Ogilby, *America*, 170.
82. Psalm 27, 1 to 3. "Ninth Station. Jesus falls a third time."
83. Howe, "Proceedings of the American Colonies."
84. "Privates of the Grenadier Regiment."
85. "Hessians"; Leffel and Barker, *American Revolution, 1775–1783*.
86. https://m.brookhavensouthhaven.org/hamlet. Colonel Smith's regiment.
87. Munsell, *History of Queens County*, 343.
88. Historical Shop, notes.
89. *Brooklyn Eagle*, "Residences Which Are Historical."
90. Ibid.
91. Onderdonk, *Revolutionary Incidents of Queens County*, 89.
92. Ibid., 92.
93. McCullough, *1776*, 179.
94. Onderdonk, *Revolutionary Incidents of Queens County*, 89–90.
95. Munsell, *History of Queens County*, 337.
96. Onderdonk, *Revolutionary Incidents of Queens County*, 104.
97. Ibid.
98. Onderdonk, *Revolutionary Incidents of Queens County*, 102.
99. Munsell, *History of Queens County*, 269–70.
100. Ibid., 270.
101. Ibid., 270.
102. Juniper Park Civic, "Newtown."
103. GAHS/LagCC Calendar, 1979.
104. Find a Grave, "John Alsop."
105. GAHS, QHS notes.
106. Munsell, *History of Queens County*, 270.
107. Kelsey, *History of Long Island City*, 19.
108. Hallett, *Hallett Family History*, 65.
109. Isaiah 43:2, NLT.
110. Held, "Brooklyn Campaign."
111. O'Donnell, *Indispensables*.
112. Onderdonk, *Revolutionary Incidents of Queens County*, 100.
113. *Brooklyn Eagle*, October 29, 1900.
114. Volo, *Blue Water Patriots*, 192.
115. Ketchum, *Divided Loyalties*.

116. Munsell, *History of Queens County*, 337.
117. Ibid.
118. Onderdonk, *Revolutionary Incidents of Queens County*, 100.
119. Heath, letter to Washington, August 31, 1776.
120. William Howe's Orderly Books.
121. Juniper Park Civic, "Newtown."
122. Micah 7:8, New International Version.

Chapter 6

123. *Long Island Star-Journal*, "Some Legends."
124. Onderdonk, *Revolutionary Incidents of Queens County*, 99.
125. "Destruction of the Alsop House."
126. Ibid.
127. QBPL. Info written on photo reverse. Captain Samuel Moore house.
128. Seyfried, "Sketch."
129. Per information given by photographer with photograph.
130. "Residences Which Are Historical."
131. Seyfried, "Sketch."
132. "Residences Which Are Historical."
133. Seyfried, "Sketch."
134. Kelsey, *History of Long Island City*, 20.
135. Onderdonk, *Revolutionary Incidents of Queens County*, 100.
136. A hypothetical quotation.

Chapter 7

137. Plaque at Lawrence site.
138. Sheehan, Lawrence family cemetery notes.
139. Kelsey, *History of Long Island City*, 19.
140. Powell, *Private and Family Cemeteries*, 27.
141. Actual gravestone in Lawrence Cemetery.
142. Munsell, *History of Queens County*, 270.
143. Ibid.
144. Onderdonk, *Revolutionary Incidents of Queens County*, p. 100.
145. Kelsey, *History of Long Island City*, 20.
146. Ibid.
147. LaGuardia Community College/GAHS historical calendar, 1981.
148. Juniper Park Civic, "Newtown and the American Revolution."
149. LaGuardia Community College/GAHS historical calendar, circa 1980.

150. Onderdonk, *Revolutionary Incidents of Queens County*, 117.
151. Faden, *Plan of New York Island*.
152. Informational plaque by "HMS" *Rose* Foundation, Bridgeport, Connecticut.
153. NYC Ferry.
154. Howe, "Proceedings of the American Colonies."
155. *Brooklyn Eagle*, "Concluding Reminiscences."
156. "Destruction of the Alsop House."
157. "Residences Which Are Historical."
158. Guerra, *NYCLPC Landmark Designation Report*.
159. Munsell, *History of Queens County*, 341.
160. Ibid.
161. "Pot of Gold," Hatching Cat NYC.
162. *New. Safeguard*, March 8, 1883. (Probably the *Newtown Safeguard*, later the *Queens County Safeguard*, a short-lived nineteenth-century local newspaper.)
163. *Brooklyn Eagle*, March 28, 1889.
164. "Pot of Gold," Hatching Cat NYC.
165. Writing on actual postcard, GAHS collection.
166. Kelley, *Historical Guide*.
167. Kelsey, *History of Long Island City*, 18.
168. Ibid.
169. *Historical Guide*, 278.
170. Seyfried, *300 Years*, 45.
171. Ibid., 41.
172. *Once Upon a Time*.
173. Munsell, *History of Queens County*, 341.
174. Seyfried, *300 Years*, 75.
175. McDonald, "Way It Was."
176. Seyfried and Asadorian, *Old Queens, N.Y.*, 9.
177. Ibid, 8.
178. *Long Island Star-Journal*, "Some Legends."
179. NYC Parks signage at Carl Schurz Park in New York City. May 1997 information.
180. History.com.
181. Munsell, *History of Queens County*, 270.
182. Duncan, *Royal Regiment*, 309.
183. Heath, letter to Washington, September 9, 1776.

184. "Forts: Montressor's Island," New York State Military Museum and Veterans Research Center.
185. Onderdonk, *Revolutionary Incidents of Queens County*, 100–101.
186. Tatum, *American Journal of Ambrose Serle*, 99–100.
187. Babcock, *Rhode Island Archives*, 516.
188. *Brooklyn Eagle*, "Additional Particulars."
189. Morgan, *Naval Documents*, 891.
190. Ibid., 892.
191. *Long Island Star-Journal*, "Some Legends."
192. Clevely, *British Troops Landing*. See image on page 166.
193. *Brooklyn Eagle*, "Additional Particulars."
194. Kelsey, *History of Long Island City*, 18.
195. Volo, *Blue Water Patriots*, 193.
196. Schenawolf, "American Revolutionary."
197. Kelsey, *History of Long Island City*, 18.
198. Onderdonk, *Revolutionary Incidents of Queens County*, 101.
199. Schenawolf, "American Revolutionary."
200. Washington, letter to John Hancock. (Heath, *Heath's Memoirs*, 70.)
201. Schenawolf, "American Revolutionary."
202. *Brooklyn Eagle*, "Concluding Reminiscences."
203. Fraunces Tavern Museum, Johnston map key.
204. Charles Blaskowitz, map key, 1776.
205. Historical signage at 34th Street East River ferry point.
206. Sethkaller.net, "1776 Safe Passage."
207. Ibid.
208. Ibid.
209. Juniper Park Civic, "Newtown."
210. Ibid.

Chapter 8

211. Kelsey, *History of Long Island City*, 18.
212. Ibid.
213. Juniper Park Civic, "Newtown."
214. Byers, *Small Town*, 1976, 6.
215. *Long Island Star-Journal*, "Some Legends."
216. "Residences Which Are Historical."

217. *Long Island Star-Journal*, "Some Legends."
218. Juniper Park Civic, "Newtown."
219. Parson, *Prison Ship Jersey*.
220. GAHS, QHS notes.
221. Skillman, *Skillmans of New York*, 25.
222. Ibid.
223. Ibid.
224. "Residences Which Are Historical."
225. *Newtown Register*, March 7, 1880.
226. *Newtown Register*, June 26, 1886.
227. "Residences Which Are Historical."
228. Skillman, *Skillmans of New York*, 17.
229. Ibid.
230. Ibid.
231. "Residences Which Are Historical."
232. Munsell, *History of Queens County*, 337.
233. Guerra, *NYCLPC Landmark Designation Report*.
234. Van Pelt, *Leslie's History*.
235. Byers, *Small Town*, 6.
236. Ibid.
237. *Brooklyn Eagle*, "Additional Particulars."
238. Juniper Park Civic, "Newtown."
239. Ibid.
240. *Brooklyn Eagle*, "Additional Particulars."
241. Ibid.
242. Ibid.

Chapter 9

243. Juniper Park Civic, "Newtown."
244. Joy, *Hudson River Passage*.
245. Governali, GAHS lecture.
246. Munsell, *History of Queens County*, 270.
247. Onderdonk, *Revolutionary Incidents of Queens County*, 101.
248. Johnston, *Campaign 1776 New York*.
249. McNamara, "Loyalist Declaration of Dependence."
250. Historical Shop, Nicholas Fish information sheet.
251. McNamara, "Loyalist Declaration of Dependence."

252. Onderdonk, *Revolutionary Incidents of Queens County*, 102.
253. Woodbridge Township Historic Preservation Commission.
254. Paine, "American Crisis Number 1."
255. Sons of the Revolution, "Uniforms."
256. Britton, "James Monroe."
257. Harris, "James Monroe," 2.
258. Ibid., 3.
259. Ibid., 4.

Bibliography

Adams, John. Letter to Hezekiah Niles. February 13, 1818. National Archives: Founders Online. https://founders.archives.gov/documents/Adams/99-02-02-6854.

Alsop, John. "John Alsop [John Alsop Jr. (1724–November 22, 1794)]." Wikipedia. https://en.m.wikipedia.org/wiki/John_Alsop.

American Merchant Marine at War. "American Prisoners of the Revolution: Names of 8000 Men." May 20, 2001. http://www.usmm.org/revdead.html.

AmericanRevolution.org. "The Hessians: Chapter VI: The Battle of Long Island, August, 1776. https://www.americanrevolution.org/hessians/hess6.php.

American Revolution Round Table of New York. Last updated January 23, 2023. https://www.arrt-ny.org/.

Babcock, Joshua. *Rhode Island Archives*. Vol. 2.

Britton, Rick. "James Monroe: Bona Fide Hero of the American Revolution." Journal of the American Revolution, January 31, 2013.

Blaskowitz, Charles. *A Plan of the Narrows of Hells-Gate in the East River, Near Which Batteries of Cannon and Mortars Were Erected on Long Island […]*. 1776. https://www.loc.gov/item/gm71000922/.

Bliven, Bruce R. *The Battle for Manhattan*. New York: Henry Holt, 1956.

Bolton, Reginald Pelham. *The Bombardment of New York and the Fight for Independence against the Sea Power of Great Britain in the Year 1776*. 3rd ed. New York: printed by the author, 1915. https://www.google.com/books/edition/The_Bombardment_of_New_York/6UXLcVDepo0C.

The Bowery Boys. https://www.boweryboyshistory.com/.

Brooklyn Eagle. "Additional Particulars About the Old Alsop Mansion." April 25, 1880.

———. "Concluding Reminiscences of the Alsop Family." May 23, 1880.

———. "Destruction of the Alsop House." March 28, 1880.

———. March 28, 1889.

———. October 29, 1900.

———. "Residences Which Are Historical." October 22, 1899. https://junipercivic.com/history/residences-which-are-historical.

Buchanan, John. *The Road to Valley Forge: How Washington Built the Army That Won the Revolution*. United States: Wiley, 2004. https://www.google.com/books/edition/The_Road_to_Valley_Forge/ebXtAAAAMAAJ.

Byers, Pam, with the Local History Committee of the Sunnyside Community Service Center. *Small Town in the Big City: A History of Sunnyside and Woodside*. New York: Sunnyside Community Service Center, 1976.

Clarke, Robert Gordon. "Henry H <?> Riker." RootsWeb. June 18, 2013. https://sites.rootsweb.com/~rclarke/page1/riker.htm.

Clevely, Robert. *British Troops Landing at Kip's Bay 1776. (painted 1777)* Royal Museums, Greenwich.

Cookinham, Fred. Interview with the author. The American Revolution Round Table of New York, May 2019.

Dayton, David E. "America's 10 Most Popular Patriotic Songs." *VFW Magazine*, December 1998.

Duncan, Captain Francis. *History of the Royal Regiment of Artillery Vol. 1 (1716–1783)*. Originally published 1872. Digital version by Andrews UK, 2012.

East View of Hell Gate, in the Province of New York. New York Public Library. 1778. https://digitalcollections.nypl.org/items/510d47db-1774-a3d9-e040-e00a18064a99.

Ellis, Joseph J. *Revolutionary Summer: The Birth of American Independence*. New York: Alfred A. Knopf, 2013.

Encyclopedia Virginia. "By the King, a Proclamation, for Suppressing Rebellion and Sedition" (1775). https://encyclopediavirginia.org.

Ephemeral New York (blog). "A Revolutionary War Sword Turns Up in Tudor City." February 20, 2017. https://ephemeralnewyork.wordpress.com/2017/02/20/a-revolutionary-war-sword-turns-up-in-tudor-city/.

Extracts from the Records of Newtown. Edited by the town clerk. Circa 1884. From a scrapbook at the Greater Astoria Historical Society.

Faden, William. *A Plan of New York Island, with part of Long Island* […]. Map. New York Historical Society Library.

Find a Grave. "John Alsop." https://www.findagrave.com/memorial/7633943/john-alsop.

Flag History. "History of Grand Union Flag." http://www.flaghistory.net/flag-origins/grand-union-flag/.

Fleming, Thomas. *1776: Year of Illusions.* New York: W.W. Norton, 1975.

Fraunces Tavern Museum. Flag room/lecture space flag exhibit placard. Accessed 2018 and 2022 and 2018.

———. Johnston map key, 1895, depicting 1776.

Gallagher, John J. *The Battle of Brooklyn 1776.* New York: Sarpedon, 1995.

Geni. "Jonathan Lawrence, Sr." Originally published in *Origin of Some New York Banks*, describing the first shareholders of the Bank of New York, 1893. https://www.geni.com/people/Maj-Jonathan-Lawrence/5025579637730036506.

George Washington's Mount Vernon. "Battle of Kip's Bay | British Military Ships on the East River 1776." *George Washington's Mount Vernon.* https://www.mountvernon.org

Governali, Joseph. GAHS lecture. February 3, 2003.

Grasso, Dr. Joanne S. *The American Revolution on Long Island.* Charleston, SC: The History Press, 2016.

Greater Astoria Historical Society. December 10, 1774 document. Document copy, Greater Astoria Historical Society collection. Original document on display at First Presbyterian Church of Newtown, Elmhurst, New York.

———. Queens Historical Society (QHS) notes, typed by G. Henke, 1974.

Greater Astoria Historical Society, Erik Baard, Thomas Jackson and Richard Melnick. *The East River.* Mount Pleasant, SC: Arcadia Publishing, 2005.

Greater Astoria Historical Society with Gary Vollo. *Long Island City (Then and Now)*. Mount Pleasant, SC: Arcadia Publishing, 2010.

Greater Astoria Historical Society with Matt LaRose, Stephen Leone and Richard Melnick. *Long Island City.* Mount Pleasant, SC: Arcadia Publishing, 2007.

Greater Astoria Historical Society with Thomas Jackson and Richard Melnick. *Long Island City.* Mount Pleasant, SC: Arcadia Publishing, 2004. https://www.arcadiapublishing.com/Products/9780738536668.

The Green-Wood Cemetery (Brooklyn, New York). Plaque on the Minerva statue.

Gregory, Catherine. *Woodside, Queens County, New York: A Historical Perspective, 1652–1994.* New York: Woodside on the Move, 1994. https://books.google.com/books/about/Woodside_Queens_County_New_York.html?id=HGCFHAAACAAJ.

Griffith, David M. *Lost British Forts of Long Island.* Charleston, SC: The History Press, 2017.

Guerra, Emilio. *1997 NYCLPC Landmark Designation Report.* Flickr, April 2012.

Hallett, Will. "1877 Description of 'The Old Hallett Burying Grounds—Astoria' from the Newtown Register." Descendants of William Hallet and Elizabeth Fones of Newtown, Astoria, Long Island, New York. December 10, 2013. http://williamhallett.com/1877-description-the-hallett-burying-grounds-astoria-newtown-register/.

———. "The Halletts of Hallett's Cove, Newtown, Astoria, Long Island, New York." November 25, 2013. http://williamhallett.com/.

Hallett, William C. *Hallett Family History.* Compiled by William C. Hallett, of Titusville, Florida, in 2014. 150-page document donated to GAHS on June 24, 2014. GAHS collection.

Hamill, John. "The British Military in New York City, 1776." John's Military History Page. January 14, 1999. http://johnsmilitaryhistory.com/revbrit.html.

Harris, Scott H. "James Monroe at the Battle of Trenton." Emerging Revolutionary War. January 12, 2016. https://emergingrevolutionarywar.org/2016/01/12/james-monroe-at-the-battle-of-trenton/.

Harvard University. "Unsullied by Falsehood: The Signing." July 27, 2016. Declaration Resources Project. https://declaration.fas.harvard.edu.

Hatching Cat NYC. "1842: The Pig That Dug Up a Pot of Gold in Sunnyside, Queens." February 19, 2019. https://www.hatchingcatnyc.com.

Heath, William. *Heath's Memoirs of the American War.* Reprinted from the original edition of 1798; with introduction and notes by Rufus Rockwell Wilson. 1904.

———. Letter to George Washington, August 31, 1776. https://founders.archives.gov/documents/Washington/03-06-02-0147.

———. Letter to George Washington, September 9, 1776. https://founders.archives.gov/documents/Washington/03-06-02-0211.

Heinl, Robert, Jr. "George Washington: General Order to the Continental Army, 2 July 1776." In *The Dictionary of Military and Naval Quotations.* Annapolis, MD: Naval Institute Press, 2014.

Held, James E. "The Brooklyn Campaign: The Battle of Long Island." Warfare History Network, October 9, 2018. https://warfarehistory network.com/the-brooklyn-campaign-the-battle-of-long-island/.

The Historical Shop (Metairie, LA). Nicholas Fish information sheet.

———. Notes. https://historicalshop.com.

History.com Editors. "This Day in History: July 28, 1776: Sargent and Hutchinson Arrive at Horn's Hook, New York." www.history.com/. amp/this-day-in-history/sargent-and-hutchinson-arrive-at-horns-hook-new-york.

Howe, William. "Proceedings of the American Colonies." Letter to George Germain, from camp at Newtown, September 3, 1776.

H., Rich. "Dr John Berrien Riker." Find a Grave. November 10, 2006. https://www.findagrave.com/memorial/16588200/john-berrien-riker.

The John Batchelor Show. Book review and discussion of *An Empire on the Edge* (2014) by Nick Bunker. WABC 770 AM, New York Radio. July 10, 2015, 12:58 a.m.

Johnston, Henry P. *The Campaign of 1776 Around New York and Brooklyn, Including* […]. Brooklyn, NY: Long Island Historical Society, 1878.

Journal of the American Revolution. https://allthingsliberty.com.

Joy, William, after Dominic Serres. *Forcing the Hudson River Passage.* October 9, 1776.

Juniper Park Civic. "Newtown and the American Revolution." *Juniper Berry Magazine.* November 28, 2011. Research from *Maspeth Our Town* by Barbara W. Stankowski, 1977. https://junipercivic.com/juniper-berry/article/newtown-and-the-american-revolution.

Kelley, Frank Bergen. *Historical Guide to the City of New York*, Frederick A. Stokes Co. for the City History Club of New York, 1909.

———. *Historic Queens.* Vol. 11 of *Excursion Planned for the City History Club of New York.* New York: City History Club of New York, 1908. https://archive.org/details/excursionplanned00kellexpchcn/page/n1.

Kelsey, J.S. *History of Long Island City, New York: A Record of Its Early Settlement and Corporate Progress* […]. New York, 1896. https://hdl.handle.net/2027/loc.ark:/13960/t6d224f8z.

Ketchum, Richard M. *Divided Loyalties, How the American Revolution Came to New York.* New York: Henry Holt, 2002.

Kitchin, Thomas. *New York in 1778. Map of New York I. with the adjacent rocks and other remarkable parts of Hell-Gate. London Magazine*, 1778. Museum of the City of New York, www.collections.mcny.org.

Leffel, Jean, and Harry W. Barker, Jr. *Uniforms of the American Revolution, 1775–1783*. Paintings by Jean Leffel, based on illustrations of H.A. Ogden and Lt. Charles M. Lefferts. Photolithos printed Zurich, Switzerland. Historical descriptions by Harry W. Barker Jr. Sons of the Revolution in the State of California, 2015.

Lennon, John, and Paul McCartney. "Lucy in the Sky with Diamonds." 1967.

Lewis, J.D. "Francis, Lord Rawdon—Colonel." Carolana. https://www. carolana.com/SC/Revolution/british_army_francis_rawdon.html.

Lippincott, E.E. "Neighborhood Report: Astoria; An Aging Custodian Worries about a Historic Cemetery." *New York Times*, September 17, 2000.

———. "Reproduction of Stolen 1930s Bank Mural Unveiled in Astoria." *Queens Chronicle*, May 10, 2001. https://www.qchron.com/editions/ western/reproduction-of-stolen-1930s-bank-mural-unveiled-in-astoria/ article_b9343019-e0c0-5780-a722-066f77b9a1c8.html.

L'Italio Americano Staff. "The Italian American Contributions to the American Revolutionary War." July 12, 2013. https://italoamericano. org/declaration-independence/.

Loeser, Peter. "Flags of the American Revolution Era." Historical Flags of Our Ancestors. http://www.loeser.us/flags/revolution.html.

Long Island Star-Journal. "Some Legends of Jack's Creek—A Part of Long Island City Which Is Rapidly Losing Its Early Characteristics—Many Relics Found of the British Occupation." Circa 1920.

Lutz, Nancy E. Brooklyn Genealogy Information Page. Edited by Steve Morse. http://bklyn-genealogy-info.stevemorse.org.

Mann, Frank Paul. "The British Occupation of Southern New York during the American Revolution and the Failure to Restore Civilian Government" Syracuse University. History—Dissertations. Paper 100. 5-2013.

Mather, F.G. *New York in the Revolution as Colony and State, Part 1 and Part 2 (1898)*. November 14, 2011.

Mather, Frederick Gregory. *The Refugees of 1776 from Long Island to Connecticut*. Albany, NY: J.B. Lyon, 1913.

McCarthy, Thomas C., ed. New York Correction History Society. http:// www.correctionhistory.org/.

McCullough, David. *1776*. New York: Simon & Schuster, 2005.

McDonald, Dan, comp. "That's the Way It Was July 1903!" Greater Astoria Historical Society, *Queens Gazette*, July 4, 2018.

McNamara, Sandra. "The Loyalist Declaration of Dependence, 1776." *Journal of the American Revolution*, December 20, 2018. https://allthingsliberty.com/2018/12/the-loyalist-declaration-of-dependence-of-1776/.

Morgan, William James, ed. *Naval Documents of the American Revolution*. Vol. 6. Washington, D.C.: Naval History Division, Department of the Navy. 1972.

Munsell, W.W. *History of Queens County, New York: With Illustrations, Portraits, and Sketches of Prominent Families and Individuals.* New York, 1882. https://hdl.handle.net/2027/nnc2.ark:/13960/t9n32m641.

Murray, Stuart. *American Revolution.* New York: DK Publishing, 2005. https://www.amazon.com/DK-Eyewitness-Books-American-Revolution/dp/0756610591/ref=dp_ob_title_bk.

National Archives. "Lee Resolution (1776)." https://www.archives.gov/milestone-documents/lee-resolution.

National Oceanic and Atmospheric Administration (NOAA). Chart #12339. 47th Ed., March 2013. Last correction: November 15, 2021. https://www.charts.noaa.gov.

Newsday. "This Date in History, July 2, 2018."

Newtown Historical Society. http://www.newtownhistorical.org/.

New York (Colony). *Committee-Chamber, New-York, Presents Forty-Three Names Ordered, April 26, 1775* […]. Library of Congress. New York, 1775. https://www.loc.gov/item/rbpe.10800600/.

New York Public Library Archives & Manuscripts. "Jonathan Lawrence Papers: 1765–1810." http://archives.nypl.org/mss/24496.

New York State Military Museum and Veterans Research Center. "Forts: Montressor's Island." https://museum.dmna.ny.gov/forts/M.

New York Sun. "Old Homesteads Doomed," December 28, 1902.

NYC Ferry. https://www.ferry.nyc.

O'Donnell, Patrick. *The Indispensables* (2021). From *The John Batchelor Show*, 710 AM Radio, New York City (podcast), May 7, 2022.

Ogilby, John. *America: Being an Accurate Description of the New World.* London, 1671.

Once Upon a Time…Long Island City Savings Bank 75th Anniversary. Brochure, 1951. GAHS collection.

Onderdonk, Henry, Jr. *Documents and Letters Intended to Illustrate the Revolutionary Incidents of Queens County, N.Y.: With Connecting Narratives, Explanatory Notes, and Additions.* Kings County, NY: 1846.

———. *Revolutionary Incidents of Suffolk and Kings Counties: With an Account of the Battle of Long Island and the British Prisons and Prison-Ships at New York.* New York: 1849. https://hdl.handle.net/2027/hvd.hx4tak.

———. *Queens County in Olden Times.* Jamaica, NY, 1865.

OSIA Blogger. "Our Italian Forefathers: Italian Contributions to American Independence." *Sons of Italy Blog,* July 3, 2012. https://osia.wordpress.com/2012/07/03/our-italian-forefathers-italian-contributions-to-american-independence/.

Paine, Thomas. "The American Crisis Number 1." *Pennsylvania Evening Post,* December 31, 1776. Viewed at New York Historical Society.

Parson, Charles. *Prison Ship Jersey.* Engraving, circa 1775–circa 1890. New York Public Library, Wallace Print Collection.

PBS. *Liberty! The American Revolution.* Six episodes. First aired November 1997.

Peale, Charles Willson (American, 1741–1827). *George Washington.* 1776. Brooklyn Museum, Dick S. Ramsay Fund.

Peterson, Harold L. *The Book of the Continental Soldier: Being a Compleat Account of the Uniforms, Weapons, and Equipment With Which He Lived and Fought.* Harrisburg, PA: Promontory Press, 1974.

Powell, Charles U., comp. *Description of Private and Family Cemeteries in the Brorough of Queens.* Edited by Alice H. Meigs. New York: Office of the President of the Borough of Queens, 1932. http://longislandgenealogy.com/QueensCem.pdf.

Raphael, Ray. *A People's History of the American Revolution: How Common People Shaped the Fight for Independence.* Edited by Howard Zinn. New York: New Press, 2001. https://thenewpress.com/books/peoples-history-of-american-revolution.

Riker, James, Jr. *A Brief History of the Riker Family: From Their First Emigration to this Country in the Year 1638, to the Present Time.* New York, 1851. https://books.google.com/books?id=YHctAAAAYAAJ&q=.

———. *The Annals of Newtown, in Queens County, New York: Containing Its History from Its First Settlement [...].* New York, 1852. https://hdl.handle.net/2027/loc.ark:/13960/t00z7fn3f.

Roberts, Sam. "Long in Repose, Last Remnants of a Founding Family Will Leave Long Island City." *New York Times,* November 3, 2014.

Schecter, Barnet. *The Battle for New York: The City at the Heart of the American Revolution.* New York: Walker Books, 2002.

Schenawolf, Harry. "American Revolutionary War Battle of Kip's Bay: An American Disaster that Nearly Cost Washington's Life—New York City,

September 15, 1776." *Revolutionary War Journal*, April 3, 2015. https://www.revolutionarywarjournal.com/kips-bay/.

Sethkaller.net. "John Hancock's 1776 Safe Passage for a Congressman Who Spurned the Declaration."

Seyfried, Vincent. "A Sketch of the Riker-Rapelje House." 1959.

Seyfried, Vincent F. *Elmhurst, From Town Seat to Mega-Suburb.* Garden City, NY, 1995.

———. *300 Years of Long Island City: 1630–1930.* Garden City, NY: V.F. Seyfried, 1984.

Seyfried, Vincent F., and William Asadorian. *Old Queens, N.Y., in Early Photographs.* New York: Dover Publications, 1991. https://catalog.hathitrust.org/Record/003836203.

Sheehan, James. Lawrence family cemetery notes. From cemetery caretaker. GAHS Collection.

Skillman, Francis. *The Skillmans of New York.* Roslin, NY, 1892.

Smith, David, and Graham Turner. *New York 1776: The Continentals' First Battle.* New York: Osprey Publishing, 2008. https://ospreypublishing.com/new-york-1776.

Smith, Marion Duckworth. The Lent-Riker-Smith Homestead. https://www.rikerhome.com/history/overview.htm.

Sons of the Revolution in the State of California. "Uniforms of the American Revolution." http://www.srcalifornia.com/uniforms/s4.htm

Stringfellow, Megan. "A Patriot: John Polhemus." Our Family History. June 30, 2013. https://thestringfellowfamilyhistory.wordpress.com/2013/06/30/a-patriot-john-polhemus/.

Stuchinski, Barbara J. *Colonial Patriots: The Remsen Family of Whitepot, Queens County, New York.* New York: B.J. Stuchinski, 2004. https://books.google.com/books/about/Colonial_Patriots.html?id=2fUEHAAACAAJ.

Tatum, Edward H., ed. *The American Journal of Ambrose Serle, Secretary to Lord Howe, 1776–1778.*

Thorburn, Grant. *Fifty Years' Reminiscences of New-York, or, Flowers from the Garden of Laurie Todd.* New York: 1845. https://hdl.handle.net/2027/aeu.ark:/13960/t3ws9r43c.

Tiedemann, Joseph S. "A Revolution Foiled: Queens County, New York, 1775–1776." *The Journal of American History* 75, no. 2; 417–44. (September 1988).

Tiedemann, Joseph S., and Eugene R. Fingerhut, eds. *The Other New York: The American Revolution beyond New York City, 1763–1787.* New York: SUNY Press, 2005.

Van Pelt, Daniel. *Leslie's History of Greater New York.* 1898

Volo, James M. *Blue Water Patriots: The American Revolution Afloat.* United States: Rowman & Littlefield, 2008. https://www.google.com/books/edition/Blue_Water_Patriots/2ekRixiWaVAC.

Warerkar, Tanay. "In Long Island City, Second Phase of Hunter's Point South Waterfront Park Debuts." Curbed New York, June 27, 2018. https://ny.curbed.com/2018/6/27/17510490/hunters-point-south-park-phase-2-opening-lic.

Washington, George. Letter to Brigadier General Nathanael Greene. June 24, 1776. National Archives: Founders Online. https://founders.archives.gov/.

———. Letter to John Hancock, September 16, 1776. National Archives: Founders Online. https://founders.archives.gov/documents/Washington/03-06-02-0251.

The Who. "Slip Kid." *Who by Numbers.* October 25, 1975, MCA Records.

Wikipedia. "Lawrence, Jonathan." http://en.wikipedia.org/wiki/Jonathan_Lawrence.

William Howe's Orderly Books, 1776–1778. William L. Clements Library, University of Michigan. Digitized 2021.

Woodbridge Township Historic Preservation Commission. General Nathaniel Heard Historical Marker, Woodbridge, New Jersey. https://woodbridgehistory.com.

ABOUT THE AUTHOR

*R*ichard Melnick served in the United States Army (1984–1992) as an airborne infantryman in Hesse, West Germany, and in seven U.S. states, achieving the rank of staff sergeant. Former president of the Greater Astoria Historical Society (2006–10), trustee (2003–18) and a licensed New York City sightseeing guide (2011–18), Richard, a night doorman in New York City, enjoys historic days and dates, lecturing and conducting fact-finding recons and walking tours. Richard has a Bachelor of Arts degree in political science from St. John's University.

Visit us at
www.historypress.com